MW01325678

CHANGE *for a* DOLLAR

To Lou Blair,

Best Wishes

CHANGE *for a* DOLLAR

A History of First Savings and Loan

Ricky N. Smith

ISBN 978-1-59715-079-8
Library of Congress Catalog Number 2011928281

First Printing

In memory of my dad

who taught me everything I know

CONTENTS

ACKNOWLEDGMENTS

To the Board of Directors of First Savings: L. Neal Smith, Dr. Steven E. Troutman, James R. Guthrie, and Bobby J. Massey for recognizing the importance of this project and allowing me to tell the story.

To the staff of First Savings: Janis Murray, Jamie Park, Amy Cannady, Denise Snead, and Rhonda Bowling for their support and encouragement.

To my wife, Juliana, for her incredible patience and assistance in making this book a reality.

INTRODUCTION

Change is one of the few constants in the world. Whether we like it or not, change defines our lives. Change is sometimes not easy to accept, and it creates in us a host of emotions both good and bad. Although our world continues on an ever changing path, we sometimes try our best to avoid change, holding on to what is comfortable. We sometimes change and fail to see it, and other times we need to change but fail to do it.

Some people will swear that First Savings may be the only financial institution that hasn't changed in the past one hundred years. It may appear that way on the surface, but the association has experienced its share of changes over the years while holding on to its roots as a small-town thrift. Although this is the story of the first one-hundred-year history of First Savings and Loan, it is also a history of Mebane. Having worked at First Savings for twenty years, I feel pretty comfortable documenting its history and telling its story. However, I am the last person qualified to write about my hometown of Mebane, North Carolina, yet First Savings and Mebane grew up together and have much in common; their stories in many ways parallel each other. First Savings and Mebane have both seen a world of change while holding on to their small-town roots.

The idea for writing this history came about in 2004 when then–*Mebane Enterprise* editor Algernon Primm was doing a story about First Savings' ninety-five years in business and asked me to put together a time line of events. I enjoyed digging through the board of director minute books that date back to 1909. History is one of my passions, and as I read through these old minutes I thought how much had changed and how different the banking world is today. It struck me just how little folks really know about savings and loans and what these institutions did for small communities across the country. Those institutions that have remained savings and loans are a curiosity to most people in this fast-paced world of Internet banking and instant loan approval. Unless you are over fifty, you probably don't know what savings and loans are, nor are you familiar with their storied past.

Another motivation for writing this history came in 2005, when I entered the Graduate School of Banking at LSU. The countless hours I spent on study projects and relationships I developed from my trips to Baton Rouge confirmed what I already knew. No one knew what a savings and loan was anymore, and what I did for a living in a small-town thrift was puzzling to a generation of bankers obsessed with the bottom line of their stock-owned commercial banks.

Today most folks assume that all financial institutions operate the same way and fall into the bank or credit union category. The lasting image that most of us have about a savings and loan is the sentimental picture conjured up by Bedford Falls Building and Loan from the film classic *It's a Wonderful Life*. Thrifts, building and loans, and savings and loans, which are all basically one and the same, have a much different story to tell than the one seen on the big screen. This forgotten sector of the financial industry financed most of the homes built in America for the better part of the twentieth century.

The banking evolution and the process of mortgage loan securitization pushed First Savings and thrifts like it to the back of the bus when it came to home lending. Still, First Savings has not only survived in its smaller financial role; it has flourished. Our nation's financial industry continues down an ever changing path that is often difficult to navigate and filled with wrong turns. Today's events have shown that this system is far from perfect, yet the nation's banking system remains the driving engine for commerce, providing America with the highest standard of living of any nation in history.

As this story is being written, history continues to be made as the financial crisis that emerged in 2008 and the recession that followed have changed our country and its financial system.

Likewise, foreign competition and the evolution of manufacturing changed Mebane from its foundation in furniture and textiles to a diverse commercial and industrial center. Tobacco fields that once blanketed the area are either overgrown with Johnsongrass or have been transformed into the latest subdivision coming to town.

For those who grew up in Mebane, my hope is that this history will trigger a memory or make you smile. If it does, then this book has accomplished its goal.

For those who are new to Mebane, I hope this story enlightens you about the rich history of the town you now call home. If that happens, then this book has achieved its purpose. If you learn something about First Savings, its legacy, its struggles, and its successes, again this book was worth writing.

From bakers to bankers, every profession has its own language, and I have tried to keep this book as simple as I can. This book was not written for the banking industry but for the folks in my hometown. History is inevitably based on facts told from the writer's perspective, and this history reflects mine. This book is by no means the complete history of Mebane, but more of an overview of events related to business and commerce. This history is not the complete story of First Savings' first one hundred years either, but it's close.

Most important, this isn't the story about a small-town institution that grew into a megabank with branches in every state and ATMs on every street corner. There are plenty of stories out there like that, and in fact First Savings' story is quite the opposite. It took one hundred years for First Savings to grow from its beginnings in 1909 to reach $55 million in assets. Hundreds of institutions in America can achieve that type of growth by the time you read a few pages of this book.

The story of local savings and loans is not unique and can be told countless times in a thousand small towns across the country where thrifts served the home loan and savings needs of its citizens. What might be somewhat unique is that by its own choice, First Savings remained a small savings and loan and did not expand, branch, or convert to a stock institution. For a century, First Savings focused on the needs of its customers, not the wants of investors. First Savings did not change for the sake of profits, a choice that has had good and bad consequences. Some consider First Savings old-fashioned and a throw back to yesterday while others see it, as one customer put it, as "an answer to prayer." First Savings is not a name you will ever hear in financial circles on Wall Street or Charlotte, and we don't want it to be. It took awhile, but as this story shows, we are quite content in the town of Mebane, North Carolina.

Ricky N. Smith
President, First Savings and Loan
November 2009

CHANGE *for a* DOLLAR

CHAPTER ONE

The Early Years

1909–1919

CONVERSING WITH NEIGHBORS is a time-honored tradition in America, and in the South this tradition has been raised to art form. Listening in on conversations of folks in Mebane, North Carolina, in the early days of the twentieth century would have been interesting. No doubt many of these friendly chats occurred around a woodstove at the local general store, or over a backyard clothesline or fence and certainly on many a front porch. More than likely these conversations ended with the standard southern farewell of "Bye, y'all." Surely folks were excited about the trainload of White Furniture that was headed for the Panama Canal or the mattress factory that was opening. The topic of conversation undoubtedly covered many subjects, but the word "change" was rarely uttered in this sleepy southern town. Besides the railroad, White Furniture Company, the Mebane Bedding Company (Kingsdown), and a few businesses, the only change residents saw on a regular basis were the turning of the leaves in the fall and the faithful blooming of native dogwood trees in the spring. Over the next century change would be something this small Piedmont town would see plenty of, and change would soon dominate any casual conversation.

Employment in Alamance County, like so many others south of the Mason-Dixon Line, was deeply rooted in agriculture and manufacturing. Small communities and towns grew up along the banks of the Haw River and Great Alamance Creek, where the local textile mill was the center of community life. It wasn't a river that brought folks to Mebane; like thousands of small towns across America, Mebane grew around and because of the railroad. Today hundreds of cars cross the tracks on Third, Fourth, and Fifth streets downtown, and few of these busy drivers recognize the significance of the iron rails beneath them. In the 1800s, a state legislator from the town that bore his name, Giles Mebane, certainly recognized how important rail transportation was to future growth and commerce. As rivers had done in previous generations, the railroad now gave birth to towns and cities and a new generation of communities. Giles Mebane's successful negotiations brought the Piedmont route of the North Carolina Railroad from Raleigh to Greensboro through Alamance County, with stops in the towns of Haw River, and Burlington, and the small depot in Mebane. The depot built on the corner of Washington and Fifth streets, where gardens and a fountain are today, was a vital link to Mebane's growth in its early days. Giles Mebane brought more than just the railroad to town, introducing legislation in 1849 that eventually separated Alamance County from its origins in Orange County.

Only 218 people lived in Mebane in 1900, and the town covered just one square mile. Life for Mebane citizens centered around the railroad, yet the predominant mode of travel was the horse and buggy, as reflected in the makeup of many local businesses. Whitt Lashley ran a blacksmith shop, and A.B. York owned a livery stable. Before there was Amick Ford and Melville Chevrolet there were local carriage dealers, A.H. Mebane and W.A. Murray. Extensive travel was a rarity for most folks, many of whom lived their entire lives within a few miles of their birth. The railroad crossings in downtown Mebane looked much different in their early years, as there were no flashing lights or crossbars—just a railroad sign that reminded the driver or pedestrian, "Stop, Look and Listen."

In 1908 Henry Ford revolutionized transportation, developing the Model T automobile, which sold for $850. Still it would be some time before the horseless carriage was a common sight as paved roads in Mebane, and North Carolina for that matter, were scarce. Folks would contend with dusty roads in the summer and mud-filled ruts in the winter until the first paved roads appeared in Mebane in the 1920s. Ironically, the patchwork of rural roads and paths that connected the state of North Carolina eventually came together to form one of the nation's best highway systems. One of the state's first main highways was Highway 10 running from Morehead City to Asheville, cutting through the Piedmont and the town of Mebane. Portions of old Highway 10 eventually became Highway 70.

If the railroad was the artery that fueled Mebane's growth, its heart was most assuredly its two largest employers, the White Furniture Company, in operation since 1881, and the Mebane Bedding Company (Kingsdown), which opened in 1904. These two homegrown businesses established and served as Mebane's manufacturing base for the better part of a century, yet when the twentieth century drew to a close, economic shifts and business decisions decided very different fortunes for these companies. Fittingly, leaders of both businesses played key roles in establishing the First Savings and Loan Association.

By 1900 there were forty-four furniture factories in North Carolina, and none had the reputation for quality like White Furniture. White had been in operation for nearly two decades and by the turn of the century was an industry leader. A.N. Scott and W.W. Corbett started the Mebane Bedding Company on the second floor of Cook's Mill just north of town. Scott's personal home sat on a wooded area where E.M. Yoder Elementary School is located today on North Charles Street. The trees from this lot were cut down and used to construct the original factory building on Third and Washington streets.

The railroad divided the town in half, running parallel with Highway 10. Most of the town's early residential growth occurred south of the tracks. Most industries and businesses settled north of Highway 10 on what is now Center Street, with the exception of the Mebane Bedding Company and a few smaller businesses near the depot. The largest retailers in the country were Sears and Montgomery Ward, but most goods and services could be found in stores and shops along Mebane's small but growing business district. Although Mebane had officially been a town for more than twenty years, in this era the town defined itself with individually owned shops such as the hardware, clothing, and grocery stores that lined Center, Clay, Ruffin, Fourth, and Third streets. Mebane had no shortage of grocery stores, as folks living on the south side of town could easily walk to John Fowler Grocery near the depot on Fifth Street. J.H. Gill Grocery did a brisk business on North Ninth Street, and John Fox Grocery opened just west of town on South Center Street. If one couldn't walk or ride to the store, Carson Thomas would gladly deliver groceries in a horse-drawn wagon.

Coal and ice could be purchased in town, and electricity was slowly moving into some homes and businesses, but would not become a reality for most of

Alamance County until the mid-1940s. Mebane had lumber- and brickyards, and feed and seed stores drawing people to town from rural communities. The Mebane Store Company at the corner of Fourth and Center streets was one of several general stores carrying a diverse line of merchandise. Although the Mebane Store faded into history, Tyson-Malone Hardware, which opened in 1906 at the corner of Fourth and Clay streets, operated for ninety-eight years, eventually becoming Ace Hardware. A straw and cotton mattress could be purchased from the Mebane Bedding Company for $1.25, and box springs for just a dollar more. H. E. Wilkinson Inc. built a stately building at the corner of Fourth and Clay streets in 1906 that remains one of the town's most prominent structures. Wilkinson's, as it was known, sold clothes, shoes, hats, and dry goods. This building became known as the Russell Building, and by the 1930s was home to Jones' Department Store. The building today carries a different line of merchandise as Solgarden.

Anyone who received an education at that time most likely attended one of the many one-room schoolhouses in the area. These historic structures have long since disappeared, although one—Woodlawn School—found a new life and renewed purpose. The original Woodlawn School was built in 1901 near Cook's Mill north of town. Later another Woodlawn School would be built in 1911 on what is now Mebane Rogers Road, becoming the foundation and source of pride for the Woodlawn Community for generations. As Mebane grew, anchored by White Furniture and Mebane Bedding Company, so did the need for larger school facilities. The wooden frame Mebane Public School was established in 1903 on South Third Street. By 1910 the original building was replaced by a larger brick structure with eight classrooms.

At the turn of the century, the United States was very rural, as three out of every five Americans lived in towns with populations less than twenty-five hundred. The work ethic in these communities was strong, and although folks prided themselves on being self-sufficient, most lived from payday to payday unable to save money. The average American worked ten to twelve hours a day, six days a week, for about twenty cents an hour, with earnings much lower in the rural South. Twenty-five percent of the workforce in southern manufacturing were children between the ages of ten and sixteen, and the hundreds of textile mills that dotted North Carolina employed children as young as six.

Mebane had few amenities in those days, but with growth came change. The Ridgeville Telephone Company began service in 1907, and in 1908 a small newspaper called the *Mebane Leader* went to press for the first time. Ridgeville became the Mebane Home Telephone Company and eventually CenturyTel, and the *Mebane Leader* became the *Mebane Enterprise*. The growth of the town could be seen in the number of churches being built. The Central Methodist Church erected a permanent structure in 1905, soon followed by the First Baptist Church at the corner of Third and Jackson streets in 1907. The original Baptist church building was destroyed by fire in the 1940s and replaced by the current structure.

Job opportunities brought people to Mebane, and the demand and need for housing grew. The financial system at the time was primitive by today's standards; money, for any purpose, was scarce. The 1900 census revealed that 46.5 percent of Americans owned their own homes, yet borrowing money to build or purchase a home was difficult as mortgage lending was a new and emerging concept.

The history of banking in North Carolina runs deep. The tradition and legacy of many of the nation's financial pioneers began in the Old North State. In 1908 Union National Bank was founded in Charlotte by H.M. Victor. What would later become First Union greatly affected banking well beyond the North Carolina border. Wachovia, with its roots in Winston-Salem, was founded in 1879. Together, First Union, NCNB (Bank of America), and Wachovia (Wells Fargo) transformed North Carolina into one of the strongest banking states in the country. Ironically, North Carolina was the last of the original thirteen states to permit banking at all.

Home financing was not a goal of banks in those days, and the nation's financial system was far from stable. The Bank Panic of 1907 saw the stock market fall 50 percent. Worried depositors in this money panic withdrew deposits en masse, causing major bank failures and leading to the creation in 1913 of the Federal Reserve System.

The need for home finance gave birth to the savings and loan industry in the mid-nineteenth century, and most of these institutions adopted a mutual form of ownership or charter. Mutual ownership is quite different from stock-owned enterprises as depositors in a mutual institution have equal control. Stock-owned companies are built and controlled by the people who invest in them or hold stock in that business. One very stark difference in mutual and stock companies is that the larger stockholders can hold significant power over the decisions of publicly owned companies. Mutuality restricts individuals and investors from gaining such influence or controlling a company.

The first building and loan association was the Oxford Provident Building Association founded in Frankford, Pennsylvania, in 1831. Its goal was to provide local townspeople who lacked financial resources a way to buy their own home. The plan Oxford adopted was modeled after mutual building societies in England and served as the foundation of the savings and loan industry. The Oxford plan was simple: members pooled their monies into the institution, allowing other members to borrow and construct a home from that pool of funds. Each member paid the institution an initial fee of $5 to join and agreed to pay the association $3 per month in dues. In April 1831 Oxford Provident extended the first ever home loan for $375 to a local lamplighter to build a house that still stands today.

Once a deposit base was established for these institutions, other members could then borrow from the deposited funds pool and repay the amount to the institution at a higher interest rate than was paid out to depositors. This spread between the interest rate paid on deposits and interest rate charged on loans was the profit the institution made.

This new enterprise of home financing gained popularity and was known by various names: building and loan associations, thrift and loans, building associations, and others that eventually evolved into the industry known as the savings and loan. Whatever the title, these institutions specialized in lending funds for home purchases and construction and in their early days steered clear of commercial ventures.

The first savings institution chartered in North Carolina was the Mutual Building and Loan Association in Charlotte, which opened in 1871. Alamance County's first savings and loan was established in Graham in 1903. A group of interested businessmen from Mebane saw the potential for such a business and began the process of organizing an association.

On Wednesday, November 3, 1909, at 3:00 in the afternoon, these business leaders met at the Businessmen's Club in Mebane and called to order the first ever meeting of the Mebane Home Builders Association. Exactly where in Mebane the Businessmen's Club met is a good question. No documentation exists in the association's records as to where the club held its meetings, but interviews suggest two places. The second floor of the old fire station at the corner of Washington and Fourth streets is one possible location, as many social and business functions were held in this building, which served as Mebane's town hall at that time. The other likely location was on the second floor above what used to be Rose's 5 and 10 Cent Store on Center Street, known as the Five Star Center today. The Mebane Home Builders Association was the first name given to the institution and reflected its limited mission of home construction. According to the minutes of this meeting, the "original incorporators of the association were present in person or by proxy."

Those in attendance that day were well-known business leaders synonymous with the town of Mebane. The original founders of the association were J. Sam White and Stephen Arthur White of White Furniture; W.W. Corbett, one of the founders of the Mebane Bedding Company; and W.Y. Malone, cofounder of Tyson Malone Hardware. Malone was instrumental in the building and early success of the tobacco warehouses that opened in Mebane. Other founders were John A. Holmes, C.O. Pickard, and Lewis Puryear, a founding member of First Baptist Church and owner of the Continental Chair Factory. The first order of business for this new venture was electing Lewis Puryear as chairman and E.S. Parker Jr. as the institution's attorney.

It is unknown how long it took to formally organize the institution, but the minutes reflect that the charter of the association "had been duly recorded in the office of the Clerk of Superior Court and a certified copy…filed with the Secretary of State" by the time of this first meeting, so the planning and organization of the institution had been going on for some time. This recorded charter was presented, approved, and formally adopted by the association, along with its first set of bylaws, which would be amended and changed countless times over the next one hundred years.

Other business transacted at this first meeting was the election of the association's first board of directors: J. Sam White, D.A. White, W.W. Corbett, A.N. Scott, A.M. Cook, J.N. Warren, W.E. Ham, J.S. Vincent, Paisley Nelson, Lewis Puryear, and W.Y. Malone.

Immediately after the first shareholders' meeting was concluded, the first "regular" meeting of the Mebane Home Builders Association was called to order. D.A. White and W.W. Corbett were elected president and vice president, respectively, and J. Sam White was named as secretary-treasurer. In those days, the secretary-treasurer was considered the managing officer, and J. Sam White received an annual salary of sixty dollars, with the other officers receiving no compensation.

In its early days, business was obviously slow as this new venture worked to get off the ground and the directors spent more time in meetings than transacting business. Oddly enough, just five weeks after the company was founded, the first annual meeting of the "stockholders" of the association was held on December 14, 1909. Already the relentless pressure of high finance took its toll as a change was made in the directors for the following year. D.A. White, Lewis Puryear, J.S. Vincent, W.Y. Malone, W.W. Corbett, Paisley Nelson, J.N. Warren, and J. Sam White were reelected from the original group of directors along with new directors J.S. Cheek, F.W. Graves, C.O. Pickard, and C.S. Harris. To clarify, the minutes often refer to members of the association as "stockholders" or "shareholders," particularly in its earlier years. Basically, the members were really shareholders as they did not technically have any stock ownership in the association.

To make the dream of home ownership possible, the Mebane Home Builders Association had the unenviable task of attracting funds in a small working-class town, which would become a constant challenge. To raise these funds, the association issued "series" stock certificates, a concept that is very different from the savings deposits that institutions have today. The series certificates were based on the Oxford Provident Building Association model where shareholders agreed to pay funds into the institution each month on an installment payment. Each shareholder was issued a Pay Day passbook to use for their monthly dues, as these installments were called. Not only did the association raise funds to lend in this manner, the series installment method forced people to save money. After a certain period this series was concluded, or matured, and the amount of the series certificate (which was the amount deposited) had increased in value. A simple example of how the series certificates worked would be that the shareholder agreed to pay in ten dollars per month for nine months, and after the nine-month period, the ninety-dollar certificate could be cashed in for one hundred dollars. This is similar to the classic Parker Brothers' game "Monopoly," in which a Community Chest Card reads "Your Building and Loan Matures, collect $100.00."

These passbooks outlined the terms of savings accounts and home loans, which were very simple in those days. Although it is unclear how much interest the certificates were paying, the payday books reflected that home loan interest rates were at 6 percent. In a time before women could vote in America, it is interesting that the passbook covers for the association read, "Women, married or single, and children twelve years old, can carry shares in their own name." The association would use the series method of raising funds until the late 1940s. Although the series-type plan raised funds, the association's board minutes reflect that the installment plan itself was a constant source of discussion and concern, as people did not always pay in their monthly installment dues as they agreed to do. Coupled with the fact that people did not always make their house payments on time, cash flows into the association became a constant monthly burden.

On December 29, 1909, six weeks after the Mebane Home Builders Association was founded, the first two loan applications were approved for J.T. Jobe Jr. and L.R. Thomas, but no amounts were specified in the minutes. Most of the earliest documented home loans were for amounts ranging from six hundred to one thousand dollars, and these loans were expected to be repaid to the association within a seven-year period.

In its early days, the association had no formal offices or full-time employees. The association operated on a part-time basis until the 1940s. The members of this new financial venture had no idea the association would survive and remain solvent. As a result, the governing body of the institution, its board of directors, was ultra-conservative in its business decisions. Since there was no staff, the association's board performed every aspect of the business, from taking in loan payments and installment dues to appraising property and approving loan applications. There is no documentation showing other individuals assisting in the day-to-day business of the institution until the 1940s.

It is unclear as to where these early applications were physically submitted since no offices existed at the time. The loan process was simple, as a member submitted an application "to the Association's Secretary." Since J. Sam White was Secretary, it can be assumed that loan applications would be taken to the White

Furniture Company where White worked. The earliest documented applications required only the member's name, address of the property, and how much the member wished to borrow. The board then inspected the property and approved or denied the loan.

Determining just how often the board reviewed loan applications is difficult. The board minutes reflect that meetings were held sporadically at various places, even in the homes of the directors.

Likewise, the association's funds were kept in various locations, including a safe at White Furniture Company. The association eventually opened banking relationships, most notably with the Mebane Bank and Trust Company (whose motto was "Reliable, Prompt, Courteous, Secure"), and later with the Commercial Farmers Bank. This was a time of little governmental regulation into the affairs of business, particularly the financial sector. There were virtually no protections for customers prior to the creation of deposit insurance in the 1930s, and depositors ran the risk of losing some or all of their funds if an institution failed.

Getting this fledgling business off the ground was a challenge for the directors as the association approved a total of just seven loans in its first year of operation. The association joined the North Carolina Building and Loan League that represented similar associations throughout the state. In 1911 there were 113 such building and loan organizations in North Carolina, serving 25,174 members with assets of $8.5 million.

The 1910 census revealed that Mebane had tripled in population from 1900, with 693 residents. Downtown Mebane saw the addition of Planters Warehouse, and other warehouses would follow. The city blocks around Clay, Third, and Ruffin streets took center stage when the fall market opened. Over time, the tobacco market grew in importance right behind furniture and mattress production, and the September ritual drew farmers from as far away as Virginia. The fall market grew tremendously over the years, adding to Mebane's overall economic expansion. The tobacco industry had been a North Carolina economic staple since its days as a colony and took on even more significance in 1913 when the R.J. Reynolds Tobacco Company introduced its first pre-rolled cigarette under the brand name of Camel.

In September 1910 Mebane Home Builders director J. S. Cheek resigned and was replaced by J.T. Shaw, then the mayor of Mebane. At the annual shareholders' meeting on December 13, 1910, most of the current directors were reelected, as was a new director, M.B. Miles. As the association struggled in its early years, the membership of the board changed frequently, and it is often unclear when some directors joined or left.

By 1914 the Great War had erupted in Europe, yet life in Mebane remained fairly tranquil as the Presbyterian church completed its stately building on the corner of Fifth and Lee streets. Thad Freshwater opened Freshwater's Store on the corner of Crawford and North First street, and by all accounts the building was painted for the first and last time. Son David would take over the family business in the 1940s, perpetuating one of Mebane's most famous and enduring landmarks. Ralph McDade built the Mebane Laundry on West Clay Street in 1915, offering horse-drawn pickup and delivery. McDade operated the laundry until the early 1940s, when he sold the business to the Isley brothers. The Masons have a long history in Mebane, and they began meeting at their new lodge at the corner of West Clay and North Third streets, a building they would occupy until 1966.

In 1915 T.C. Carter replaced E.S. Parker Jr. as the association's attorney, beginning one of the longest relationships in the institution's history, lasting until 1970. In preparing this history, obtaining information from the earliest years of the association was very challenging, and unfortunately for some substantial periods of time little or no information is available. The period from 1914 through 1919 is one such period, as very little in the way of board minutes has survived. The information that does exist from that period is handwritten and often illegible. Given this limited information, it is difficult to determine just how financially solvent the early association was, as no balance sheets, financial records, or statements remain from that time. The earliest known written financial record—from a December 1, 1916, audit—revealed the association's assets stood at $30,218, with $25,273 in home loans and $4,945 in cash. One of the original founders of the association, D.A. (Dave) White, general manager of White Furniture Company, was killed in an car accident in 1916, but no mention of White's death appears in the minutes, and who, if anyone, took his place on the board is unknown.

While America cautiously observed the war in Europe, its population, spurred on by immigration, reached 100 million in 1915, with most of the growth in the large population centers in the Northeast.

As savings associations grew in America, so did home construction, and those looking to build in Mebane could find most building materials in local factories, lumber mills, or brickyards. If something had to be shipped in by rail it could be sent to the depot downtown. But what arrived on a train in 1917 was a bit unusual. An entire home kit was shipped from the Alladin Home Company in Bay City, Michigan, through Sears, Roebuck. The home came ready for construction, including precut lumber and nails, for the unassembled price of $1,217. The home on South Fourth Street remains a topic of conversation nearly a century later.

By 1917 the United States had entered the conflict raging in Europe, and Alamance County records reveal that 1,096 men from the area served in World War I, suffering 110 casualties. The war was a major stimulus for growth as the U.S. economy boomed during and after the war years. The world's financial center shifted from London to Wall Street as European countries looked to the United States for resources during the conflict. When the war ended in 1918, returning soldiers came home ready to get on with their lives, sparking an economic boom that lasted a decade.

Mebane, like so many communities, was on the brink of an incredible period of growth and transformation. Homes were springing up just south of the depot on South Third, Fourth, and Fifth streets, and on Holt as well as Jackson and Lee streets. The north side of town saw more homes built on Cloud (Wilba), Crawford, and Graham Streets. Boardinghouses were common, and the construction of multifamily units increased after both world wars as duplexes and triplexes became popular.

In 1919 General Motors formed the General Motors Acceptance Corporation, allowing consumers to finance the purchase of an automobile. The introduction of installment buying was a huge step for the average American, who could now buy a car and spread payments over time. Automobile sales naturally exploded.

The Mebane Home Builders Association somehow survived its first ten years of existence and after a slow beginning established itself as a solid funding source for home building. After originating just seven loans in 1909 the association was regularly approving four to five loans a month by the end of the decade. Still, the association was a part-time venture, and its long-term future was far from certain.

The institution made the dream of owning a home possible for its members, yet the association had no home of its own. Board meetings were still held at different locations, including the Melville Drug Company where A.J. Thompson was elected secretary-treasurer in 1919. The prosperity of the 1920s and a man named John McIntyre added much-needed stability and leadership to this fledgling business, setting the course for its future.

Center Street around 1910 shows the depot on the right and a few stores. Note the unpaved streets. The road crossing the tracks on the near side of the depot is Fourth Street. *Courtesy Mrs. J.J. Carroll*

A train loaded with White Furniture heads for the Panama Canal in 1906. The picture shows the intersection of Center and Fifth Streets with the original White Furniture factory in the background. *Courtesy Don Bolden*

The Mebane Bedding Company and White Furniture fueled Mebane's early growth and need for housing. *Courtesy Mrs. J.J. Carroll*

Looking east at the intersection of Clay and Fourth Streets. Wagons and stoves are for sale at Tyson Malone Hardware on the right. A few stores and livery stables line Clay Street on the left where Dollar General is located today. *Courtesy Mrs. J.J. Carroll*

The intersection of Third and Center looking north shows the Mebane Fair was being held. Veterans Garden is now located in the wooded lot to the right and Davis and Humbert Attorneys now sits in place of the billboard on the left. *Courtesy Mrs. J.J. Carroll*

W. Y Malone, W.W. Corbett and J. Sam White were among the Association's original founders. *Courtesy Luanne Jobe Nicholson, Kingsdown, Sam White*

James Shaw Vincent, Dave White and A.N. Scott were members of the Association's first board of directors. *Courtesy Jane Iseley, Sam White, Kingsdown*

CERTIFICATE

FOR

5

SHARES

Mebane
Home Builders' Association

ISSUED TO

Lacy Jobe

DATED

May 1910.

The Association raised money in its early days by selling "shares" which were essentially certificates of deposit. This certificate issued to Lacy Jobe in 1910 shows Jobe has five "shares" or $500 on deposit.

Street No.................

Series No.................

No.................

OFFICE OF THE

Mebane
Home Builders' Association

OF MEBANE. N. C.

SEP 29 1910 19.......

APPLICATION FOR LOAN

By Mrs. J. L. Johnson.

..........Shares, $.........., for.......... years.

.... 19.......

Referred to Committee of Inspection for examination.

L. Puryear
J. T. Shaw
P. Nelson
Com.

D. A. White [illegible]
President.

Mrs. J. L. Johnson submitted this loan application in 1910 for $600 to purchase a house and four acres on Fifth Street. The loan was to be repaid in 7 years with a 6% interest rate and a monthly payment of $8.77. The loan committee of Lewis Puryear, J.T. Shaw and Paisley Nelson inspected the property and president Dave White approved the loan.

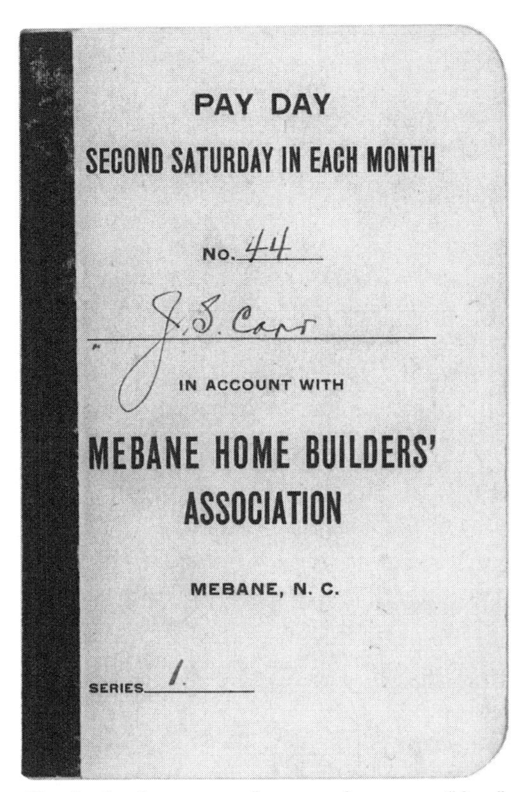

PAY DAY

SECOND SATURDAY IN EACH MONTH

NO. 44

J. S. Carr

IN ACCOUNT WITH

MEBANE HOME BUILDERS' ASSOCIATION

MEBANE, N. C.

SERIES 1.

Pay day books were used to record customer "dues" or monthly deposits. This book issued to J. S. Carr was number 44 from the first group of deposit shares in 1909. Note that deposits are to be made on the second Saturday of the month.

The Farmer's Warehouse can be seen on the left looking south from Graham Street down N. Second Street around 1920. *Courtesy Mrs. J.J. Carroll*

Facts About

Mebane Home Builders Association

It is purely a mutual Company,
It takes your monthly savings and puts them to work at 6 per cent.
It gives you back $100 for $83.00 paid in.
It is as safe as first mortgage on real estate can make it.
It creates the habit of systematic saving.
It lends your savings and collects your interest for you.
It creates and makes avavilable, a fund for building homes in your town.
It helps you if you want to buy, build, or repair your home.
It enables you to borrow, on easy terms without extra charge.
It gives you seven years to pay back, if you want it
It pays the taxes and pays you good interest.
It helps a young man to create a working capital with what he would "Blown In"
It is a good proposition if you want to Save, Invest, Borrow, or Lend.
It has done much good in Mebane.
It is growing, and will soon become one of the greatest agencies in the growth and development of our Town.
It's Mutual; It's Safe: It's Profitable.

For information ask those who are in it, for they believe in it.

Get ready for the next Series

Mebane Home Builders Association

A. J. Thompson, Sec. & Treas. **S. G. Morgan, President**

A brochure from 1919 explains the new concept of the Mebane Home Builders Association.

CHAPTER TWO

The Roaring Twenties

1920–1929

THE WORLD WAS RECOVERING from the ravages of war as the new decade began. The United States was spared the brutality and destruction left by four years of fighting, being separated from the rest of the world by two large oceans. Still, a foreign invader landed in the United States by the early 1920s, and no bullet could stop it. The influenza pandemic that spread through Asia and war-torn Europe reached the shores of the United States. Entire families were often lost, and Mebane did not escape the horror of the disease. Future First Savings president Neal Smith's father Carl Smith lost his first wife and infant daughter to the illness. Carl Smith soon fell victim himself, and doctors, unable to do much for him, waited for him to die so all three family members could be buried at the same time. Smith survived, but the deadly influenza outbreak took the lives of 15 million people worldwide, killing 13,644 in North Carolina.

A population shift occurred in the United States in the early 1920s, as more people lived in urban areas than in rural communities. The exception to this trend was in the agricultural South. The nation's postwar economy expanded through the decade as Americans bought houses, cars, and appliances in record numbers. The Dow Jones Industrial Average began its postwar surge in August 1921 at 63.90, rising 500 percent by 1929. Henry Ford's successful assembly-line method of manufacturing drove American factories, quenching the thirst of consumer spending. The average American family income reached $1,518, and although Americans were earning more, finding a safe place for one's savings posed some risk. Between 1921 and 1931, six hundred of the nation's thirty thousand banks failed each year.

A postwar building boom produced over 20 million owner-occupied homes by 1920 that averaged five rooms in size but offered little privacy to the typical five-member family. These homes were usually wood frame houses with no indoor plumbing, and tin roofs were common. Fireplaces, built for aesthetics in homes today, were essential for cooking and heating. House fires were so common that many homes were constructed with the kitchen separated from the main house. Since most fires started in the kitchen the thought was that the main house could be saved during a fire and only the kitchen would be lost. The American home in the early twentieth century had no insulation and was cold in the winter and hot in summer. First Savings' Neal Smith grew up in just such a house. "In the winter, Mom would pile quilts a mile high on you when you went to bed, and how you laid down was the way you woke up, 'cause you couldn't roll over with all that weight on you. We had a tin roof, and in the summertime the house would heat up like an oven. All the windows were opened. A lot of times we would go outside and sit on the porch at night and wait for the house to cool down before we went to bed."

Like the rest of postwar America, Mebane was booming and times were good. The town's population reached 1,351 by 1920, forcing the city to make necessary improvements to accommodate the demands of a vibrant and growing community. The town accumulated bond debt that reached six hundred thousand dollars during the 1920s, establishing basic amenities that made growth more certain and attractive to businesses and home owners. Water and sewer services were introduced, and Mebane paved some of its major streets and constructed sidewalks. The town's main water supply was water piped from Mill Creek and deep wells. The town's filtering plant and water reservoir was located on North First Street where the fire station is today.

As Mebane grew, so did the Mebane Home Builders Association. The board took on a group of new directors in early 1920 that influenced the future of the association for decades to come. S.G. Morgan was elected chairman of a board of directors that included A.J. Thompson, J.A. Williams, Paisley Nelson, A.N. Scott, J.S. White, B.F. Warren, U. S. Ray, J.C. Hall, and W.C. Weatherly. Another board member elected that day was John M. ("Mr. Mac") McIntyre.

Although Mr. Mac did not actually start the Mebane Home Builders Association, for all practical purposes, it is fair to say that he did. The early directors were novices at this new financial venture, groping in the dark for direction like a ship without a rudder. Since its founding eleven years earlier, the institution had elected three board chairmen, changed managing officers twice, and gone through twenty-five directors. The association never truly got off the ground until the election of John McIntyre. To describe McIntyre as a take-charge kind of guy is an understatement, as he rarely took no for an answer, making his own decisions that the board essentially rubber stamped. McIntyre was indeed a one-man show, which was exactly what the Mebane Home Builders Association needed. John McIntyre took the helm of this sleepy small-town institution and pushed it down the road to success.

Also elected to the board was C.R. Grant, but in early 1921 he withdrew all his stock (savings certificates) from the association and was relieved of his directorship. The vacancy was filled by one of the association's most beloved directors, A.B. Fitch, who served until his death fifty-one years later. Fitch owned the successful Fitch-Riggs Lumber Company located at the corner of Holt and Third streets beside the Mebane United Methodist Church. The lumber company was destroyed by fire in the 1940s and now is a parking lot for Kingsdown. Like fellow directors W.C. Weatherly and John McIntyre, Fitch lived on South Fifth Street across from the Presbyterian church, and his former home can be identified by an ivy-covered plaque that reads "Fitch House circa 1921."

The board experienced little turnover in its membership during the 1920s, finally achieving much-needed stability for the institution. Beginning in the 1920s, once elected, most directors rarely left the board, serving the institution for years and in many cases decades. In doing so they became seasoned, and with McIntyre at the helm, the association found direction and began to grow.

The 1920s is another period of the association's history that is difficult to document. Records are very incomplete, and what information is available reveals a tremendous growth in home loans. An example from the board minutes of February 1921 shows that eight loans totaling $15,800 were approved at that meeting alone.

A significant event in the life of the association took place on March 2, 1922, as the board minutes mentioned for the first time that a meeting took place at the Reliable Furniture Store on Clay Street. Beginning in the 1920s, Reliable Furniture became synonymous with the association as the institution operated inside the store until the early 1950s. Although this was the first mention of a meeting held at the furniture store, the association had not settled on this location exclusively and still met in other places, including the Town Hall and Chamber of Commerce Hall. There is no documentation as to when the association actually moved into the furniture store, but by the late 1920s the institution was regularly transacting business there. Director John McIntyre owned Reliable Furniture, and by providing the institution its first home, McIntyre created customer traffic for both the store and the association.

In 1920 American Legion Post 95 was organized in Mebane, and its membership elected Coy Patton as the first commander. As the town grew so did the need for more services, including fire protection. In 1922 the town commissioners authorized W.T. Dillard to organize the Mebane Volunteer Fire Department. Mebane's all volunteer department had a fire chief, an assistant and twenty-five fire fighters. The town purchased its first fire engine in August 1923 and kept it parked in a garage on West Center Street (Washington St) where the first fire station would eventually be built. The department had no way to summon volunteers to an emergency and the whistle at the Mebane Iron Bed Company, next to White Furniture, was used as the department's fire alarm.

That alarm sounded on December 21st, 1923 as a horrific fire swept through the White Furniture Company and Mebane's largest employer burned to the ground. The original White factory built in 1881 was a wooden structure, and the blaze quickly overwhelmed any efforts to fight it. Many Mebane residents were now unemployed and feared the company would not reopen. Being so close to Christmas, owner Will White gave everyone at White Furniture their Christmas bonus and stated that those who could wait until the plant was rebuilt would be hired back. White Furniture Company resumed operations just seven and a half months later.

Perhaps tragedies and events like the White Furniture fire and the influenza outbreak brought people together and molded Mebane's early identity. Being a small town, everyone knew each other, worked together, and worshiped on Sunday together. Children played and went to school with each other and formed lifetime friendships. Men hunted and fished with each other, and women formed social clubs that improved the community's quality of life.

This resilience and community spirit allowed the town to recover from the White Furniture fire, and by 1924 life was returning to normalcy. Mary Jobe became the manager of Rose's 5 and 10 Cent Store, and John Trollinger's brickyard and cotton gin on West Holt Street were busy as ever. On Graham Street in Burlington, the Pioneer Plant of Burlington Mills began operations, resulting in the birth of what would become textile giant Burlington Industries.

This was a time of little regulation and oversight of financial institutions, and the association's board had plenty of latitude in running the business. Director A.N. Scott, co-owner of the Mebane Bedding Company, docked the pay of one of his workers five dollars when Scott learned at a directors' meeting that the worker was delinquent on his dues to the association. Board members were expected to be civic-minded and were involved in the community. When the Mebane Kiwanis Club was formed in 1924, every member of the institution's board was a charter member.

The richest man in America in 1928 was Al Capone, whose illegal income was estimated at $100 million a year, compared to the average citizen who earned $2,470. Still the decade had been one of promise and prosperity, with most Americans earning more than ever, pushing average home prices to a record high of $7,782. The association's directors thought this was a good time to set up a reserve account to "take care of any unforeseen losses." With the events that were about to unfold, the timing could not have been better.

In nearby Haw River, the Granite Mill, so named for the natural granite foundation of the site, was purchased by textile giant Cone Mills. The plant would evolve into the Granite Finishing Plant, one of Cone's largest components in North Carolina's thriving textile industry. At a time before environmental laws, manufacturing plants of all kinds routinely discharged waste from their operations into the air and local waterways. The Granite Plant's location on the Haw River provided memorable aromatic experiences for anyone crossing the narrow two-lane bridge through the small mill town.

C.S. Loftis, owner of the Mebane Feed and Flour Mill, joined the association's board in February 1929, but it was discovered that Loftis did not own any shares in the association and he was relieved as a director. In April the board filled the vacancy with a gentleman who provided constant and consistent leadership for the next thirty-eight years. That man was S.M. Hupman Sr. Hupman had purchased the Ridgeville Phone Company from D.W. Ledbetter in 1922, changing the name to the Mebane Home Telephone Company.

No documentation is available as to the asset size and strength of the institution at this time, but collectively building and loan associations in North Carolina had total assets of $95 million by the end of the decade. By the late 1920s, the association was consistently holding board meetings and transacting business at the Reliable Furniture Store. It took twenty years, but the Mebane Home Builders Association finally had a roof over its head, albeit someone else's roof. It is unclear at this time if the association had regular hours inside the furniture store, but it can be assumed that any business requests came through Reliable Store owner and now managing officer of the association, John McIntyre. Still a part-time endeavor, the association was moving in the right direction, thanks to McIntyre's leadership. The strength of that leadership was about to be tested.

The 1920s had been a period of prosperity not only for the country but for the town of Mebane. In 1929 Young's Jewelry Store opened on North Fourth Street, and the Mebane Music Club was founded by Mrs. W.A. Harper of Elon College, becoming a lasting Mebane institution.

The Mebane Bedding Company expanded by purchasing the Silkheart Mattress Company in Sanford, Florida. In 1928 the company merged with Royall and Borden Manufacturing Company of Goldsboro and the Cotton Belt Manufacturing Company of Rocky Mount, changing its name to the Mebane-Royall Company. The Mebane-based mattress maker now maintained five manufacturing plants.

The United States was on the brink of a horrible economic disaster and was totally unprepared for it. There were no safeguards, no deposit insurance, and no health or retirement benefits. The role of government in the 1920s was entirely opposite from its dominance of American life in 2009. Americans of the 1920s believed in the ability of the individual to succeed or fail, and the populace saw the government as somewhat of a nuisance and often an intrusion. "The less government the better" was the feeling of most Americans. Former president Calvin Coolidge once remarked that "if the United States government ceased to exist, no one would notice," as seen in the isolationist position the country took after World War I, when the United States pulled away from foreign affairs and concentrated on its own situation.

And it was a good situation. The high times and good life of the decade spurred speculation in stocks. As the market continually moved higher, banks jumped on the bandwagon, lending money to fuel the buying frenzy. Investors could borrow up to 75 percent of the value of a stock purchase, and nearly 40 percent of all bank loans, as the decade drew to a close, were made to buy stock. The Dow Jones Industrial Average continued unabated, reaching a peak on September 3, 1929, of 381.17. Unsuspecting investors confident in the market's stability would not see the Dow at this level again until 1954. The party finally ended on October 29, 1929, when the U.S. stock market crashed and $30 billion of investment evaporated, plunging the country into the Great Depression.

The Clay Street business district looking west from Fourth Street was undergoing change around 1910. *Courtesy Mrs. J.J. Carroll*

By the 1920s, Clay Street took on its familiar appearance known today. The sign in the middle of the intersection was common in town cautioning drivers. The sign says to "go right." *Courtesy Mrs. J.J. Carroll*

A woman crosses the unpaved intersection of Third and Clay Streets around 1920. The Mebane Bedding Company is in the background and the Mason's Building stands on the right. *Courtesy Mrs. J.J. Carroll*

One hundred years later, Kingsdown's walkway over Third Street remains a downtown fixture. IT Express now occupies the former Mason's building across the street from The Melville Trading Company.

The intersection of Fifth and Center Streets as it appeared around 1920. A portion of the depot can be seen to the far right. *Courtesy Mrs. J.J. Carroll*

Today the corner of Fifth and Center Streets still remains one of the busiest intersections in Mebane.

Center Street begins to take shape as the picture looking north on Fourth Street shows. The Rose's 5&10 Cent Store is on the right. Roses and the old fire station are possible locations where the first meeting of the Mebane Home Builder's was held in 1909. *Courtesy Mrs. J.J. Carroll*

The Five Star Center now occupies the old Roses's store reflecting downtown's evolution.

Looking west on Washington behind the depot around 1915 shows the two-story municipal building and the fire department in the background. Mebane's current city hall would be built in the lot on the left. *Courtesy Mrs. J.J. Carroll*

The old fire station on Washington Street as it appears today.

From 1920 to 1961, John M. McIntyre's leadership brought the Association through the Great Depression and World War II. *Courtesy Mrs. W.R. Hupman*

Looking east from the intersection of Clay and Third streets, this photo shows the Piedmont Warehouse on the left. The outline of a horse can be seen under the trees to the right. *Courtesy Mrs. J.J. Carroll*

The Reliable Furniture Company closed in the 1990s and this photo shows the building today. The Association operated inside the Clay Street business from the late 1920s until 1952.

A businessman's businessman. President of the Mebane Home Telephone Company, Sam Hupman Sr. served on the board of directors from 1928 to 1966. *Courtesy Bob Hupman*

This picture of Fifth Street looking North from the 1920s shows homes that the Association financed in its early years. The house on the far right belonged to Association director A. B. Fitch. *Courtesy Mrs. J.J. Carroll*

The Fitch Riggs Lumber Company can be seen on the right of the photo looking east on Holt Street. The site of the former lumber company is now the parking lot for Kingsdown. *Courtesy Mrs. J.J. Carroll*

CHAPTER THREE

The Depression Era

1930–1939

BY 1930, ONE IN EVERY TEN AMERICANS was foreign-born, proving that the United States was truly a land of diversity. In a few short years, the waves of immigrants who had come to America seeking a better life, settling mostly in the urban areas of the Northeast and Midwest, would question if life in America held true promise. The dreams of these newcomers and all citizens soon become a decade-long nightmare.

Mebane entered 1930 with a population of 1,568, and the good times of the 1920s had produced a meager unemployment rate of 3.2 percent. The economic effects of the market crash were not immediately felt, but factories and businesses gradually closed and unemployment worsened.

The banking system of the day was fragile, to say the least, with only a handful of meaningful laws and little oversight. There were 11,777 savings institutions nationwide in 1930, but only 7,500 survived the financial turbulence of the next ten years.

Somehow the financial sector survived the trauma of the market crash, making it through the new year with only minor problems. A year later, in October 1930, 600 banks nationwide closed their doors in rapid succession as panic gripped the industry, bringing the total bank closings for the year to 1,352. In North Carolina, 88 banks failed along with 233 building and loan associations. The real catalyst for consumer panic occurred on December 11, 1930, in the heart of the nation's financial district in New York City when the Bank of the United States shut down. The Bank of the United States was not owned by the government but its very name suggested otherwise, and the failure of the largest commercial bank to date had a tremendous psychological effect.

Nationwide, over twenty-six thousand businesses failed in 1930, and home foreclosures soared. As fear rose, depositors rushed to withdraw their savings from banks as quickly as possible. These massive withdrawals or runs on financial institutions became common as fear eroded confidence in the banking system. Before deposit insurance, savings deposits could be lost if an institution failed. Runs were devastating and often fatal as institutions were not liquid enough or prepared to deal with such heavy withdrawal demands all at once. Worried depositors took no chances, lining up outside institutions waiting for them to open and hoping to withdraw their money. In most cases, depositors who arrived at an institution first received their funds while others weren't so fortunate. Just as the stock market crash destroyed the financial fortunes of large investors, the subsequent bank failures of the Great Depression hit people of every economic position and status, and many folks lost everything.

Locally one of the early bank casualties was the Commercial Farmers Bank, which had opened in 1919. This distinguished building, highlighted by two prominent columns, still graces the corner of Clay and Fourth streets. Mebane music legend Joe Thompson was on Clay Street that day when rumors were flying that the Commercial Farmers Bank was in trouble. As a young boy Thompson recalled a line of desperate and worried customers stretching down Clay Street waiting their turn to go in the bank. These people weren't Wall Street investors; they were farmers and mill workers in a small working-class town, and what little savings they had were inside the vault at Commercial Farmers Bank. The Thompsons, like so many families, lost their family farm during the hard times of the Great Depression.

The association maintained accounts with the Commercial Farmers Bank for a decade, but it is not mentioned in the board minutes if these accounts were still open at the time the bank failed or if the association suffered a loss due to the bank's closing. It is almost certain that the Mebane Home Builders Association experienced a high rate of withdrawals during the early 1930s, but whether the association experienced any panic runs by its depositors is unclear.

Robert Mason grew up in Mebane and moved to Virginia, becoming the editor of the *Virginian-Pilot* newspaper. He later recounted this story, which was printed in the *Mebane Enterprise*:

> John McIntyre ran a sort of desktop building and loan association in his furniture store. Let me tell this: Dad put his savings in the S&L only to transfer them into his checking account at the [Commercial and Farmers] bank when it was time for my older brother and me to enter or return to college. On Friday morning in September, 1929 (I think it was) he went to Reliable to collect his money for deposit before banking hours closed at 2:00 pm. McIntyre seemed to have left the store just as Dad approached it. Dad waited for him to return probably irritated, he gave up and left. He figured to complete his business Monday. But on Monday the bank did not open. It was a dead duck. Our college funds meanwhile were secure in the Reliable vault.

The bank runs of the day gave rise to a story that has circulated in the banking industry ever since. Wachovia Bank had several branches throughout the state, and rumors were flying that a run was about to take place in its Asheville location. The nervous manager from Asheville phoned Wachovia's home office in Winston-Salem explaining the situation. Two of Wachovia's top officers loaded thousands of dollars in bags, threw them in the back of a Model A Ford, and drove all night to Asheville, which took several hours in those days. The two men arrived at the Asheville branch early the next morning before the bank opened. A long line of nervous depositors had already formed, confirming the bank manager's fears. The men unloaded the cash, piled it in the vault, and were able to meet the withdrawal needs of its customers. The story goes that since the bank went to such great lengths to protect its customers, confidence was restored in the bank, and a full-blown and possibly fatal bank run was avoided.

The association may not have experienced bank runs but still could not maintain consistent deposit inflows and loan production. The few loans that were made during the 1930s had the added clause, "when funds are available." Customers approved for mortgages often had to wait for months until the institution took in enough money to fund loans. As the local economy deteriorated, the association's loan delinquencies rose dramatically with a barrage of homes on the brink of foreclosure. Foreclosure was bad enough, but with plummeting real estate prices, the association faced the possibility of foreclosing on property that was rapidly declining in value. To avoid such a calamity, the institution waived and extended mortgage payments to members in serious trouble. With a decade of hard times still ahead, it is not surprising that the association's best lending year of the Depression era was 1930, as fifty-six loans were extended with a volume of $83,300. Worried that its members might lose their jobs in uncertain times, the directors denied most loan applications for the year 1931. As the local economy worsened, members fell further behind on mortgage payments and monthly dues installments, placing further strain on the institution.

The fast-paced commercial and residential activity of the 1920s all but disappeared for Mebane, and economic growth was at a virtual standstill. White Furniture was one of the few local factories able to stay open during the Depression, operating with reduced wages and shorter hours. The association's directors had seen the institution through the good times of the 1920s, but now the pendulum was swinging the other way and the association now faced a very uncertain future.

At the February 1931 annual shareholders' meeting, Director A.N. Scott asked the membership to allow him to step down from the board after his name was placed in nomination, stating that there are "other good men" who could serve in that capacity. After some discussion, Scott's request was denied. He was elected to the board anyway—with Scott casting the only "no" vote against himself—and he reluctantly served for another term on the board. Beginning in the 1930s, the institution's board minutes became more consistent. The records were in typed form and revealed that loan payments of members were falling woefully behind as nine loans were slated for foreclosure in August alone. By September the association had twenty-seven mortgage loans that were three months past due, including a loan to Director J.C. Hall.

The catastrophe and ensuing panic surrounding the banking system was partly due to the nation's economic collapse, but one of the main catalysts for global uncertainty was gold. The world's monetary system based its security on the gold standard for decades, and the strength of a nation's currency was directly related to that country's gold reserves. The global economy had been wavering, but when

Great Britain, a worldwide financial anchor, abandoned the gold standard in September 1931, a worldwide financial panic ensued. Investors rushed to liquidate their holdings, fearing that other countries might follow Britain's lead. This fear and uncertainty created a domino effect, and 2,293 U.S. banks failed.

By 1932 the unemployment rate hit 25 percent and another 1,453 banks failed. Construction of new homes had dropped 95 percent since the market crash in 1929. In those days, banks and savings and loans were basically businesses unto themselves with little supervision, access to liquidity, or deposit insurance. That year alone, twenty thousand businesses went bankrupt and twenty-one thousand people committed suicide, forcing the government to act.

Congress passed a series of laws and regulations in the early 1930s that transformed the financial system and, in the process, the government itself. In a effort to restore public confidence, Congress passed the Federal Home Loan Bank Act, creating the Federal Home Loan Bank. On October 11, 1932, the association passed a resolution to become a member of the FHLB and submitted an application referring to the association as "The Mebane Home Building and Loan Association." Although the resolution was passed, the association did not pursue membership in the FHLB at that time and would not become a member until the late 1940s.

Although money was scarce, the Mebane Kiwanis Club was doing its part to restore confidence by forming a committee "to get hidden money back into circulation." Franklin D. Roosevelt was elected president, promising a "New Deal" to a nation in economic ruin. The banking system would be one of his first great challenges.

By January 1933, mortgage loans that were three months past due for the association reached critical levels, including the loans of Director J.C. Hall and attorney T.C. Carter. Even with these delinquencies, Hall and Carter were reelected as director and attorney, respectively, at the annual shareholders' meeting, which had been permanently moved to the third Thursday in February. Also at this annual meeting, Director A.N. Scott, who had voiced his displeasure at being nominated as a director one year earlier, was not reelected and was replaced by J.E. White.

Despite the hard economic times, some Mebane entrepreneurs made a go of it as the City Market grocery store opened on Clay Street and pharmacist James S. White established the Carolina Drug Company on Center Street. Local dairy farmer C.M. Ray purchased the Melville Chevrolet Company, hoping car sales would soon pick up.

As these new enterprises were forming, the Mebane Home Builders Association found its very existence in jeopardy. By March, mortgage loan delinquencies climbed to thirty-four, and the directors worked with members in financial trouble trying to avoid foreclosure if possible. Many of the banks in the area had closed, and the directors called a special meeting to discuss what bank "could be considered safe." The association opened an account with the National Bank of Alamance in Graham.

With so many of its members unemployed, payments of membership dues and mortgage loans naturally fell behind. The institution's liquid funds ran dangerously low, forcing the association to pledge twelve thousand dollars in mortgage loans to the National Bank of Alamance in order to borrow six thousand dollars. There is no documentation of the reason for raising six thousand dollars, which was quite a large sum at the time. More than likely this money was needed to meet high withdrawal demands on series certificates, as new mortgage loans were nonexistent.

One out of every four Americans remained out of work during the winter of 1932. The Dow Jones Industrial Average reached its Depression-era low of 41.22 and had fallen 89 percent in three years. Full-scale panic hit the financial system again in February, and this time the paranoia ripped uncontrollably through the country, causing four thousand banks to fail in just two months.

By Inauguration Day on March 1, 1933, the first order of business for newly elected president Franklin Roosevelt was restoring order to a financial system on the verge of collapse. Roosevelt declared a nationwide bank "holiday" on March 6, and all banks in the country closed for a four-day period. On March 9, Congress passed the Emergency Banking Act of 1933, allowing banks to borrow funds from the Federal Reserve, which provided much-needed liquidity to meet panic withdrawals. The government continued to refine financial laws, and the Banking Act of 1933 passed in June, creating the Federal Deposit Insurance Corporation.

This legislation began a long process that put the broken financial system back together, regaining the public's confidence by insuring savings deposits. This insurance plan was originally designed to be temporary, insuring losses up to twenty-five hundred dollars.

The Banking Act of 1933, also known as the Glass-Steagall Act, set in motion other laws that would remain the foundation of the industry for half a century. Multiple bank failures resulted from the relationships between commercial banks that were involved with Wall Street investment banks, relationships that Glass-Steagall now strictly prohibited. The act established rate ceilings that controlled the interest rate paid by banks on certain forms of deposits. This rule, known as Regulation Q, was designed as a defensive tool to reduce bank failures by reducing interest costs. Still on the books in the 1960s, Regulation Q was extended to the savings and loan industry, contributing to its downfall in the 1980s.

The Reconstruction Finance Corporation (RFC), formed during the Hoover administration, pumped money into failing banks and kept them afloat. From 1933 to 1935 the RFC purchased more than $1.7 billion in preferred stock in the nation's slumping banks. By the program's end in 1935 the RFC had substantial interest in half of the nation's commercial banks. The government took a similar approach in 2008 by taking stock in many of the country's financial institutions, which is just one of many common threads between the Depression and the financial crisis of 2008.

Although the nation's savings institutions were extending few loans, the process of home lending had changed very little by the 1930s. Most mortgages were extended by local lenders with a ten-year maturity and required a 20 percent to 30 percent down payment with an interest rate that hovered near 7 percent. With 40 percent of the nation's mortgages in default, Congress passed the Home Owners Loan Act of 1933, regulating savings and loans and authorizing the Federal Home Loan Bank Board (FHLBB) to charter and regulate federal savings and loan associations.

The Great Depression paralyzed the country, reducing any international role the United States had in world affairs. The nation, licking its wounds, drifted further into isolation. Roosevelt's first one hundred days in office saw an unprecedented creation of government agencies. Until that point, government intervention in the lives of most Americans had been minuscule. Suddenly, government programs and laws influenced many areas of American life. Some saw Roosevelt's New Deal as an answer to a prayer while others resented the government's newfound role, fearful the nation was moving toward socialism.

The economic pain hit close to home as mortgage loans for the association that were three months past due peaked at a Depression-era high of thirty-nine. Never having faced such harsh economic times, the association extended and waived payments for troubled customers. But times were getting desperate, and by 1933 the association began a risky policy of not only extending payments but loaning extra money to members who were already in loan default to bring their loan balance current. This move was very dangerous as the association was basically lending more and more money to a delinquent and sometimes unemployed borrower who may not have been able to repay the debt. These loans were extended on properties declining in value with no real short-term hope that prices would rise. The intent was to buy time, and the decision to extend credit in this manner was a huge gamble with potentially fatal consequences if the economy and these delinquent loans continued to deteriorate.

For an ultra-conservative association to implement such a radical strategy certainly reflected the desperate times of that period, but in truth the association had no choice. It was either take a chance on the borrower and hope the economy improved or proceed with foreclosure and lose money on real estate the institution could not sell.

Fortunately this questionable and unconventional strategy worked. Although certainly dangerous, the extension of more credit allowed members to keep their homes, avoiding foreclosure and creating goodwill with customers who were in dire straits, many of whom became longtime, loyal customers.

With the high number of loans headed for foreclosure, it is difficult to interpret the board minutes regarding homes that actually reached the point of a foreclosure sale. Many times, the minutes mentioned that "foreclosure be initiated" sometimes on multiple properties, but subsequent minutes seldom mention if foreclosure actually occurred and if the property was sold or owned by the institution. The customer could have paid off the loan entirely or, in the most likely scenario, worked out a loan restructuring.

Many individuals, including the association's John McIntyre, profited during these difficult times as he and other opportunistic investors took over properties from distressed owners as real estate was going at fire-sale prices. McIntyre had an inside track, knowing what properties were on the brink of foreclosure and often took over payments of delinquent customers. While McIntyre certainly profited from this, the Mebane Home Builders Association did as well. By taking properties over from folks facing foreclosure, he enabled the Association to get these troubled loans off its books.

The only positive local economic news in 1933 was that Virgil Warren bought Pickard's Drug and Seed and changed the name to Warren's Drug Store. One of Mebane's most famous businesses was born.

Although the creation of deposit insurance quelled the wave of bank failures and panic runs, the near collapse of the financial system in America in the early 1930s created a general mistrust of financial institutions that took decades to heal. Many individuals took their chances hiding money in their homes in sometimes unsafe and often creative places. Neal Smith recalls a man who came into First Savings during the 1950s wanting to set up a deposit account. The man brought in money tied up in bundles that smelled like turpentine. When questioned, the man admitted he had placed the money in empty paint cans and buried them in his yard for years rather than risk placing his money in a financial institution.

More than half a million families nationwide had lost their homes to foreclosure over a three-year period, and Christmas 1933 was a bleak holiday for most Americans. The country was glad to say good-bye to 1933 as it had been a brutal, cruel year. With most Americans experiencing such misery, Congress decided the nation could use a drink to drown its sorrows and it repealed the Volstead Act, ending Prohibition. North Carolina didn't lift its ban on alcohol until July 1935. Some locals didn't seem to care if Prohibition was repealed, as home-built stills gave rise to North Carolina's moonshine industry.

As 1934 began, radio was king and families enjoyed the nightly ritual of sitting in their living rooms listening to news broadcasts and other programs, as well as President Roosevelt's Fireside Chats.

On July 14, 1934, association director Dr. J.M. Thompson died suddenly, and the following month, A.H. Jobe was elected to fill the vacancy. Very little information is available regarding Thompson's legacy as a director, having served just four years. Jobe, however, served a long tenure until his death almost forty years later. A.H. Jobe began working for the White Furniture Company in 1907 at age thirteen, where he labored in the sanding room. By age seventeen, Jobe advanced to the veneering department, where he stayed until he retired in 1962.

New laws and regulations poured out of Washington restoring stability to the nation's financial system. These laws may have helped the banks but did little to change the nation's economic condition. Lending reached its low point of the Depression era for the association in 1934, as just thirty-four loans were made, totaling $23,700.

Several bank robbers gained national attention during this period for their bold and daring holdups, becoming legends in American folklore. Although many of these thieves were also killers, they attained some measure of respect in the hearts of many Americans who had been financially ruined by bank failures. Some folks viewed the sometimes deadly exploits of these criminals as payback for a corrupt industry. In May 1934 Bonnie Parker and Clyde Barrow were killed by authorities in Louisiana, ending their crime spree, and John Dillinger, dubbed "Public Enemy Number One" by FBI Director J. Edgar Hoover, was killed outside a movie theater in Chicago.

In 1931 Haw River Bank cashier J. A. Long was carrying a one-thousand-dollar payroll for a local factory in his car when he was robbed at gunpoint. The Haw River Bank itself was robbed a few days later, as a masked gunman made off with five hundred dollars.

The toll that the Depression had taken on the nation's housing market was staggering. The average cost of a home had fallen to $3,400, down 57 percent from its high in 1928. The American worker saw his paycheck shrink to an average of $1,600 a year, down 36 percent in this same period. North Carolina lagged behind the nation in home values. At that time, the Mebane Home Builders Association was extending new home loan amounts at 75 percent of value, suggesting the average home in the Mebane area was worth approximately $2,133.

Another piece in the financial puzzle was put back together when Congress passed the National Housing Act (NHA) of 1934 in an effort to stabilize housing. Many felt that if the housing industry could recover, so would the entire economy. Until that point, most financial reform had been focused on banks, and the NHA created the Federal Savings and Loan Insurance Corporation (FSLIC), broadening deposit insurance to the thrift industry. The FSLIC was supervised by the Federal Home Loan Bank Board (FHLBB), offering the insurance to "approved institutions" and insuring deposits up to five thousand dollars.

When deposit insurance came available through the FSLIC, it is not clear whether the association's deposits automatically fell under the new deposit insurance program. Most likely they did not. The institution did not become a savings and loan association at the time, nor did it apply for insurance coverage. Institutions were required to be examined for safety and soundness to be approved for deposit insurance, and such an examination of the association was never mentioned or documented. Insured deposits of the association became official fifteen years later when the institution adopted a savings and loan charter.

The combination of government assistance and low real estate prices breathed new life into the housing industry. The new Federal Housing Administration provided long-term mortgage insurance. With less risk to lenders of buyers defaulting on loans, mortgage rates fell. Regulations setting home appraisal standards were established, and lenders accepted lower down payments on home purchases. Loans were amortized over longer periods, reducing monthly payments and making home ownership more affordable.

That the Mebane Home Builders Association survived this bleak period in American history is surprising. The fact that the association was a part-time venture certainly worked in the institution's favor. The few mortgage loans that were approved during this period were often stipulated with the statement that the home "required" work, such as painting, or replacing a roof or a porch.

By the mid-1930s, most bank runs that occurred in the early days of the Depression had disappeared. Apparently, increased demand for deposit withdrawals had ceased as John McIntyre reported that the association had thirteen thousand dollars of cash on hand to lend and suggested that "members of the association should advise friends and neighbors that now is the time to buy or remodel their homes." Hoping to capitalize on these funds, the association adopted the slogan, "Mebane Home Builders Association, Home Financiers, Turn your rents into homes." The association managed to survive for a century, and thankfully that catchy slogan did not.

On April 2, 1935, a series of storms and tornadoes ripped through the Piedmont, killing twelve in Greensboro. As the storm moved east through Alamance County, fire broke out in the Mebane Motor Company on Center Street, spreading quickly to the theater next door and completely destroying both buildings. These buildings were located where the Welcome Finance building is today. The fire was so massive that assistance was needed from the Graham and Durham fire departments to subdue the blaze. The Mebane Motor Company was a two-story building with an elevator that carried cars to the second floor for storage, and as the building burned, cars came crashing down through the ceiling of the first floor.

In June, Dr. H.C. Carr of Durham, "owner of the New Hollywood Theater," met with the directors of the association to obtain financing for a new movie theater building. Dr. Carr requested a loan of ten thousand dollars for the theater's construction. Loan approval was initially given for five thousand dollars, but the directors reconsidered, approving a seventy-five-hundred-dollar loan. This is a good example of the different loans made by the association at that time. In those days, loans were extended on a variety of properties, such as farms, garages, funeral homes, retail stores, and businesses, even the Mebane Fair Association.

The Mebane Fair or Four County Fair brought folks from Person, Orange, Caswell, and Alamance to Mebane and was a cross between a circus and state fair. From high-wire trapeze artists and baby contests to livestock, the fair was a popular tradition in Mebane up until the 1940s. The fairgrounds were west of the town on Highway 70 where Craftique is located today. Although the Fair Association loan was approved, the directors were not that desperate, rejecting a five-hundred-dollar loan request from a member offering his slaughter pen as collateral.

Home loans were the association's bread and butter, and although the lending policy at that time on certain types of property was somewhat liberal, the institution was known to be very conservative on how much risk it would assume when making a loan. This applied not only to the property used for collateral but also the individual requesting the loan. Director S.M. Hupman Sr. discovered firsthand that this conservative approach applied to directors as well when he submitted an application for a loan. Hupman was required to put his business, the Mebane Home Telephone Company property, in the loan as extra collateral.

In June 1935 J.C. Hall resigned from the board having served thirteen years, and was replaced by Paisley Nelson, who had apparently also left the board at some point during the 1930s, but no mention is made as to when he left or for what reason. Although his service had not been continuous, Nelson was the only remaining founding director of the institution who remained on the board.

Government's role in the lives of Americans grew larger in 1935 with the passage of the Social Security Act. Deposit insurance was made permanent by the Banking Act of 1935, establishing "assessments" or premiums to be paid into the insurance fund by banks and savings and loans. This time of massive government intervention and legislation reinvented the banking system, as only 373 banks failed in the eight-year period from 1934 through 1941.

The economic nightmare that gripped the country was far from over, yet Mebane seemed to be on the move in 1935. Bob Jones opened Jones' Department Store in the Russell Building at the corner of Clay and Fourth streets, establishing one of Mebane's most popular businesses. Dixie Yarn purchased Durham Hosiery on West Holt Street, changing the name of the operation to Rockfish Mebane Yarn. The Junior Woman's Club was formed, and Mrs. Carl Sykes and J.E. Barnette opened Ruby Mae's Dress Shop at 104 Clay Street.

A local literary club known as the Reviewers were seeking community support for the establishment of a library. Mayor June A. Crumpler and the White family contributed generously to the community-wide effort. The Mebane Public Library had its humble beginnings in the summer of 1936 at Mebane High School. The new principal of the school, E.M. Yoder, offered the use of a room at the school until a permanent location could be found.

America turned to various diversions to forget about their economic woes as the golden age of Hollywood was beginning and folks packed local movie theaters. Baseball had a strong local following, and Mebane native and sports legend, Lew Riggs, made it to the big time. Riggs was traded from the St. Louis Cardinals to the Cincinnati Reds, where he played for six seasons, appearing in one All-Star Game and the 1939 World Series.

By 1937 the local economy was on the mend and confidence was returning to prospective home buyers. Loan demand improved to the point that the association had to borrow $4,000 from the Durham Bank and Trust Company, which at that point had a branch in Mebane.

In January 1938 the board minutes reflected that the assets of the institution stood at $211,360; this was the first written financial statement in print since 1915. The board included a printed financial statement in its monthly minutes for a brief time but unfortunately ended this practice in the early 1940s.

These statements shed some light on the association's financial situation, but may not be a true indicator of the institution's financial condition. The system of accounting used at the time is somewhat confusing as some of the entries on these monthly statements list items as assets that would be considered liabilities on financial statements of today and vice versa. The statements often show sudden and tremendous shifts in assets, which is quite puzzling. For example, in December 1938 the financial statement indicated that the association's assets had more than doubled during that year alone, totaling $429,256. Interestingly, one year later in December 1939, the monthly statements indicate the association had lost about half of its assets and was $246,761 in size. Such a drastic and sudden change in the financial condition of the institution would seem to be a major concern, yet there is no explanation, comment, or statement as to the cause of this rapid shift. The fact that no documented explanation of these shifts exists may in itself confirm that these fluctuations were a regular occurrence and a reflection of the volatile times.

As 1939 drew to a close, renewed loan growth forced changes to the association's loan policies. "After a quite a bit of discussion the directors voted unanimously in favor of making long term loans, that is, twelve year loans on new well constructed buildings, or mighty good old dwellings. The dwellings must be in number one condition to qualify for this loan." This simple statement is a prime example of how most institutions of the day operated. Everything from property inspections and decisions were very subjective and left to the sole discretion of the board to determine value and risk that the property posed to the institution.

The board also amended the association's rules concerning stock ownership and instructed attorney T.C. Carter to research and prepare the requested bylaw changes. After a few months, Carter submitted the requested bylaw changes along with a bill to the association for seventy-five dollars. Apparently the directors felt that Carter's attorney bill was a bit too high and authorized payment to Carter of only fifty dollars for his services. The directors contemplated making loans that were insured through the Federal Housing Administration (FHA). Incredibly, the board debated this issue for six months before deciding not to offer such loans.

Improvements to the economy had been painfully slow over the past ten years, but there seemed to be light at the end of the tunnel. Businesses were opening, factories increased operating hours, and people were returning to work. The Fair

Labor Standards Act was passed, and the first-ever minimum wage was established at twenty-five cents an hour.

The depressed real estate market and bank closings of the 1930s created a strange relationship between banks and customers that would be repeated in 2008. It took decades for Americans, still smarting from bank failures, to trust the long-term stability of the nation's financial system. Likewise, the harsh economic times forged an ultra-conservative management style for most institutions that had been lucky enough to survive the decade and which viewed potential loans with tighter scrutiny. Depositors, fearful of losing money, often kept their savings at home while lenders were reluctant to lend.

Consumers and lending institutions had been devastated over the decade, and although America had been preoccupied through the 1930s with its own internal economic problems, war was looming. The country's armed forces were woefully inadequate, and President Roosevelt began to build its military capacity and in turn created jobs.

At the 1939 shareholders' meeting, Secretary-Treasurer John McIntyre addressed the membership and did not mince words, stating "that now was the time to get rid of all or any of the old directors that they do not want." After some discussion the membership got the same old directors who were once again reelected. The association borrowed another seven thousand dollars to meet the strong mortgage loan demand, raising hopes that an economic revival was on the horizon.

Confident that the economy was indeed turning around, E.E. Hodge opened C&H Motor Sales, and the new post office opened its doors on Center Street where the Mebane Police Department is today. The economy was on the verge of unprecedented growth, but it would come at a high price. The Depression changed the lives of every American, and the war years that were to come would do the same. On September 1, 1939, Germany invaded Poland, and the country fell to the Nazis in a month. France and England declared war on Germany, and although the United States was not directly involved in the conflict, the nation began to prepare for war. Burlington Mills raised wages by 15 percent, producing fabric for parachutes, uniforms, tents, and other war-related articles. North Carolina's textile mills turned out sheets, towels, canvas, socks, blankets, and even shoelaces for the military. Once America entered the conflict, one government official stated that North Carolina's textile production was so vital to the war effort "that every soldier and sailor in the service of the nation either wears or carries some article manufactured in North Carolina."

President Roosevelt, believing that a longer Christmas shopping season would boost the economy, proclaimed that Thanksgiving would be celebrated on the fourth Thursday of November, and the controversial shift in the holiday became law.

The Mebane Home Builders Association survived a decade of economic chaos and was now a thirty-year-old business. The last available financial statement from February of that year indicated the association ended the 1930s with total assets of $246,761 and $203,238 in total mortgage loans. The economy, depressed home values, and limited building coupled with frugal borrowers are revealed in lending numbers for the decade as the average loan extended by the association was just $909, a figure that changed very little during the ten-year period.

The despair of this era produced what journalist Tom Brokaw described as "the Greatest Generation"—Americans who, out of necessity and adversity, developed an incredible work ethic and value system with survival skills that somehow sustained them through this miserable period of American history. Tough and resourceful, this generation of Americans would step from the shadows of isolation to the center stage of world affairs. In less than a decade, the country went from the depths of the Great Depression to the most powerful nation the world has ever known.

The Mebane Home Builders Association inside the Reliable Furniture Store *Courtesy Mebane Enterprise*

West Center Street is seen from this shot of the depot from the 1930s. The two story house was the original home of the White family, owners of White Furniture, and was located where Kerr Drug is today. The infamous magnolia tree can be seen beside the house. *Courtesy Don Bolden*

A car passes over the tracks at Fourth Street in the 1930s. Several businesses on Center Street can be seen in the background including the City Café. The large building in the center was the Hollywood Theater. (Welcome Finance today). The post office, now the police department, was built in the vacant lot next to the theater in 1939. *Courtesy Don Bolden*

Customers say goodbye at the closing of the Quality Store on Clay Street in 1938. To the left of the store is Ruby Mae's Dress Shop and the double doors lead to the Tyson Clinic. The building with the columns is the Commercial Farmer's Bank that failed in 1930. *Courtesy Don Bolden*

A crowd gathers at an accident on the tracks at Third Street. Across Center Street a Sinclair station is open where Veterans Garden is today. The white building across the street is Eagle Oil Company and next to it is Melville Chevrolet. The second house past the dealership is the Cooper house where First Savings built its current location in 1960. *Courtesy Mebane Historical Museum*

The depot in 1935 shows the building sits only a few yards from Fifth Street. The Mebane-Royall Company (Kingsdown) water tower is seen in the background. *Courtesy Don Bolden*

Downtown Mebane bustles with activity as the fall market begins at the tobacco warehouses. *Courtesy Mebane Enterprise*

Despite the hard economic times of The Great Depression, cars line Mebane's vibrant downtown business district. *Courtesy Don Bolden*

A concerned crowd in front of the Raleigh Bank and Trust Company during the financial uncertainty of the 1930s. This was a common sight as "bank runs" caused many of the nation's financial institutions to fail. *Courtesy of the North Carolina State Archives*

CHAPTER FOUR

It's a Wonderful Life

1940–1949

SELECTING A DECADE FROM THE TWENTIETH CENTURY that truly captures the American spirit, one would have to look no further than the 1940s. Americans entered the decade full of uncertainty as the economy slowly improved. In a few short years, the nation went from the dark days of the Great Depression to fighting a world war. By the middle of the 1940s, most Americans truly believed that they could accomplish anything. The prosperity of the late 1940s gave birth to the baby boom generation, a consumer-driven middle class, and a home-building bonanza for the savings and loan industry. It was the decade the Mebane Home Builders Association made the final transition from a part-time endeavor to a full-time, thriving business, placing the final bricks in the foundation of what would become the First Savings and Loan Association.

The association entered the new decade having survived its toughest challenge in its thirty-year history, and its leadership having earned the confidence and loyalty of its members. The customer base the institution forged during this period became its foundation for generations to come, and the institution would reap the benefits when it became a stand-alone business.

Veteran board members A.B. Fitch, A.H. Jobe, S.M. Hupman Sr., John M. McIntyre, Paisley Nelson, J.E. White, and W.C. Weatherly were reelected. The same officers were appointed as John McIntyre remained secretary-treasurer; W.C. Weatherly, president; and S.M. Hupman Sr., vice president. The same leadership who led during the hard times of the 1930s would see the association through a world war and the prosperity that followed.

The Mebane Home Builders Association jumped out of the gate in 1940 with its best lending year in ten years, closing seventy-five home loans totaling seventy-seven thousand dollars. What was encouraging was that the foreclosures and mortgage delinquencies that had plagued the institution for a decade were declining.

Since the association operated in the Reliable Furniture Store, overhead was low, and it can only be assumed that other individuals who may not have been actually employed by the association assisted in the day-to-day business. The first indication of others working on behalf of the institution was recorded in the minutes from December 1940. The directors—obviously in a generous holiday spirit, but not wanting to go overboard—ordered boxes of candy for Miss Pauline Nicholson and Mrs. Van White "in appreciation for the work they did during the past year." An impressive compensation package to be sure.

The economic cloud that hung over the country for the previous eleven years was lifting, and people were working again. But another problem was on the horizon. The nation was at peace, but war was breaking out everywhere as Denmark, the Netherlands, Belgium, and France had fallen victim to the Nazi Blitzkrieg. Hitler focused his war machine on England, and a full-scale air war was under way. Asia was in turmoil also, as the empire of Japan was flexing its power in the Far East.

Mebane crossed an important milestone in 1940 with 2,060 residents. A 31 percent population growth during the Depression years was quite remarkable and showed the town's resilience. The twenty-four graduates of Mebane High in 1940 saw changes to their school as a gymnasium, science, and library buildings were added to the campus. This class was the first in the school's history to have a printed annual named *The Trumpet*, organized by English teacher Annie Crawford. Around 1940 the Mebane teacherage was started at 212 West Jackson Street across the street from the Mebane Public School. The teacherage offered a place for the school's single female teachers to live.

By 1941 Mebane's economy returned to life as J. S. White acquired the hotel above his drugstore—the Carolina Drug Company located on Center Street, where the Five Star Center is today—and aptly named it the White Hotel. The Mebane Library that opened five years earlier in a room at Mebane High School was in desperate need of larger facilities and looking for a permanent home. Mrs. W.S. Harris, the driving force in making the library a reality, once again saw an opportunity as the vacant bank building, once home to the Commercial Farmers Bank, was for sale for three thousand dollars. Harris began a campaign to purchase the building, bringing her case before the Mebane Town Commissioners. Members of Mebane's governing body at this time were referred to as "commissioners," but later the name was changed to the Town Council. The commissioners were reluctant to "use taxpayer money for such an endeavor." Undaunted, Harris and the community pulled together with assistance from the Kiwanis Club and private donations. John McIntyre chaired the fund-raising committee, and Mrs. Harris served as secretary. Sam White led the way, pledging twelve hundred dollars, and L.P. Best acquired money from both Alamance County and the Mebane Community Chest. The Town Commissioners soon relented and with funds secured, the building was purchased in December 1941 and deeded to the town. The library moved to its new home in 1942, where it remained until the mid-1970s.

Home lending was back, particularly construction loans, and by November loan applications were so strong that John McIntyre stated that the association's bank balance was "depleted." This is a prime example of how quickly funds could be loaned out in a short period of time as the association relied solely on local deposits to fund loans. The association turned once again to Durham Bank and Trust Company to borrow funds to meet this sudden and welcome demand.

The nation was climbing out of the Depression, yet any hope for good times came to an abrupt end on December 7, 1941. Japanese forces attacked the U.S. naval base at Pearl Harbor, and America officially entered the war. A nation mired in economic misery for over a decade was suddenly full of economic activity as the country geared up for a worldwide conflict. Burlington Mills and other local textile factories operated at full capacity, producing items for the war effort. The Fairchild Aircraft Plant located on Graham Hopedale Road in Burlington produced the AT-21 Trainer airplane for the army. Over five thousand residents from Alamance County entered the various branches of the armed forces.

World War II was fought on several fronts, including the home front, as the war touched the lives of every American, not just those in uniform. People who were not involved directly in the military were employed in factories making equipment, ammunition, or some item related to the war effort. What was strikingly different in the workforce from times past was the strong presence of women in jobs traditionally reserved for men. "Rosie the Riveter" became a wartime icon, revealing the importance and contribution of women in the workplace. Rationing of everything from food to gasoline to tires forced Americans to again sacrifice as they had during the Depression years.

In 1942, 80 percent of the U.S. federal budget went to the war effort, and a nation ravaged by unemployment rolled up its sleeves and went to work. The demand for transportation of goods encouraged Burlington-based Barnwell Brothers Trucking Company to merge with several other regional carriers to form Associated Transport. German U-boats torpedoed ships off the North Carolina coast, and there was fear that the U.S. mainland could come under attack. The N.C. Building and Loan League encouraged associations to purchase war damage insurance. The directors passed on the insurance as Mebane was not exactly a high-priority target. Those on the West Coast weren't as confident. Fearful of an attack, the Rose Bowl was moved from Pasadena, California, to Durham, North Carolina, where Duke lost to Oregon State 20-16 in the New Year's Day football classic.

The U.S. Treasury issued Liberty Bonds to fund the war's massive cost. War bonds were being offered in schools, post offices, and most financial institutions, including the Mebane Home Builders Association. The war years presented a different challenge for the association as the demand for mortgage loans that showed promise in 1941 fell sharply. Unemployment during the Depression stymied loan demand and prevented consistent deposit inflows for the association. Ironically, the nation came close to full employment over the next three years, but the war itself now stood in the way of loan demand as building materials and other items were in short supply due to rationing. Such was life in America until the war ended.

As the war economy kicked into high gear and with people steadily working, mortgage payments and monthly dues were paid on a more consistent basis. What the war economy took away in loan demand, it gave back in savings deposits. Money flowed into the association like never before, and the institution found itself with an abundance of cash. Unfortunately, the association had no place to put the money to work locally as loan demand vanished. In years past, the institution had little excess cash as deposits stayed loaned out for home mortgages. The economics of war allowed the association to regularly invest in government bonds that paid a reasonable return. The association purchased war bonds of ten thousand dollars in February, eleven thousand dollars in June, and fifteen thousand dollars in September. These were substantial amounts for that time, given that the average home loan for the association in the early 1940s was one thousand dollars. The abundance of cash prompted a notice from the Durham Bank and Trust Company stating the bank could not guarantee deposit insurance because the association's balance exceeded five thousand dollars.

In February 1942, two "employees," Miss Marie Thompson and Mrs. Frances Terrell, were mentioned in the board minutes. One year earlier, the board had expressed appreciation to Miss Nicholson and Mrs. White for their work, but it is not clear if they were still assisting the association. Miss Thompson's relationship with the association was apparently brief, but "Miss Frances," as she was affectionately known, built a career spanning nearly six decades. Terrell served in several capacities, including corporate secretary, and continued her relationship with the institution until her death in 1993.

The association's low point in lending for the decade occurred during 1943 as only thirteen loans were closed, totaling $21,300 for the entire year. Put in perspective, this was the lowest loan total on record since the early 1920s. Before the decade was over, the association would close more loans in one month than it did in the entire year of 1943. Delinquent installment dues payments that averaged twenty per month dropped to just eight by August.

First Savings had a total of $55,000 in war bonds on its books and, despite the simplicity of its operations, saw the need to hire a bookkeeper. Miss Marie Thompson was elected for this position, and Mrs. Frances Terrell was appointed as assistant bookkeeper. Their salary, according to the minutes, was quite unusual at "$1.00 a year and other such amount as may be prescribed." It can be assumed that the work performed by these "employees" was voluntary.

The association's reserve account set aside for emergency contingencies reached $13,500, and the abundance of cash prompted the directors to look for ways to revive home loans. The association lowered its interest rate on future mortgages to 5 percent and introduced a rate reduction loan. This was essentially a contract between the institution and existing customers that reduced the interest rate temporarily on mortgages that the association currently held. This type of loan modification was new territory, and the board enlisted attorney T.C. Carter to research the idea. In April, the rate reduction loans went into effect with a 5 percent interest rate. The promissory notes were drawn at a 6 percent interest rate, and the contract stated that the institution could increase the rate up to the original note rate of 6 percent. A form of this loan contract is still offered today.

Health care changed for Mebane in 1944 when doctors George McLamb and W.E. Cook purchased the Tyson Clinic from Drs. T.D. Tyson and Woodrow Tyson. The new doctors changed the name to the Mebane Clinic, and the practice operated at its familiar Clay Street address until the 1980s. This location is now home to Martinho's Restaurant.

The war took a dramatic turn on June 6, 1944, as the Allies stormed the beaches of Normandy; the nation began planning for postwar America. Just as the invasion of France on D-Day altered the course of the war, events later that month shaped the economy of postwar America in dramatic fashion. On June 22 President Roosevelt signed into law the Servicemen's Readjustment Act of 1944, better known as the G.I. Bill. This legislation provided enormous benefits ranging from health care and housing to education for returning servicemen and women. The G.I. Bill would not only repay part of a huge debt the nation owed its veterans, but the benefits sparked a postwar boom in housing. More than 15 million veterans were eligible for these benefits, and lenders across the country recognized the potential for lucrative returns. This opportunity was not lost on the Mebane Home Builders Association, as John McIntyre and attorney T.C. Carter worked through the details to set up Veterans Administration (VA) loans. On July 19, 1945, the association approved its first ever VA loans to James Tate and Patrick Jones.

As 1944 drew to a close, President Franklin D. Roosevelt was elected to an unprecedented fourth term. As the nation began to think about life after the war, Hitler launched a bold German counterattack in the Ardennes Forest, igniting the costliest battle in U.S. history. More than eighty-one thousand Americans fell in the cold Belgian snow that December in what became known as the Battle of the Bulge, briefly deflating hopes for an end to the war in Europe.

America had focused on nothing but war for five years, but the nation and Mebane were on the verge of another economic explosion. For fifteen years, the town had experienced very little growth, and with the war winding down, optimism grew. Local folks must have anticipated a building boom as Crumpler Lumber Company, soon changed to Crumpler-McLeod Lumber Company, became the third lumber mill operating in town, joining Fitch-Riggs Lumber Company and Builders Supply. T.L. Jefferies and J.J. Carroll opened Central Motors as a Desoto-Plymouth dealership, and Mr. and Mrs. D.L. McBane opened McBane's Store just east of town on Highway 70. The Village Store opened on Clay Street, becoming a downtown business landmark for over sixty years.

Roosevelt had been president of the United States for over twelve years, leading the nation through arguably two of the most difficult periods in its history: the Great Depression and World War II. But Roosevelt would not see the final Allied victory. The ailing president passed away in April, and the completion of the war effort fell on the shoulders of Vice President Harry Truman. Just one month after Roosevelt's death, Germany formally surrendered on May 8, and the conflict in Europe ended. War still raged in the south Pacific as the Marines and navy continued to island-hop closer to Japan.

During its early years, the Mebane Home Builders Association was regulated by the State of North Carolina Commission of Insurance. Auditors from the state arrived unannounced, and minutes reflect that the association was usually examined each November. An audit normally lasted from one to two weeks, and upon completion the examiners usually met with the board of directors to present their findings. Minutes indicated that only minor issues were brought to the board. One auditor who examined the association on several occasions was J.D. Taylor. Familiar with the association's practices, Taylor began making suggestions to improve the institution.

The Mebane Home Builders Association had operated on a part-time basis, never straying far from the basic Oxford model for the previous thirty-five years. In July 1945 Taylor and the directors initiated changes that charted a new course for the association. Taylor recommended that the association switch from the antiquated series savings installments, which had been in place since 1909, to regular passbook savings accounts. The board approved this recommendation on July 21, 1945.

After making the switch to passbook accounts, the directors made a critical decision, one they would later regret. They restricted these savings accounts to accepting one-hundred-dollar limits per month per family. For most families in a working-class town like Mebane, saving one hundred dollars a month during the 1940s was not realistic. Still somewhat puzzling is why any restrictions would be placed on accepting deposits, given that securing deposits had been an ongoing challenge since the institution began. At the time, the institution was flush with cash, which could have been one factor. The main reason deposit limits were imposed was control. The amount of money a person had on deposit at the institution determined the number of voting shares that an individual had as a shareholder, and board members were the largest shareholders. Having more voting shares assured their continued position on the board, and limiting deposit amounts kept other shareholders from gaining any more votes. The decision, however, had a detrimental effect of slowing the growth of savings account monies, which were desperately needed to fund a soon-to-be-exploding demand for home mortgages. Some fifteen years later, differing philosophies and control of the association's votes came to a head.

In August 1945 the Japanese cities of Hiroshima and Nagasaki were destroyed with the first-ever use of atomic weapons. World War II officially ended, and by the end of 1945 veterans returned home ready to pursue the American Dream of owning a home. That dream and consumer spending drove the economy forward for the next twenty years.

The average cost of a home jumped to $4,625. Home values in North Carolina lagged behind the national average, as one entry in the association's board minutes states that the association made a loan for $2,575 "to construct a new three-bedroom house," which would have to be considered on the high end of the cost spectrum.

The birth rate in the United States increased by 20 percent in 1946 as the baby boom generation was born. Relations between the United States and the Soviet Union deteriorated and brought on the Cold War that lasted over forty years.

Americans were earning more, as the average annual wage climbed to $2,390. The business of making home loans that had been dormant sprang to life, aided by the popular VA mortgages. The increase in loans prompted the appointment of June A. Crumpler as assistant attorney to T.C. Carter. By April, Carter and Crumpler were very busy as the highest number of loan applications in four years was approved.

Mebane was once again bustling with activity, which had been pent up for a decade. On Highway 70, west of town, the first piece of mahogany furniture rolled off the assembly line at Craftique Inc. Craftique developed a worldwide reputation for quality furniture that was a reflection of company owner L.P. Best's attention to detail. The upscale furniture found its way into some the nation's finest homes and institutions, including the White House, the Smithsonian museums, and the Library of Congress.

Walker's Funeral Home opened in 1945 on West Center Street. In those days the role of a funeral home included not only traditional burial services but also ambulance service. The creation of emergency medical services, or EMS, was still decades away.

F.L. Duncan purchased the local feed mill on East Center Street, changing the name to Mebane Flour and Feed Mills. The local American Legion Post 95 had more than two hundred active members and the following year purchased nineteen acres of land at the end of West Clay Street. J.A. Isley and C.H. Cates opened the Country Store on Highway 70, and W. Conrad Sutton and Howard Kirkpatrick purchased the Mebane Laundry on West Clay Street from the Isley brothers. Apparel Inc. purchased the old Continental Chair Factory building at the corner of Fifth and East Center (now Washington) streets, where the city of Mebane planning offices are located today.

Unfortunately, one longtime Mebane business would not take part in the economic prosperity that was to come. On October 2, 1945, the Fitch-Riggs Lumber Company, located at the corner of Holt and South Third Street and owned by association director A.B. Fitch, burned to the ground. The fire threatened nearby homes for a brief time before firefighters could subdue the blaze.

Home building caught fire in a figurative sense, and the association—flush with cash a year ago, but operating with self-imposed savings account limits—was rapidly running out of money to lend. By late October the association borrowed twenty thousand dollars from Durham Bank and Trust "to meet the loan activity until we can get some...government bonds cashed." One reason loans were strong was the popularity of VA loans that now composed a large portion of the association's loan portfolio. Concerned that the association might be originating too many of these mortgages, the board contacted the State Building and Loan Association to determine the appropriate percentage of VA loans an association should have as part of its total loan portfolio. The state responded that "40 percent is about right."

With the postwar building boom officially under way, new and modern methods of development emerged. Levittown, a middle-class suburban housing development, was built on Long Island, New York, and by 1970 more Americans lived in suburbs than in cities. Confidence had returned to the nation's financial system, as just twenty-nine institutions failed between 1942 and 1946.

Like other returning veterans, Mebane native David Freshwater was looking for a job. He assumed the family business, Freshwater's Store, when his father passed away in 1946. Freshwater's, at the corner of Crawford and North Second streets, was one of many local general stores operating in their heyday. Freshwater had a unique style of running his business as he never used a cash register and did all the figures in his head. The store didn't even have a telephone.

The local housing boom prompted the Crumpler-McLeod Lumber Company and Builders Supply to merge, forming the Mebane Lumber Company. G.N. Hoover and his son Leo opened the Hoover Sash and Door Company just east of town.

The downtown tobacco warehouses had a record year in 1947 as 9.5 million pounds of tobacco were sold. Civic activities came to life once again as the Mebane Exchange Club was formed.

The First Baptist Church on South Third Street completed its new sanctuary following a devastating fire, and the association approved its largest loan to date of $20,000 for the church. The association enjoyed record loan production as $180,000 in VA loans were extended in just two years. Too much of a good thing was hard to take, and the directors again expressed concern that too many VA loans might be risky. After complaining of no loans a few years earlier, the association now had more loans than it had money to lend. After just two years of extending VA loans, the association discontinued accepting VA applications. It was becoming clear that the Mebane Home Builders Association could no longer operate in part-time capacity and meet the needs of a growing community.

The association had never loaned out more than $100,000 in one year in its history. In 1946 and 1947, loan totals of $270,900 and $312,100 were made, respectively, reflecting the incredible housing market. The Home Builders Association extended more home loans in these two years than in the decade of the 1930s.

Demand for home loans came from outside the Mebane community as well, as home loans were approved for Burlington, Hillsborough, and Efland. The board raised mortgage loan rates to 6 percent, and the abundance of loans quickly ended the need for rate reduction loans.

When searching for a home loan, customers in Alamance County had a choice of four savings institutions: one in Graham, two in Burlington, and the Mebane Home Builders Association. What these customers didn't have was a choice of loan products. Mortgage rates were highly regulated, and savings institutions offered identical terms. All thrifts were virtually the same, but what set them apart was the availability of money. Hampered by small deposits, the strong loan demand of the time caused some institutions to literally run out of money to lend, forcing customers to seek loans from other lenders. The key to retaining customers over the long haul was local savings deposits, and customers who were lost to another institution that had money were most likely lost for good.

After forty years in operation the board was convinced that the institution simply could not continue operating on a part-time basis. In 1948 many changes that impacted the future of the institution were put in place. The community had associated the institution with the Reliable Furniture Store, as the association had operated in the Clay Street business since the 1920s. The association's attachment to the store was necessary in its early days and perhaps its saving grace during the Depression. But now it was obvious that the association had to cut the cord from the furniture store and establish its own identity in a separate location. Still, it wasn't that simple. Before this independence could be achieved, numerous internal changes were necessary.

The first change was set in motion in early January 1948 when examiner J.D. Taylor returned to discuss the results of the last examination performed in late 1947. Taylor was the driving force for change and a friend to the association who provided much-needed advice and guidance. On this visit he suggested that the institution insure its savings accounts under federal deposit insurance. The association was still operated by a board of directors who were good businessmen and community leaders, but in all honesty they were not full-time savings and loan executives.

After decades of sleepy existence, the association was on the verge of tremendous change, but W.C. Weatherly, who served as the association's current president and a board member since 1920, would not live to see these changes. He passed away suddenly on April 17, 1948. The board paid its formal respects to Weatherly at the monthly meeting as a resolution was read recognizing his accomplishments. Weatherly's death created the first vacancy on the board in thirteen years, and local dentist I.C. Clark was elected to replace Weatherly. Clark was appointed vice president, and Sam M. Hupman Sr. became president.

Following Taylor's lead, the association applied to the Federal Home Loan Bank Board (FHLBB) for deposit insurance in June, and by September the insurance was approved with strings attached. The FHLBB's approval stipulated that the institution adopt the bylaws and charter of a savings and loan association. On September 16, 1948, the Mebane Home Builders Association officially became a savings and loan, adopting the required bylaws and becoming a member of the Federal Home Loan Bank on October 13, 1948. Individual deposits were now insured up to five thousand dollars through the Federal Savings and Loan Insurance Corporation.

Just one week later another meeting was called to find a separate office location from the furniture store. The minutes stated that the board be "resolved that within a reasonable time the office quarters will be so rearranged as to provide separate identity of the association and that it may be clearly discernable to the public as a financial institution." After nearly forty years, the association was ready to stand on its own.

Getting its own office was more important to the institution than ever, as mortgage lending in 1948 was setting records. The association could not attract enough deposits to fund these loans and was again forced to borrow funds from its dependable source, the Durham Bank and Trust Company.

Americans now earned more money than ever, averaging $2,936 a year, further driving the economy forward. The impact of the nation's building boom can be clearly seen in the cost of housing; by 1948 the average home in the country cost $7,700, up 67 percent in just three years. It took the nation twenty years to recover to pre-Depression home price levels following the free fall of home values during the 1930s.

Attorney June Crumpler hired a young associate for his law firm who would have an incredible impact on the history of the association. Lee W. Settle was a navy veteran whose World War II experience included Omaha Beach on D-Day. Settle returned to North Carolina following the war, graduating from Wake

Forest and completing his law degree at UNC. Over the next fifty-six years, Settle provided priceless legal advice and counsel to the association, maintaining a close relationship that continued until his death in 2004.

Mebane continued to flourish, and as the town grew so did businesses. W.W. Corbett, an original founder of the Mebane Home Builders Association, reorganized the Mebane-Royall Co., changing the name of the mattress maker to the Mebane Company. F.M. Southerland opened Southerland Dyeing and Finishing Mills as Mebane remained firmly entrenched in textiles. The award-winning careers of photographers William and Harriette Lynch began on the top floor of the Eagle Oil Company. A few years later, William Lynch Studios moved to the Lynch home on South Fifth Street.

The postwar years were a swinging time for teenagers, and *the* place to be was the Teenage Club. Every week, Mebane High School students gathered on the second floor above Rose's Department Store on Center Street. Local teens had a great time in the large open room that featured a jukebox, where many learned to dance to big band music.

America was enjoying the good life, too. In 1948 over 1 million television sets were sold, compared to just five thousand in 1945. The profound influence of this new technology on American culture was hard to imagine at that time, as grainy black-and-white pictures filled the airwaves and were often interrupted by "technical difficulties." Despite these problems, Americans loved every minute of it, and television antennas were as common as chimneys on rooftops across the country—unless one had the popular rabbit ears on top of the television.

By the late 1940s the American Dream of owning a home was finally coming true for a generation that had known very little material wealth. Americans were buying new cars, something that they had been unable to do during the war as production had been temporarily discontinued. Still, the idea of debt was something most folks frowned upon—with the exception of a home. But by the end of the decade, the convenience and ease of installment buying had gained a solid foothold, strengthening consumer spending.

The building boom of the late 1940s was unlike anything the association or the financial industry had experienced, placing new demands on Mebane's newly formed savings and loan.

Like every savings and loan, the Mebane Home Builders Association relied on local deposits to fund loans whenever possible, but this source of funds had always been unpredictable and frustrating, made worse by its self-imposed deposit limits. By becoming a savings and loan and a member of the Federal Home Loan Bank, a more stable and consistent source of funds was now available. FHLB members could meet their liquidity needs through loans called "advances," repaying these funds with interest at a later date. On May 19, 1949, the association obtained twenty-five thousand dollars, the maximum the institution could borrow, on its first-ever advance.

The 1940s was an incredible time for the association, Mebane, and the country. The association was basking in the economic prosperity that followed the war and confirming the need to stand alone as a full-time financial institution. Forty years old, the Mebane Home Builders Association entered the golden years of the savings and loan industry. Home construction, returning veterans, and the baby boom drove the housing industry like never before, and the association found that it had to change to meet the demands of its customers and community.

It could be argued that the story of First Savings truly began in the late 1940s with the adoption of the thrift charter. Yet its future would be dictated by its past. The Mebane Homebuilders Association that gave birth to First Savings was ultra-conservative, and regardless of changes that lay ahead, this new association would cling fast to its roots. The 1950s would see the trials of the last forty years clash with inevitable change, creating division and strife on the board and altering the association's future.

Unlike the association, Mebane's story did not begin following World War II, but the town was certainly a much different place than before, as the postwar economy changed Mebane's commercial and residential identity. The period after the war gave birth to some of the town's most recognizable and enduring businesses.

Charlie McAdams Sr. was serving up barbecue at a new restaurant on Highway 70 called the A&M Grill. On July 3, 1949, the first worship service was held in the newly constructed Mebane United Methodist Church on Fourth Street. Mebane High School students slipped across the street for a quick snack or soft drink at Clark's store, hoping that Principal Yoder wouldn't catch them. Celebrating forty successful years, the tobacco warehouses were now the focus of a festival each fall, complete with the crowning of a Tobacco Queen. Attorney June Crumpler left his law firm to work full-time at his lucrative building business, the Mebane Lumber Company, while his associate attorney Lee W. Settle continued the law practice.

The railroad now ran more freight traffic than passenger service. Competition from long-distance trucks slowly eroded the once-dominant railroad industry. This growth prompted trucking giant Associated Transport to construct a new terminal at the corner of Beaumont Avenue and North Church Street in Burlington. Trucks and the exploding automobile industry placed more strain on North Carolina's two-lane highways. The 1950s would see the construction of the nation's interstate highway system, again altering the future of commerce and changing North Carolina.

Alamance County celebrated its centennial in 1949 with a population that had reached sixty-seven thousand residents. Despite the economic prosperity of the postwar years, North Carolina, like many southern states, still lacked many amenities that other states enjoyed. Alamance County only had 225 miles of paved roads, mostly on major highways and streets in the towns of Burlington, Graham, and Mebane. The county was still dominated by 650 miles of dusty dirt roads that wound their way through countless tobacco fields and dairy farms. Alamance County produced mostly tobacco, corn, hay, and dairy products on its 2,739 farms. Textiles was still king as fifty hosiery mills blanketing the county provided the bulk of local employment. Indoor plumbing, electricity, and telephones were finding their way into more homes and businesses, at least in cities and towns, but oil lamps and chamber pots were still common in homes along the county's country roads.

The decade began and ended at opposite ends of the economic spectrum. Americans were enjoying prosperity for the first time in nearly twenty years. American consumers had a higher standard of living than past generations, with excess money to spend. As America entered this period of prosperity, its people carried with them a value system forged during the Great Depression and World War II. Those who survived the 1930s and 1940s understood that the country was indeed resilient and could endure the toughest of times. Americans emerged from these experiences with a strong value system and work ethic, and they knew the importance of saving money. Although the sky seemed the limit for a country on the move, the scars of the Depression remained just below the surface. The Depression not only robbed Americans of homes, jobs, and finances, it stole their dignity and self-worth. Many of those who had suffered so much for so long approached life with guarded pessimism, and for them the glass would always be half-empty, adding to their sense of frugality. These survivors were now confronted with the virtues and vices of capitalism and a newfound materialism. Determined that future generations would never face the hardships they endured, members of the Greatest Generation gave to their children many of the material possessions they never had, sowing the seeds for a new and very different type of consumer, whose purchasing power would be driven by credit. The baby boomers, like no other generation before them, forever changed the face of American commerce.

Mebane High School was more than a school building to generations that grew up in Mebane before 1960. *Courtesy Don Bolden*

An eastbound train passes Dixie Yarn in 1940. *Courtesy Mebane Historical Museum*

By This Faith We Live

OUR Association is a fellowship of human beings for human beings. We exist for the common man, for those who work, economize, and save. We are educators in habits of saving, trustees for savings, and merchandisers of homesteads in behalf of families without homes.

Our Faith

WE believe in Savings and Loan Associations as cooperative institutions for safety of savings, promotion of thrift, protection of capital, and establishment of homes.

We believe in the sanctity of the home, in the sturdy patriotism centering in a home, in the right of every family to earn and own a home, and that the supreme test of an Association is the measure of its service in teaching thrift habits and making families investors in America through investment in homes.

We believe a Savings and Loan Association is a public trust, that all in its service are trustees for others, and that consent to any lesser service than public service is a violation of our trust.

We believe that careful appraisals, sound investments, conservative dividends, ample reserves, and adaptation of policy to changing social needs are fundamental to fulfillment of our stewardship as a Savings and Loan Association.

We believe that safety of savings is the first responsibility of a Savings and Loan Association, that income and dividends are secondary, and that any disbursement of funds except for safe income or the welfare of members and the community is indefensible.

We believe the Association that serves best, and best deserves success holds honor above gain; cherishes equal ethical standards in business and personal life; accepts and meets its responsibilities to its community; respects its shareholders, its employees, and itself; guides and advises its members selflessly; protects them in the profits of thrift; guards them in ownership of their homes; is fair with borrowers, patient with delinquents, but never neglectful of duty; serves all men without bias of religion or race or politics; is not moved by ambition for influence or lust for power; is not balked by censure nor bought by praise; is an Association of humanity, of and for the people of today in the United States of today.

Our Pledge

TO this faith we dedicate ourselves and our Association. In this faith we serve and hope. By it we live.

This pledge was common in thrifts throughout the country and a reflection of how savings and loans operated. This pledge still greets customers as they enter First Savings today.

A parade heads east on Clay Street in 1949. The Duke Power company is seen on the right and the two large buildings in the distance are the tobacco warehouses that burned in 1960. *Courtesy Don Bolden*

Clay Street today is a mix of antique stores and specialty shops. Brick Alley Antiques, The Elegant Relic and Xtreme Dance Academy can be seen on the right.

CHAPTER FIVE

The Nifty Fifties

1950–1959

IN 1950, FUTURE FIRST SAVINGS AND LOAN PRESIDENT NEAL SMITH graduated from Mebane High School and no doubt exchanged written well wishes with his thirty-nine fellow graduates in the school's yearbook *Furmacotto*. The fact that the school named its yearbook for the four major industries—furniture, mattresses, cotton, and tobacco—shows how important these industries were to Mebane residents and its future leaders. The name paints an accurate description of life in Mebane during the 1950s. The tremendous growth in business ventures following the war redefined the town's commercial environment and set the stage for residential development that would follow suit during the 1950s and 1960s. First Savings ended the 1940s with an incredible loan demand. Interestingly the 1950 census reveals that, despite the housing boom, Mebane's population growth remained flat during the 1940s and stood at 2,068 in 1950. Level population growth and First Savings' strong loan demand reveal that existing Mebane citizens were becoming home owners for the first time.

The country entered an extended period of prosperity in the late 1940s, courtesy of the postwar economy. With the dark days of rationing and unemployment lines behind them, Americans began to discover the open road. The love affair with the automobile was in full bloom. Businesses responded to the nation's shift to a mobile society, offering curb service as customers enjoyed a hamburger and milkshake without leaving their car. Drive-in theaters sprang up, and moviegoers could watch the latest Hollywood blockbuster for sixty-five cents. Changing with the times, the banking industry introduced the drive-through window.

Railroad passenger service continued its decline even while Americans' love for travel grew. An interstate highway system was under construction, and the sooner the better. Highway 70 and other two-lane roads that ran through small towns like Mebane were antiquated, carrying more and more traffic for a growing and mobile population. Interstate 85, running from Petersburg, Virginia, to Montgomery, Alabama, was built during the 1950s and 1960s, cutting through Alamance County just south of Mebane. Just as the railroad brought growth to the Piedmont and Mebane one hundred years earlier, the interstate opened new opportunities for future growth and expansion.

The world remained a very dangerous place in 1950. The Soviet Union developed nuclear weapons, and the spread of Communism became the newest threat to the American way of life. Constant fear of nuclear war became ingrained in the nation's psyche as civil defense shelters were built in communities across the country. Underground bomb shelters were the latest option for home owners. The fear of nuclear annihilation passed to a generation of American schoolchildren who participated in air-raid warning drills and were told to "duck and cover." North Korea's invasion of South Korea brought the United States into another armed conflict.

Despite the Korean War and global uncertainty, the U.S. economy steamed full speed ahead. By 1950, demand pushed the average cost of a house in America to $8,450, up 116 percent in ten years. The housing boom created a nation of home owners, as a record 55 percent of Americans now owned their own homes. A new car listed for an average $1,511, and gas sold for eighteen cents a gallon.

The average family income rose to $4,237 a year, a 178 percent increase since the mid-1930s. With decent wages and low inflation, Americans had it both ways during the Nifty Fifties as folks had discretionary money to spend and at the same time saved 10 percent or more of their income. This stable period of financial prosperity was quite a change from the previous twenty years, giving consumers a sense of financial security and the confidence to take on more debt. By 1952 the average consumer had amassed 40 percent of his or her annual income in outstanding debt. Placed into perspective, this ratio would rise to 126 percent of income by 2006.

The Mebane Home Builders Association began the decade with familiar faces, as directors John McIntyre, A.H. Jobe, A.B. Fitch, S.M. Hupman Sr., Paisley Nelson, J.E. White, and I.C. Clark were reelected. McIntyre remained as managing officer and secretary-treasurer, while Hupman and Clark continued as president and vice president, respectively. The success of the Mebane Lumber Company left attorney June Crumpler with less time for the association, and Lee W. Settle was hired as an assistant to attorney T.C. Carter.

The goal of becoming a full-time financial institution was emerging as a reality, and several key decisions made at the February 1950 shareholders' meeting charted a new course for the institution. John McIntyre suggested the association change its name to "be more in line with the associations in the state." From these meeting minutes, a clearer picture of the association's financial condition emerged. For the first time since the early 1940s, a record of the assets of the institution were now available in print. Attorney T.C. Carter addressed the meeting and "spoke on the progress that had been made during the past 30 years" stating "that [the association] had grown from $19,000 in 1920 to $563,000" today. McIntyre made a motion to establish a building fund and set aside "from $1000 to $2000 to build a home or office for the association at some future time ... [and] this is to be added to from time to time as the stockholders see fit."

Events swiftly unfolded, and four days later on February 20, 1950, the directors selected the name of "First Savings and Loan Association." The position of executive vice president was created for McIntyre, and two weeks later on March 3, a special meeting was held to discuss the hiring of a full-time secretary-treasurer. McIntyre—who had served as secretary-treasurer for decades in a part-time capacity—now stated that Reliable Furniture was demanding more of his time. Also present at this meeting was State Examiner J.D. Taylor, whose previous recommendations and guidance had placed the association on its path for future growth. Taylor was the obvious choice to lead the association forward. The board offered him the position of executive vice president and secretary-treasurer and agreed to hire "a girl to help ... part time." Later that month, Taylor accepted the position, replacing John McIntyre, who remained a powerful and influential voice on the board.

Taylor's first official day on the job was May 2, 1950. The hiring of J.D. Taylor as a full-time executive officer was a significant event in the life of the institution in several ways. Taylor's employment brought First Savings one step closer to realizing the goal of becoming a full-time financial institution. His appointment as managing officer changed the association administratively, shifting day-to-day operations away from the board. It would appear that this shift in control would be a welcome change, yet it resulted in conflicts with the board.

In fairness, McIntyre and a veteran board of directors ran the institution for twenty-eight years and had survived the struggles of the Depression. The association was now a thriving business, and for them to relinquish control to anyone, even someone as skilled as Taylor, would be difficult. The board had made First Savings what it was, and the directors had earned the right to run it. Thus it was understandable that McIntyre and the board continued to micromanage operations.

Taylor's tenure at First Savings came at the best possible time as lending hit the ground running. Between 1950 and 1954 the association averaged closing 151 loans a year. Even more striking about these numbers was that the average loan amount climbed to $3,210, a 40 percent increase from 1949.

Mebane's business environment grew when Walton Lumber Company, a supplier for the furniture business, opened with Stephen A. White as its secretary-treasurer. T.E. Pender and W.C. Amick opened Pender and Amick clothing store on Clay Street.

T. D. Jones and W.D. Sykes became the first letter carriers for the Mebane Post Office in 1950. Until then, folks had to come to the post office on Center Street and personally pick up their mail. Jones and Sykes delivered their routes entirely on foot. Jones's route measured 12.1 miles and included between six hundred and seven hundred homes. In a newspaper interview, Jones recalled that most mail sent to the Mebane Post Office was simply addressed with a person's name and the town. The mail still made it through because everybody knew everybody. Jones and Sykes coordinated their daily routes to meet each other at Freshwater's Store for a break.

In the fall of 1950 the state examiners paid a visit to First Savings and found a loan they did not like. The association had made a 100 percent home loan that was guaranteed by White Furniture Company. The loan was made to one of White's employees with the understanding that if the borrower defaulted, the furniture maker would make the payments, preventing foreclosure. This type of creative financing would have been routine in the past, but now the association was closely regulated by the state. Although still very minimal by today's standards, the reality of government regulation was making its presence felt. First Savings was required to set up a pledged savings account as collateral until the customer had paid the loan down to 80 percent of the property's value.

The self-imposed deposit limitations placed on savings accounts continued to take its toll. In September the board borrowed more funds from Durham Bank and Trust. Although determined to limit savings deposits from the community, the board was more than willing to borrow funds to meet loan demand, a practice that eventually drew criticism from regulators.

The liquid position or available cash equivalent of funds that regulators required of savings and loans at that time was 6 percent of its total deposits. In other words, if an institution had $100,000 in deposits, it needed $6,000 in liquid funds. The association's excessive borrowing and high loan demand resulted in a liquid position of only 5.31 percent of its deposits. The examiners stated that although 6 percent was required, "20 percent is considered desirable." The directors weren't too concerned over this issue and hoped to build up the association's cash position "as loan requirements were met," mostly through monthly payments made to the institution.

Now that First Savings had a full-time managing officer and regular office hours, access to home loans became easier for customers, and the process created more loan closings than ever. Total accounts held by the institution in 1950 topped one thousand for the first time. By October no loans were reported past due, a major accomplishment. The association added new staff as Betty Carden and Frances Miller worked as full-time tellers, along with J.D. Taylor's wife Clara, who worked part-time.

Directors Paisley Nelson, S.M. Hupman Sr., and A.B. Fitch were appointed to an office building committee, and by year's end they recommended purchasing a lot "owned by the [Reliable] Furniture Store located between Dr. Malone's office and Pender and Amick's for $3,500." Building a permanent office could not come fast enough. Assets of the association had reached $776,646 with $727,563 in mortgage loans by the end of the year, while savings deposits topped $690,267.

Until 1951 the 6,004 savings institutions in America, unlike its banks, had the benefit of tax-exempt status. Savings and loans focused on housing and were considered less stable and secure than the banking industry. That Depression-era thinking quickly disappeared as the postwar building boom made savings and loans more profitable than ever. Congress repealed the tax-exempt status of the savings and loan industry, placing thrifts on the same tax level as banks.

Credit unions, however, retained their tax-exempt status. This segment of the financial services industry was designed to serve a certain membership of customers who had a common bond, such as state employees. Like thrifts, credit unions had the reputation of serving the working class and those with limited financial options. Congress felt credit unions were looking after the little guy and allowed the tax-exempt status to continue. The importance of the credit unions' tax exemption is important to note here. Credit unions in the 1950s operated in a different manner than banks and savings associations and thus were not competing directly with traditional tax-paying institutions. Tax exemption would become a hot-button issue by the mid-1990s as credit unions stepped from the shadows and began competing directly against banks, offering the same sophisticated and diverse banking services while enjoying tax-exempt status.

As consumers took on more debt, the idea of charging when dining out produced the Diner's Club card. The card was issued to two hundred members for use at twenty-seven select New York City restaurants. Although the event occurred with very little fanfare, this product innovation led to the now-ubiquitous credit card and changed the direction of American consumerism.

Mebane's downtown retail base expanded in 1951 when Mr. and Mrs. W.A. Corbett opened Corbett's Infants and Children's Wear on Clay Street and R.M. Noble established Noble Oil Company. After a successful Major League Baseball career, Lew Riggs returned to his hometown and opened Riggs Shoe Store on Clay Street, hiring nineteen-year-old Neal Smith as a salesman. A few doors down from Riggs's store, doctors at the Mebane Clinic were seeing an average of sixty patients a day, and house calls were an everyday occurrence. The busy clinic added to its staff Dr. George M. Bullard, who would become part of the First Savings story a decade later.

Western Electric began operations in the abandoned Fairchild Aircraft facility on Graham-Hopedale Road in Burlington, creating jobs and a housing boom on the east side of the city. Town and Country, one of the largest residential subdivisions in Alamance County, was opened and became home to many Western employees.

First Savings reached a major milestone in 1952 as its total assets topped the million-dollar mark, reaching $1,045,637. The board finally eliminated the restrictive policy of limiting monthly deposit amounts placed in passbook accounts.

With a building lot purchased and a floor plan approved, the association was ready to begin construction on a new office. The contract was awarded to local builder Linwood Albright for $26,446.25, and construction was soon under way. In an interview in 2005, Albright smiled when he talked about the construction of the building. "That thin brick we used on the front of the building took forever to lay. But you know we must have done a good job 'cause that building is still standing." On December 5, 1952, First Savings and Loan formally opened its new office building at 124 West Clay Street to much fanfare. After forty-three years of supplying funds for home loans, First Savings finally had a home of its own. The building was modern for its day, complete with a night deposit box, a large vault, and adequate office space.

It seemed the pieces were finally coming together for the association as more internal changes had taken place for the institution in the last seven years than in the previous forty put together. First Savings was now a chartered savings and loan with full-time staff and insured deposits. Considering the conservative nature of the directors, these monumental changes came very quickly and set the institution on firm ground going forward. Before the year was over, another employee came on board when Betty Roundtree was hired as a teller.

The Mebane Public School was the center of education for the town, housing all twelve grades in one building. That changed in 1952 when an elementary school was built on nine acres of land on Charles Street purchased from the American Legion. The new school was named for longtime Mebane educator E.M. Yoder. That same year, optometrist A.T. Glenn opened a clinic at 105 Clay Street, and Henry Loy served up hot lunches at the Mebane Sandwich Shop on Center Street. On West Holt Street, Mebane Manufacturing was established by W.R. Wilkinson, W.B. McClean, and J.R. Cecil.

Having served as Supreme Allied Commander in World War II, Dwight D. Eisenhower was elected president of the United States in 1952. President Eisenhower ironically cut defense spending and finalized legislation creating the Interstate Highway System that would one day bear his name.

At the annual shareholders' meeting, the directors who had become synonymous with First Savings—A.B. Fitch, S.M. Hupman Sr., John McIntyre, A.H. Jobe, I.C. Clark, Paisley Nelson, J.D. Taylor, and J.E. White—were reelected to the board. This was the last time J.E. "Ed" White was mentioned as a director of the association, and he was not in attendance at any of the regular board meetings for the remainder of the year. White was first elected to the board in 1932 and had served for over twenty-one years.

Ed White was known as a quiet and reserved man who spoke very slowly and distinctly. Director Jobe confirmed White's slow southern drawl in a story that took place on a trip the two took to High Point. The story goes that on their way back to Mebane, Ed White began telling a story to Jobe as they left High Point. Jobe stated that after they arrived at White's house he had to wait another fifteen minutes in the driveway for White to finish telling his story.

Despite the elimination of deposit restrictions, high loan demand forced the association's continued dependence on borrowed funds. In March, "The Secretary was directed to send to the Federal Home Loan Bank in Greensboro any funds in excess of $20,000.00." It is not clear if this amount was a required reserve or a repayment of an FHLB advance.

Indicative of the times, Taylor suggested "hiring of a male assistant Executive Officer." Taylor explained that the association "should be training someone capable of becoming the managing officer if and when there is a need." After just three years with the association, Taylor had shorter work hours and indicated he would be absent occasionally from the office. After taking the managerial reins, Taylor chartered a new direction for First Savings. Even so, this was still McIntyre's association, and Taylor appeared to be losing patience with McIntyre managing from the sidelines.

At the May 21, 1953 board meeting, twenty-one-year-old L. Neal Smith was hired as a service representative. Smith's long tenure with the association officially began on June 10. The hiring of Neal Smith was quite a departure for this veteran group of directors. Unlike Taylor, Smith was born and raised in Mebane, and he was from a younger generation than any of the sitting directors. It was also at this meeting that Lee Settle was named as the association's trustee, replacing T.C. Carter. Beginning in 1953, regular and consistent financial statements were printed and given to members annually.

The fighting in Korea came to an end in July, after claiming the lives of more than thirty-three thousand U.S. servicemen and women. The war in Korea demonstrated to the world that the United States was determined to stop communism, setting the stage for a deeper and costlier involvement a decade later in Southeast Asia.

The building boom seemed to have no end in sight, and mortgage loans continued to soar as well as loan amounts. The association approved a home loan for eleven thousand dollars, an amount unheard of a few years earlier. The association's business hours during its days at the furniture store were never clear, but by the mid-1950s, First Savings was open from 9 a.m. until 4 p.m. Monday through Friday, and 9 a.m. to 12 noon on Saturday.

Two enduring American icons emerged in 1955 as Ray Kroc bought a hamburger franchise from the McDonald brothers and launched an empire of golden arches. Entertainment giant Walt Disney opened Disneyland in Anaheim, California.

More changes took place at the February shareholders' meeting as Neal Smith was named assistant secretary-treasurer to J.D. Taylor. By now, Smith was handling most of the loan closings, which remained strong as twenty-six loans totaling ninety-seven thousand dollars were closed in the month of February alone. The association staff grew as Joyce Bradshaw joined the institution and First Savings joined the U.S. Savings and Loan League, the national trade association for the savings and loan industry.

New subdivisions were under way on Jackson Street, Circle Drive, White Drive, Carr Street, and North Fifth and Sixth streets, among others. Most new construction was the brick ranch–style home that would remain a staple in home building for the next twenty years. Most of these homes had three bedrooms, two bathrooms, and a carport or garage, and were around eleven hundred square feet. This residential growth sparked the town of Mebane to establish a stable long-term water supply, and Lake Michael was created north of town.

The Federal Savings and Loan Insurance Corporation (FSLIC) notified the association that it must set up a reserve account to cover possible losses on loans. The association had established such an account in the late 1920s for this purpose, but apparently the amount that had accrued was not sufficient. Regulators required that ninety-eight thousand dollars be placed in the reserve account with "future additions [to] be made," indicating that the association was growing too fast and that more safeguards needed to be established.

By the mid-1950s several employees had been hired at different times by First Savings, but no information exists as to when employees left the institution. In June 1955 the financial statement noted full-time employees as Neal Smith, Joyce Bradshaw, Frances Miller, and J.D. Taylor. First Savings was now averaging twenty-five loan closings a month, and by September another thirty-thousand-dollar advance was obtained from the Federal Home Loan Bank. This remarkable period during the 1950s and into the 1960s was a time of unmatched growth as the incredible loan demand caused the association's assets to triple in just five years.

On June 23, 1955, President Clark regretfully accepted the resignation of J.D. Taylor as managing officer. Taylor took a position at a larger savings and loan in Florida. Although his tenure had been short, having served since 1950, Taylor's influence on the association is unmatched. As a state examiner, Taylor had offered recommendations to the institution in the 1940s, well before becoming part of the organization. Taylor advocated regular savings accounts, discontinuing the antiquated series plan, pushed for federal deposit insurance, and was responsible for the association becoming a chartered savings and loan. J.D. Taylor was the right man at the right time in a period of significant change for the institution, forever establishing his legacy.

Neal Smith was promoted to secretary-treasurer and executive vice president, and named to replace Taylor on the board. Although Smith had been with First Savings just two years, he learned the business essentially from Taylor. J.D. Taylor's departure after just five years as executive officer was due in part to McIntyre's interference, as both men had very different views of the association's future. McIntyre was more conservative, favoring slow growth and resisting change, while Taylor was somewhat progressive. These differences created obvious philosophical clashes. Taylor's departure would serve to widen a division in the board that was forming by the mid-1950s.

During the association's first one hundred years, many individuals influenced the institution and contributed to its success. But three key people shaped First Savings into the institution it has become today. Elected to the board in 1920, John McIntyre established the original identity and operations of the association, creating a successful business while building its loyal customer base. His leadership brought the institution through the Depression and saw it prosper through the postwar boom. J. D. Taylor went a step further, taking the successful part-time venture that McIntyre built and positioning the business to take full advantage of the economic prosperity of the 1950s. Through Taylor's initiatives and leadership, the institution became a full-time savings and loan with huge potential. Neal Smith took that potential, reestablished the institution's mission, and guided the association forward for the remainder of the century.

The loan demand of the 1950s had Neal Smith closing several home loans a day, simple transactions by today's standards. At that time, loans were approved based on a person's income, debt, and value of the property used for collateral. Before the use of licensed appraisers, most small institutions determined the value of property being secured by a home loan. This simple evaluation was done by a loan committee, usually made up of board members. Basically these "appraisals" consisted of the committee performing a visual inspection of the property and making a subjective opinion of value. Once the value was established, an attorney performed a title search and the loan was closed. Before the deluge of government regulations that changed everything by the early 1970s, the process from application to closing could often take less than a week.

The appraisal committee not only determined the values of real estate loans but provided some of First Savings and Loan's lighter moments. These weekly trips were more of a social outing. Some of the tales that are suitable for print center around new cars that committee members were eager to show off to fellow directors during home inspections. One such story from Neal Smith happened in 1955 when Dr. I. C. Clark took the committee on its rounds driving his brand-new blue 1955 Buick. The committee was inspecting a home in Hillsborough. Neal Smith and A.B. Fitch were inside the home while A.H. Jobe and Clark were outside measuring the long ranch-style home. Jobe ended up in the shrubs holding the middle of the measuring tape. The home owners had several outside dogs, as Jobe realized when a strong odor tipped off what was caked to the bottom of his shoe.

"My goodness, what am I going to do, Doc?" cried Jobe.

Clark replied with a straight face, "Oh, don't worry. By the time you walk back to town, it'll be done wore off." Thanks to a rather embarrassed home owner, Jobe put his shoes in a brown grocery bag and placed them in the trunk of Clark's car for the return trip.

A similar episode involved John McIntyre, and the event reveals the few regulations that counties placed on home owners during the 1950s. At that time, septic systems were not designed to receive water from sinks or washing machines. This wastewater was funneled into the yard, usually into a ditch, where the water could drain away from the home. One morning as the loan committee was inspecting a house, Mr. Mac was walking backward in the yard looking back at the home. McIntyre inadvertently found the drainage field as his foot sank into the ground up to his knee in a messy combination of water, grease, and mud. On this day it was A.B. Fitch who was the chauffeur in his brand-new Dodge. After a few minutes, McIntyre pulled his leg out of the smelly muck and retrieved his shoe. Once again a home owner came to the rescue, supplying a burlap sack for Mr. Mac to wrap around his leg for the trip back to Mebane.

Members of the loan committee would appraise a house by a simple walk-through inspection, examining room sizes and the condition of the property. On one such inspection, the committee was greeted by the home owner, who proceeded to show a few of the members the outside of the house while Mr. Mac inspected the home's interior. Many of the older homes at that time added a bathroom by enclosing back porches that were usually adjacent to the kitchen. Mr. Mac opened the door to the newly added bathroom without hesitation. To his horror, McIntyre discovered that the toilet was occupied by the lady of the house, who promptly screamed. A totally embarrassed McIntyre slammed the door, apologized profusely, and retired quickly to the safety of the car, knowing he would receive a good dose of ribbing from his fellow directors. On subsequent appraisals, the practice of knocking on all doors before entering became a standard practice of the appraisal process.

On December 1, 1955, a black seamstress named Rosa Parks refused to give up her seat to a white passenger on a city bus in Montgomery, Alabama, and was promptly arrested. The incident led to the boycott of the city-owned bus company, led by a young pastor named Martin Luther King Jr. This simple but defiant act by Mrs. Parks ignited the civil rights movement, setting the stage for monumental social change in America.

At this point of the 1950s, the housing boom seemed to have no end in sight, much to the delight of the savings and loan industry. A stable economy, predictable interest rates, and an incredible housing market pushed home prices higher to a nationwide average of $10,950, a 30 percent rise in just five years. Mortgage loan rates had remained at or near 6 percent for over a decade while the savings rates held fast at 3.5 percent. In 1956 mortgage rates fell to 5 percent, fueling more home buying.

At the annual shareholders' meeting in February 1956, the directors had a lot to smile about. After crossing the million-dollar mark in assets just four years earlier, the association had eclipsed the $2 million level, reaching $2.3 million by the end of 1955. The financial statement at year's end also revealed that the cash or liquid position had improved. John McIntyre and T.C. Carter were presented with thirty-five-year service awards at the meeting.

First Savings was a reflection of a town that was growing commercially and residentially. Drs. G.Y. Mebane and William Aycock moved to the newly constructed Medical Arts Building on South Fifth Street that would later become home to Coldwell Banker Real Estate Company by the late 2000s. South Mebane Elementary was completed on South Third Street, becoming the second elementary school to be built in town in just five years. The Mebane Wesleyan Church completed its new building on the corner of Fourth and Crawford streets. Alton Huey built a Mebane landmark in 1957 as Huey's Restaurant opened just east of town on Highway 70. Huey's was built on the site of the old Shady Oaks Drive-In, which had been another famous Mebane eatery to an earlier generation.

On March 16, 1957, Zeke Ray and Gene Compton led the Mebane High School Tigers to a state basketball championship, defeating the Jonesville Blue Jays. Coached by the legendary George Shackelford, the Tigers capped a perfect 28-0 season with the win. This seemed to be the year of perfection as Coach Frank McGuire's University of North Carolina Tar Heels won the National Championship in men's basketball with a triple-overtime win over Kansas and finished the season with a perfect 32-0 record.

In 1957 two Charlotte institutions, the American Trust Company and the Commercial National Bank, merged to form the American Commercial Bank. Three years later, American Commercial merged with Security National Bank of

Greensboro, and North Carolina National Bank was born. By the late 1980s and into the 1990s, NCNB became one of the largest banks in the nation through aggressive mergers and acquisitions. Known as Bank of America today, NCNB not only transformed the banking industry but also the city of Charlotte.

Several dates in the association's history mark multiple events that shaped the future of the institution. January 16, 1958, is one of those red-letter days. The board of directors on that day accepted with regret the resignation of Director Paisley Nelson. Nelson was the only remaining member of the original founding board of directors. His remarkable forty-nine-year relationship with the association earned him tremendous respect from customers and staff. The board named him an "honorary director in recognition of his long and loyal service." Attorney Lee W. Settle was appointed to fill the directorship vacancy, which could not have come at a more crucial time as Settle's counsel would be called upon in earnest in the next few years.

Also on this date Shelby O. Murphy began an incredible forty-eight-year career of her own at First Savings that would last until her retirement in 2006. Mebane was a small town where everyone knew each other, and Murphy took that small-town friendliness and set the standard for customer service. Murphy and others who worked the teller lines had a much different job at that time, as financial transactions in those days were recorded by hand.

At the 1958 shareholders' meeting, director A. B. Fitch received a thirty-five-year service award. With the resignation of Paisley Nelson, the board now consisted of I.C. Clark, A.B. Fitch, A.H. Jobe, S.M. Hupman Sr., John M. McIntyre, Lee W. Settle, and L. Neal Smith. The association's full-time staff rose to four when Shirley Oakley joined the institution in February.

The association originated 262 mortgage loans totaling $1,037,800 in 1958, marking the first time First Savings exceeded the $1 million mark in loans. The institution would end the decade with back-to-back million-dollar lending years, setting the stage for another successful decade to come.

Deposit insurance rose to ten thousand dollars, marking the first increase since the mid-1930s. The credit card industry was still in its infancy in 1958 when the American Express card debuted, along with the BankAmericard, forerunner of the Visa card.

After just five years in the Clay Street location, a few directors felt that First Savings should expand to a larger office. The Clay Street location was designed and built to serve the association's needs for many years, but no one could conceive of the institution's incredible growth that began after World War II and continued unabated through the 1950s. First Savings, which started the decade with one thousand members, had twenty-three hundred members by 1958. The board, however, was not unanimous on the idea of expanding.

After years of relative unity, differences of opinion and conflicts within the board surfaced during the 1950s. First Savings and Loan had survived fifty years in operations with little controversy, but the growing pains of the prior ten years were taking its toll and the seeds of confrontation were being planted. In some ways conflict was inevitable. The association's transition to a full-time business over the previous ten years created changes that came fast and furious. These changes meant giving up both control and management of day-to-day operations, which was difficult for some board members. J.D. Taylor's departure in 1955 was the first casualty in an internal struggle among the directors. The significant age differences created friction, and the differing philosophies of veteran members versus new board members often clashed. The enormous demand for mortgage loans that created this growth proved to be profitable. Still, change is always hard to contemplate when the status quo is working.

Putting differences aside, the association began 1959 with plans to celebrate First Savings' fifty-year anniversary. Although the official date was in November, the celebration was held from June 15 to July 11. The theme of the event was the Gold Rush, and the association planned numerous activities, with special replica golden coins minted for the occasion. Each coin was individually numbered and engraved with a picture of the First Savings office building. Customers received a coin each time a deposit or transaction was made, becoming eligible for prizes drawn that matched the corresponding numbers on the coins. Neal Smith arranged for an old western-style covered wagon to be parked outside the offices on Clay Street. While parked there, the wagon caught fire one night, and the *Mebane Enterprise* ran the headline "Indians Attack First Savings," complete with pictures of the destroyed wagon. Smith was jokingly accused of setting the wagon on fire to gain publicity for the anniversary, but the actual cause of the fire was never determined.

Although references were made to the need for a larger facility, it was never noted in the board minutes that the association had been in the market for purchasing land for such use. Apparently some directors had been pursuing such efforts, as the minutes of the June 18, 1959, board meeting authorized the purchase of the "Cooper Property located at the corner of Highway 119 and 70A for the sum of $15,000. Attorney Lee Settle was authorized to negotiate the purchase of this property for the above sum and if it could not be purchased at this price, he was to obtain option on said property." The land being considered for purchase is the current office location at 206 West Center Street.

On June 30 the directors authorized the purchase of the land for $17,100. Once the purchase became a reality, the division in the board finally came to a head. John McIntyre made a motion seconded by S.M. Hupman Sr. "that the votes cast for and against the Association purchasing the Cooper property be recorded. Those casting votes against the purchase of the property were J.M. McIntyre, S.M. Hupman Sr. and A.H. Jobe and those voting for the purchase of the property were A.B. Fitch, I.C. Clark, L.N. Smith and Lee W. Settle. And this is to be recorded in said minutes to show to succeeding generations that J.M. McIntyre was opposed to the purchase of this property." Obviously from the language and tone of the minutes, there was a significant difference of opinion on this issue, particularly with McIntyre. Ironically, ten years earlier, McIntyre had been the driving force behind the institution obtaining a new building. But McIntyre felt he was losing control of the association and was fighting back.

The board authorized "the secretary to negotiate a sale of the present office building for the sum of $28,000-$31,000." On September 11, the directors authorized "that Charles C. Hartman be employed as architect on the new office building to be constructed on the Cooper property and that it be announced immediately that construction would begin in the Spring of 1960, according to plans submitted by Charles C. Hartman."

As the decade came to a close, Alaska and Hawaii attained statehood, and Russian Prime Minister Nikita Khrushchev visited the United States. Little girls were excited as the first Barbie doll was introduced. The decade of the 1950s had been a period of peace and prosperity, and Americans had more material wealth now than any previous generation. But that peace was about to end. The upheaval facing the country could hardly be imagined in the late 1950s in the sleepy southern town of Mebane, where the big news was that Pender Auto Parts opened for business.

In 1959 Mebane remained the self-sufficient little town it had always been. From thriving businesses and industry to health services and a movie theater, Mebane had everything most of its residents needed, even its own phone company. And it didn't take much to satisfy that generation of citizens. Its residents were mostly natives whose families grew up in Alamance and Orange counties. That trend stayed pretty much intact until the early 1970s, when multinational companies located in the area, bringing with them unprecedented growth, diversity in population, and a changing culture. Years later, Neal Smith went down the list of loans made by the association during the 1950s, commenting that he either knew the applicant or the family personally long before they had ever applied for a loan. Mebane, like most small southern towns of that era, was a comfortable and balanced mix of factory workers, shopkeepers, and small business owners. The town was close-knit, bound together by the common threads of White Furniture, The Mebane Company (Kingsdown), Dixie Yarn, Mebane High School, church and family.

The golden age of the savings and loan industry in the 1940s and 1950s financed the postwar building boom. Home ownership rose from 43.6 percent in 1940 to 61.9 percent by 1960, and they did it the right way. There were no gimmicks or subprime loans to contend with, and foreclosures were rare. The nation's mortgage industry would try to improve on this accomplishment forty-five years later with disastrous results.

The Nifty Fifties had been good to First Savings, but unlike the town it served, the association was far from self-sufficient. Assets reached $3.5 million by 1959 as First Savings grew five fold in ten years, with over twenty-seven hundred members and a reserve of $235,453. First Savings averaged 241 loan closings a year, with lending volume averaging $1,030,120 annually. The average loan amount grew from $2,968 in 1950 to $4,274 by 1959.

These numbers were great but somewhat deceiving. First Savings, like many associations around the country, were besieged with loan applications that far exceeded their deposit base. For most of the decade, the board made matters worse by limiting the amount of money its own customers could deposit. Every institution subscribed to the standard strategy of borrowing short and lending long. In other words, the association borrowed short-term money, usually through advances from the Federal Home Loan Bank, and would lend this money on long-term mortgages. This strategy worked perfectly for savings and loans until the 1970s.

But the numbers weren't the association's most pressing problem. The board was hopelessly split on the association's future direction. Over the next two years, board meetings became a battleground threatening the association's future. The association had faced many challenges over the previous fifty years. These experiences taught this veteran group of directors valuable lessons during some the worst and best of economic conditions. Still its greatest challenges would lay ahead. The decade to come would be a turbulent time and turning point for the nation and for First Savings.

The Association moved from a part time venture to full time business opening its first office building at 126 West Clay Street in 1952. *Courtesy William Lynch Studios*

Although designed to serve the Association's needs for many years, the Clay Street office became too small in less than a decade. *Courtesy William Lynch Studios*

A revealing photo from December 5th, 1952 at the open house for the Clay Street office. FRONT ROW L-R Betty Miller, J.D Taylor (first full time managing officer), Clara Taylor, Frances Miller (employee) Nellie Nichols, Marie Thompson (employee), Jack Oliver, Ed Kuykendall Jr. (N.C.Savings and Loan League) BACK ROW L-R Lee Hooks, Walter Cooper and R.D White (Community Federal), D.R. Fonville (First Federal), W.C. York (N.C. Insurance Commission), three unidentified people, Wade Key (Hillsborough Savings). *Courtesy William Lynch Studios*

This brochure from the 1950s was a miniature sewing kit.

The Gold Rush was the theme for the Association's fiftieth anniversary in 1959 and a covered wagon was used for advertising. The money bags represent the institution's assets in 1909 compared to 1959. *Courtesy Mebane Enterprise*

Special coins were used to commemorate both First Savings fiftieth and one hundred year anniversaries.

Neal Smith receives a gavel at the Mebane Toastmaster's Club in 1955, the same year he became managing officer. On Smith's immediate right is R. Nelson Pender and Smith's immediate left is future chairman of board, Jack Phelps. *Courtesy William Lynch Studios*

This home on Jackson Street was typical of homes First Savings financed during the 1950s. Variations of the ranch style home set the standard for home construction in America from the 1940s to the 1970s.

The Mebane Company's (Kingsdown) iconic building during the 1950s. *Courtesy Kingsdown*

Kingsdown's modern manufacturing plant today on I-85/40. *Courtesy Kingsdown*

CHAPTER SIX

Times They Are A-Changin'

1960–1969

IN 1964 SONGWRITER BOB DYLAN PENNED THE WORDS "The times they are a-changin'," and in doing so he captured the essence of the 1960s. After ten years of good economic times Americans entered the decade full of optimism. Nothing appeared on the radar screen that would seem to alter that view. The decade of the 1950s has the distinction of a tranquil, almost boring time in American history, but after two decades of turmoil, the Nifty Fifties offered a welcome respite. The Norman Rockwell view of the 1950s may be somewhat naive, but Dylan's descriptive statement of the 1960s was certainly on target.

Americans had good reason to be optimistic, as the average family earned $6,691 a year. The savings and loan industry was at its pinnacle, boasting forty-eight hundred institutions nationwide. The postwar housing boom had hit its peak. This twenty-year period saw the American Dream of home ownership rise faster than at any other time in history, and housing had come a long way. Homes were larger for growing families and had more amenities than ever before. The cost of a house appreciated 50 percent during the 1950s, reaching an average of $12,675 by 1960. North Carolina was slow in joining in this national prosperity, as one out of every three of its citizens lived below the poverty level. Being in the rural South, homes in Alamance County were priced 33 percent lower than the national average, selling for around $8,400.

The oil-producing countries of Saudi Arabia, Iran, Iraq, Kuwait, and Qatar met in Baghdad, Iraq, and formed the Organization of Petroleum Exporting Countries (OPEC) in an effort to force up oil prices. The formation of OPEC barely made the newspapers in 1960 as oil was selling for three dollars a barrel. Everyone seemed to be moving their hips in the early sixties, either dancing to Chubby Checker's smash record "The Twist" or trying out the latest fad called the hula hoop. Berry Gordy Jr. started Motown Records in Detroit and built a music empire with groups such as the Temptations and the Supremes. Alfred Hitchcock shocked moviegoers in the classic thriller *Psycho*, giving a new perspective on taking a shower.

Like Hitchcock's deceptive character Norman Bates, everything on the surface appeared to be running smoothly at First Savings. But as Mr. Bates demonstrated, sometimes things aren't always what they appear to be. The association welcomed Ann Sykes, who began a twenty-year career with First Savings as secretary in 1960. Sykes assisted Neal Smith with the growing loan demand, and the timing was perfect. First Savings had its best lending year to date, closing 290 loans totaling $1,581,400. While the association's future looked bright, controversy was brewing.

For fifty years, First Savings had weathered any storm that came its way. Even facing the Great Depression and World War II, the association always rose to the challenge. A new and different kind of threat now confronted the institution. This time the source was internal, as the division among the board that began in the late 1950s continued to widen. The split among the leadership that came to a head when the plans were finalized for its new office building was not about expanding. The problem was control, opposing philosophies, how the association should be managed, and who should manage it. The directors fell into two camps, with one side being the old-guard members supporting John McIntyre and the younger board members aligning with Neal Smith and I.C. Clark.

The members of the board and shareholders loyal to McIntyre's agenda had good reason for their loyalty, and history was on their side. McIntyre, now in his late sixties, served as managing officer from the 1920s until 1948, and his proven track record through both prosperous and difficult times had garnered support from the institution's earliest customers. Smith and Clark, compared to other members of the board, were newcomers and reflected a more progressive style in the footsteps of J.D. Taylor. Clark, in his fifties, had been on the board for twelve years and was a dentist by occupation. At twenty-eight, Smith was managing officer but had only been with the association for seven years. Smith and Clark's support came from the majority of the membership that became customers during the incredible growth of the 1950s.

Change was something the old guard willingly accepted as long as they were in charge. After struggling along for the first fifty years of its existence, Taylor's changes and Smith's guidance had put the association on sound footing. The newcomers also had the advantage of the postwar boom and the economic prosperity that came with it. McIntyre, who saw the association struggle during the Great Depression and the war, had to feel a sense of entitlement, having invested forty years in the association. Both groups had contributed significantly in the achievements of the business, but now there were too many cooks in the kitchen. Although McIntyre voluntarily had left his position as managing officer in 1948, he maintained his influential seat on the board and could sense he was losing control. Any business, large or small, cannot survive with multiple leaders, and the association was headed for a showdown.

The philosophical differences that had simmered for two years came to a full boil at the February 1960 shareholders' meeting. A year earlier, McIntyre opposed the purchase of the Cooper property and a new facility, but he lacked support from other board members. This year would be different. As usual, the incumbent members were reelected for another term at the meeting. The association's inadequate bylaws allowed McIntyre's supporters to increase the number of board members with two new directors supporting the old guard's position. The election of R.A. Wilkinson Sr. and John Henry James increased the board to nine members, and battle lines were drawn.

Winter weather hit North Carolina with a vengeance as snow fell on three consecutive Wednesdays in March 1960. The legendary storms are still a topic of conversation every winter. These unusual weather systems that dumped eleven, seven, and two inches of snow, respectively, are still etched in the minds of the schoolchildren from that time, who spent several days sledding and building snowmen rather than sitting in the classroom.

There was a definite chill in the air at First Savings as the conflict widened and tempers flared. The directors tried to compromise at a special meeting on March 23.

At the request of the board, W.C. York, deputy commissioner of insurance of the Savings and Loan Division and the association's regulator, attended the meeting to mediate the crisis. York felt that "the existing controversy could be settled by increasing the number of directors from nine to eleven." The reason for adding two more members to an already fuming board is unclear, but the existing members went along with York's recommendations, electing June A. Crumpler, former assistant attorney for the association, and Dr. George M. Bullard Sr. to fill these positions. A week later on March 28, the now-eleven-member board met in another called meeting hoping to iron out its differences. The minutes of that meeting stated, "A discussion was held relative to the general policies of the institution and the consensus of opinion was that every effort should be made to increase the services of the association and to the public wherever possible." Exactly how to accomplish these goals and who should lead these efforts still went unresolved.

The differences on the board had no real effect on the operations of First Savings as mortgage loans were being extended at a record pace. In April alone, thirty-seven loans were closed following a banner first quarter. McIntyre's opposition to a new office for the association had apparently softened as in April the board "unanimously" approved a bid from Charles C. Hartman to construct the new office for $108,570.30.

Graham-based Alamance National Bank was opening a branch in Mebane, and thirty-four-year-old Ned M. Gauldin would be its manager. First Savings agreed to lease the association's former location on Clay Street to the bank, but construction delays on the new building prevented First Savings from moving when Alamance National was ready to open. Neal Smith contacted Insurance Deputy Commissioner W.C. York in Raleigh with a proposal. Smith requested that First Savings and Alamance National move in together, in the Clay Street location, until the new First Savings building was ready. Smith stated, "York said it was illegal but to go ahead and let the bank move in with us but suggested writing a letter to the Office of the Comptroller of the Currency in Washington explaining the situation. York said the OCC won't agree to this arrangement, but by the time they review the request and tell you not to do it, you'll be in your new building anyway." York was right. Alamance National opened and operated in the same building alongside First Savings for a brief time. First Savings moved into its new offices some three months later, and both the bank and the association received stern letters from the OCC stating that under no circumstances were First Savings and Alamance National Bank to operate in the same location.

Mebane entered the new decade on the move with a population of 2,364, a 15 percent increase during the 1950s. Downtown Mebane remained the center for manufacturing and small business, and the future looked strong. From appliances at Reliable Furniture, to shoes at the Village Store and medical care at the Mebane Clinic, the residents of Mebane could find most anything they needed in the businesses on Clay and Center streets. But on one spring night in 1960, these historic buildings and the town's business district were almost lost.

For fifty years, the tobacco warehouses were downtown fixtures that came alive during the seasonal fall market. Other times during the year, the large buildings were used for storage for local industries and businesses. Mebane FCX Service stored its fertilizer in the Piedmont Warehouse and across the street Planter's Warehouse was packed full of cotton bales used for mattress production by the Mebane Company. On May 30, 1960, at 2:15 a.m., Mebane police officer James McLeod was making his customary rounds when he noticed smoke coming from the Piedmont Tobacco Warehouse and reported that the warehouse was on fire.

The volatile contents of the buildings created a massive blaze that could be seen for miles, and nine fire departments responded to the inferno. Several businesses suffered damage, including Parker's Shoe Store, Melville Chevrolet, Mebane FCX Service, Piedmont Café, and Kirkpatrick's Feed Building. Downtown business owners, including Neal Smith, feared the worst. At 4 a.m., Smith entered the chaos on Clay Street, stepping over water hoses to reach the association's offices less than fifty yards from the blaze. Years later Smith reminisced how he could feel the intense heat from the fire as he unlocked the door of the association and made his way inside. Smith put anything of value laying out in the office into the fireproof vault. The overnight blaze severed power lines, cutting electricity to more than three thousand people. By daybreak, the blaze was finally controlled, and all that remained of the warehouses were smoldering ashes. The town offered a $175 reward for information on Mebane's worst disaster yet. The actual cause of the costly fire remains a mystery.

The warehouses, like White Furniture and the Mebane Company, were vital to Mebane's economy. The first warehouse had opened the same year as First Savings in 1909. Farmers from surrounding counties brought tobacco to auction in the fall, and buyers representing large tobacco companies such as R.J. Reynolds and Liggett Myers came to town. The warehouses were so important that construction on the new Piedmont Warehouse on Highway 70 just west of Mebane was completed in three months, just in time for the September Tobacco Market. Joe Dillard started Farmers Warehouse on Ruffin Street while Jule Allen opened a warehouse on Mattress Factory Road. The destruction of these buildings forever altered the appearance of downtown. The loss left a gaping hole in the once-vibrant downtown landscape that for years simply sat vacant until a coin Laundromat was built on the Third and Ruffin street corner. These empty lots were finally brought back to life when the Sports Center of Mebane and Farm Bureau Insurance opened in the late 1990s.

The severely damaged Mebane FCX Service opened a new building on the corner of Charles and West Center. This business, which would later become Southern States, operated at this location until 2009 when a new facility was constructed on Highway 119 south of town. Byrd's Food Store opened across from the new FCX building, expanding its presence from its home offices in Burlington. The former Byrd's store became home of Ace Hardware for many years until it closed in 2009.

Despite the warehouse fire, business on Clay Street soon returned to normal. The Colonial Grocery Store at the corner of Fifth and Clay streets completed a major expansion, and Warren's Drug Store, a Clay Street fixture since the 1930s, opened its new location at the corner of Fourth and Clay. Operating seven days a week with free home delivery, Warren's employed pharmacists Calvin Oakley and Doug Isaac.

Just east of town, Playland skating rink made its debut. The rink was located behind Huey's Restaurant, and was popular with the junior high crowd as Top 40 music blared from the large sound system. This building plays to a somewhat older clientele today as home to Mebane Antique Auction Gallery.

Several stately homes once occupied the section of Mebane along Center Street where the association's new office was being constructed. The continued development of Mebane's business district eventually replaced these houses. A large two-story house once stood on the property adjacent to First Savings and was home to Sam Morgan, one of the association's founding members. Central

Carolina Bank had purchased the Morgan property and was putting the finishing touches on its new Mebane branch in 1960. Walker's Funeral Home is the last home from this era that still stands today.

Small towns have their sources of pride, and for Mebane in 1960 it was the Tigers of Mebane High School. From basketball to football and other sports, the school produced more than its share of championship teams, which locals followed with a passion. Football coach Archie Walker continued this storied tradition as Jimmy Copeland, Johnny Reeves, and Tommy Amick led the Tigers to their sixth straight Mid-State conference championship.

There was no cheering going on at First Savings as the controversy on the board continued to build. The board agreed that changes were needed to the institution's bylaws, namely to address the election of board members. A committee was formed to draft these revisions. Both factions hoped to gain an advantage before the next election, and changing the rules could swing the votes in their favor. Despite its problems, the board remained united on one issue: extending home loans. The strong demand required a hefty $150,000 FHLB advance during the summer months, followed by another $50,000 advance in the fall.

On October 3, 1960, the country gathered in their living rooms to watch the debut of *The Andy Griffith Show*. Griffith was from Mount Airy, and the show itself was centered around life in a small southern town in North Carolina called "Mayberry." It was no surprise the show became an instant hit, beloved by everyone in his home state and millions around the country. Before Griffith became a television star, he was known for his down-home country humor, and he even spoke at Mebane High School's Senior Banquet in 1947.

On November 15, 1960, the association officially opened the doors to its new office at 206 West Center Street and held an Open House on Friday, December 2. The building basically is the same today at it was originally constructed, with only cosmetic changes made over the years. The large teller counter is the same today as in 1960. The lobby was originally one very large room with a small sitting area surrounded by iron railings used as dividers. An additional office was added during the mid-1960s. The large window that faces Second Street originally had a large planter at its base, filled with artificial plants. Major interior and exterior improvements were made in 1988 and 2005.

As 1961 began, John F. Kennedy was sworn in as president of the United States after defeating Richard Nixon in the November election. The University of North Carolina hired thirty-year-old Dean Smith as head basketball coach, replacing Frank McGuire, who left for the University of South Carolina. The Berlin Wall was constructed, dividing the German city as the Cold War was at its peak.

There were no visible walls at First Savings, but the division among the board pushed confrontation to the top of the agenda at the shareholders' meeting in February. The issue of control, complicated by a set of vague bylaws, left the institution vulnerable particularly during the election of directors. The meeting opened with a heated discussion on the committee's proposed bylaw revisions. McIntyre's supporters refused to change any of the rules before voting on directors for the coming year. It is important to note that when voting at a shareholders' meeting, a member of the association could cast his vote in one of two ways. The member could either attend the meeting and vote in person or vote by proxy, the preferred choice of most members. A member voting by proxy assigns his vote to another member of the institution or a representative. An individual with large numbers of proxy votes can vote these proxies however he or she wishes.

The bylaws went unchanged, and the next order of business was the election of the board of directors. As the nominations for the board began, several motions were made from the floor. One motion, to disallow any votes in the election that were represented by proxy, was soundly defeated. If passed, this motion would have allowed only members present at the meeting to vote, essentially ignoring the wishes of the majority of the membership. A motion to reduce the number of directors from eleven down to nine passed, and things got heated.

To avoid further controversy, R.A. Wilkinson and John Henry James both requested that their names be withdrawn during the balloting, but both were reinstated during the voting. The decision to reduce the number of board members made the difference. The nine members receiving the highest number of votes were A.H. Jobe, S.M. Hupman Sr., I.C. Clark, A.B. Fitch, L.N. Smith, G.M. Bullard, June A. Crumpler, John Henry James, and Lee W. Settle. Remarkably, John M. McIntyre, a member of the board for forty-one years, was not reelected. After the smoke cleared, "A short talk was made by Mr. McIntyre asking the shareholders to join him in supporting the institution to make it an even larger and better institution." The election results were stunning. The board thought this would end the situation once and for all, but this was not to be the case.

The ousted McIntyre and his supporters pursued legal action, and in March, "The President was authorized to employ [counsel] at his discretion to answer charges and demands of a group... and to follow action recommended by [counsel]." It seemed unbelievable that the situation was being taken to such lengths and could not be resolved or mediated. More incredible was that this was happening at a small-town thrift in Mebane, North Carolina.

The sticking point for everyone remained the bylaws, and W.C. York, commissioner from the state insurance office, sent a suggested set of bylaws to the association in another effort to keep the peace. By year's end, with York's help, the bylaws of the association had been revised. These changes played a key role in the next shareholders' meeting.

By summer, the association enlarged its lending territory, extending loans in surrounding counties. The loan data suggests that the association had all the business it needed in Mebane, as another hundred-thousand-dollar FHLB advance was authorized to meet loan demand. First Savings was extending loans at a rate that greatly outpaced savings deposit inflows, and advances from the FHLB continued to climb. This was a universal problem for most associations, and it was not unusual to run special promotions to draw in potential customers. Institutions offered everything from china to glassware to toasters in an effort to entice new deposit accounts. The standard advertising slogan of the day was "Deposit by the Tenth, Earn from the First."

Advertising itself took many forms, and one of the most popular was sponsoring youth sports teams. In the early 1960s, the association sponsored pee-wee and midget baseball teams. First Savings provided T-shirts carrying the association's logo and the name of the team. At that time recreational activities were limited, except in the summertime, and were reserved mostly for boys with very little available for girls. The town's recreational department divided the town into four teams, and boys from all over Mebane proudly wore their new uniforms representing the Northeast Pirates, Northwest Cardinals, Southwest Indians, and Southeast Tigers.

Family recreation made significant strides in 1961 when Thompson Heights Swimming Pool on North Fifth Street and Dogwood Swimming Pool on South

Fifth Street opened. This was quite an improvement from the days of swimming in Back Creek or the holding pond at Cook's Mill.

Another popular spot was the Dogwood Golf Course, which was the place to be particularly on Wednesday afternoons when most of the town's businesses closed at 1 p.m. Dogwood was a nine-hole course built in the 1930s that closed during the 1960s when Arrowhead Golf Course opened on Mebane Oaks Road. The greens and bunkers of the old Dogwood course were later replaced by houses in the 1970s when the Brookhollow subdivision was developed. The only remaining building from the old course is the former clubhouse, which became home to Kiddie Kare Child Care and Development Center.

As 1962 began, all eyes turned to the annual shareholders' meeting. A year had passed since the eleven-member board was reduced to nine and McIntyre had been forced off. The year had been full of legal challenges and maneuvering by McIntyre supporters, called "The Shareholders' Group." The legal action brought by the Shareholders' Group finally reached the North Carolina Supreme Court. McIntyre's supporters had requested the names of all depositors of First Savings. The association had refused to honor this request, citing that such disclosure violated a member's privacy. The Court disagreed, ruling in favor of the Shareholders' Group and forcing the association to publicly release the names of its members.

The annual shareholders' meeting was delayed until March, allowing each side an extra month's time to prepare. It had been a long and painful struggle, and a final showdown was at hand. On March 15, 1962, 154 shareholders and several newspaper reporters packed the offices of First Savings. Over twenty-four hundred proxies were submitted, and an incredible eighty-three names were placed in nomination for just nine director positions. Judge L.J. Phipps from Chapel Hill was asked to oversee the elections. It took examiners two and a half hours to count and inspect the ballots, with the results not known until midnight. McIntyre's group fell short, and the membership reelected the incumbent board of Clark, Jobe, Bullard, Settle, Fitch, James, Crumpler, Hupman, and Smith. The Shareholders' Group had gone to great lengths to oust the association's leadership but simply did not have the support of the general membership and were outvoted in the elections five to one.

This would be the last challenge from the Shareholders' Group. The shareholders' meeting of 1962 finally brought to a close a difficult and painful but perhaps necessary period of the association's history. It was necessary because it forced the institution to adopt proper and specific bylaws that would prevent similar actions of a few individuals from jeopardizing the desires of the entire membership. The experience also initiated the change to a one-vote policy, giving each member an equal voice when voting and ending the practice of wealthy members having more votes than those of modest means.

This ongoing controversy never negatively impacted the association's business. In fact, First Savings experienced an incredible period of growth during this time, and when the dispute ended, the association had reached nearly $5 million in assets. Directors Jobe, Hupman, and James, members of the Shareholders' Group, put the issue behind them, fully backing the institution's management and uniting the board for the first time in a decade.

The second-guessing was over. The closing of this chapter in the association's history took Neal Smith from the lingering shadow of John McIntyre and thrust him into the main leadership role of the association. The proxy fight not only changed First Savings, but it had a long-lasting effect on Neal Smith and his management style. Although Smith had been with the association for nearly a decade, the lessons learned over the previous three years stayed with Smith a lifetime. Fifty years later, Smith recalls this period often with vivid detail and great emotion.

It was time to move on and return to the business of lending. Loan demand continued at such a torrid pace that four hundred thousand dollars in FHLB advances were needed by June. The association increased its lending limit from 80 percent to 90 percent of the property value, further generating loan activity.

First Savings was certainly changing, but this was nothing compared to the evolution of America's social fabric. Missile sites discovered in Cuba forced a tense standoff with the Soviet Union as the Cuban Missile Crisis tested President Kennedy's resolve. Racial tensions escalated in the South as the civil rights movement gained momentum. Federal troops were sent to enforce integration at the University of Mississippi after rioting occurred. Sam Walton opened the first Wal-Mart store in Arkansas, and the United States took the lead in the space race when astronaut John Glenn became the first man to orbit the earth.

The ever-present problem of retaining deposits had been a thorn in the side of the association since it opened its doors. This problem was common for most savings and loans. FHLB advances kept monies flowing to institutions to fund mortgage loans, thus driving the housing market forward. The value of these advances to the savings and loan industry during the postwar building boom cannot be overstated. Still these advances were a debt that had to be repaid, and they often impacted smaller institutions that were more dependent on these advances. Neal Smith and his friend Wade Key came up with an alternative.

Key, formerly with Hillsborough Savings and Loan, went to work for Home Federal Savings and Loan in Palm Beach, Florida. Smith and Key remained friends and corresponded frequently. It turned out that Key's institution had the exact opposite problem, as mortgage loans were dead in South Florida and Home Federal had more money coming in to its institution than it could lend. Smith and Key entered into a loan participation agreement that helped both institutions. The agreement allowed Home Federal to "buy" mortgage loans from First Savings, thus providing money for First Savings to lend. The loans purchased by Home Federal served as an investment for its excess cash on hand. First Savings sold three hundred thousand dollars in mortgage loans to the Palm Beach thrift in October. Loan participations are common today but were somewhat rare in the early 1960s. The primary purchasers in today's environment are the government-sponsored enterprises—the Federal National Mortgage Association and Federal Home Loan Mortgage Corporation, which supply the liquidity needed for the nation's mortgage market. In 2008 the government took over both the FNMA and FHLMC as the mortgage crisis surfaced.

School consolidation in Alamance County was in full swing, and in its wake many storied rivalries between local schools disappeared. The rivalry between Haw River High School and Mebane High School went so deep that some folks from Mebane objected to sending their children to school with those living in Haw River and vice versa. On August 29, 1962, Haw River's school colors of green and white merged with Mebane's blue and gold, forming the now familiar green and gold of Eastern Alamance High School. In the transition, the old Mebane High School building became Mebane Junior High School. The school was more than just brick and mortar to those who passed through its doors. When Mebane High School ceased to exist, part of the town's heritage disappeared.

First Savings extended its first-ever scholarships to high school graduates in

June 1962. Recipients were Linda Richmond, William Larry Rogers, and Judith McGowan James from the last graduating class of Mebane High School. Although this program has changed over the years, a four-year scholarship is still given to a graduating senior from Eastern Alamance.

Eastern Alamance did not have a football stadium when the school was first constructed. The Eagles played their home games at the Mebane Ball Park, the same field where the Mebane Tigers provided decades of memories. A wooden fence surrounded the field, which had a unique scoreboard featuring a large round clock at the field house end of the stadium. The facility would later be named Walker Field in tribute to Mebane High School's legendary football coach, Archie Walker. Walker Field is still used for city recreation activities.

Archie Walker was a football legend during the 1950s and 1960s who began coaching at Mebane High School in 1945, compiling an impressive record of 148 wins, 38 losses, and 13 ties. His Tigers won eight consecutive Mid-State Conference Championships in the late 1950s and early 1960s. Walker was the coach of the Eastern Eagles, who began their first football season on the road at Graham High School in the fall of 1962. This first football game for Eastern also began a tradition for First Savings as well. The association provided miniature footballs that cheerleaders threw out at halftime. This tradition continued for years at home games.

As 1963 began, management of First Savings wondered what surprises the year's annual shareholders' meeting would bring. The past two shareholders' meetings had been some of the most difficult and trying times in the association's history. Compared to those experiences, the shareholders' meeting of 1963 was quite boring. One year earlier, 154 members packed the association's lobby for a proxy fight, but only 27 members showed up at the meeting in 1963; 9 of those in attendance were directors. The highlight of the meeting was the presentation of a twenty-five-year service award to Director A.H. Jobe. Hoping for the best, but preparing for the worst, the board again invited Judge L.J. Phipps to monitor the election of directors. Phipps, who supervised the 1962 marathon meeting, presided over a very routine affair, much to the board's relief. The storm had finally blown through, but another hurricane was forming as the events of 1963 shaped a generation and changed the world.

Over two hundred thousand people gathered at the Lincoln Memorial in Washington, DC, to hear Dr. Martin Luther King Jr. deliver his "I Have a Dream" speech. Communist forces stepped up their aggression in the unstable country of South Vietnam. Thirty years earlier, President Franklin D. Roosevelt shaped the ideals of the Greatest Generation, and the current president John F. Kennedy inspired their children, the baby boomers. President Kennedy—asking "What you can do for your country"—developed the Peace Corps, and the country was on the verge of space exploration. The chaos of the Kennedy assassination on November 22, 1963, sent financial markets reeling and thrust Vice President Lyndon Johnson into the presidency.

Despite the unstable times, the association grew 67 percent in assets in three years and stood at $6 million. The first four years of the decade, although tumultuous, were some of the association's best lending years. First Savings averaged 292 loan closings a year with an average annual volume of $1,683,775. The average home loan amount extended by First Savings in the early 1960s was $5,766, an 80 percent increase in ten years. First Savings' borrowing from the FHLB to meet this demand reached a total of $700,000 by 1963.

Since becoming a director in 1948, Dr. I.C. Clark spent very little time at the institution, outside of attending monthly board meetings. Clark, now semi-retired from his dental practice, worked part-time with the association, assisting Neal Smith with closing loans. Smith had been closing all mortgage loans himself for years, along with managing the business. Clark's assistance was welcomed. When Clark came to work, Smith resigned his position as treasurer, deferring this position to Clark, but retained the position of executive vice president.

Charles C. Hartman, the association's original building contractor from four years earlier, added an office for Clark. To project a professional image, uniforms were ordered for the staff, much to their dismay.

Monthly board meetings at that time were held in the evenings on the last Thursday of each month at the association's offices. These meetings in the early 1960s were notoriously lengthy and a forum for heated debates, some lasting well into the night. After the proxy fight, these meetings became less confrontational and more productive. Director June Crumpler suggested moving the meeting to a daytime lunch meeting, and the idea was an instant hit. Arrangements were made with Charlie McAdams at the A&M Grill. The association's monthly board meetings continue at the Grill today. Directors rarely missed a meeting after this change, prompting Neal Smith to comment, "Feed 'em and pay 'em and they'll show up."

The year 1964 marked the end of the careers of two local sports legends. Football coach Archie Walker retired from Eastern High School, and longtime basketball coach, George Shackelford, left Mebane to take a position at the Department of Public Instruction in Raleigh. Shackelford set an incredible standard in basketball at Mebane High School during the 1950s as his teams won fifty-one straight Mid-State Conference games, including a State Championship in 1957.

Mebane's downtown business district bustled with activity and looked much the same as it had for generations. Jones' Department Store at the corner of Clay and Fourth was busy as ever, as was Rose's 5 and 10 Cent Store. Boxcars lined the auxiliary tracks near the depot, loaded with furniture, mattresses, and textile goods made in Mebane. The high-pitched White Furniture whistle blared at lunchtime, followed by the deep diesel horn from the Mebane Company. The familiar siren of the Mebane Fire Department promptly sounded every Thursday night at 7 p.m., calling volunteers to their weekly meeting. Before sunrise a Melville Dairy truck delivered milk in glass containers to homes across the county. Local schoolboys tossed the morning paper in driveways, dodging neighborhood dogs in the process.

Many of the businesses along Center and Clay streets grew up around and in support of industry giants White and the Mebane Company. But by the 1950s, these businesses had their own identities and customer base. An erosion of that customer base began in the 1960s as the new four-lane interstate made travel easier to other cities. Fearful of losing consumer dollars, local businesses began a "Shop in Mebane" campaign.

The town itself was slowly but surely growing toward the interstate as Arrowhead Golf Course opened off Mebane Oaks Road behind Junior Madden's Texaco. By 1965 land surrounding the interchanges attracted more development. The Arrowhead Restaurant and Motor Lodge opened, and A&M Grill's Charlie McAdams leased the restaurant. Builder James Freeland stated that all the materials used to construct the restaurant and motel were purchased in Mebane. One mile west, work continued on the Stuckey's Restaurant that was being built at the Trollingwood Road exit. As these small businesses sprang up on I-85, no one at that time imagined that these were the beginnings of a new business district that would later alter Mebane's commercial identity.

As Mebane basked in peaceful southern tranquility, tensions grew in Southeast Asia. A controversial incident in the Gulf of Tonkin prompted Congress to pass the Gulf of Tonkin Resolution, and officially the Vietnam War began.

After seventy-five days of filibustering by southern senators, the Civil Rights Bill passed, legislating an end to racial discrimination. The bill paved the way for more laws protecting minorities in the purchase of a home. As part of his Great Society program, President Johnson signed the Medicare Act, providing health care to seniors. In November, Johnson easily won reelection over Republican challenger Barry Goldwater and announced his War on Poverty.

The Vietnam War and an aggressive legislative agenda for social programs from the Johnson administration impacted the nation's economy. The extended inflationary period that the country was about to enter placed severe pressures on the housing industry. Americans were earning an average of $6,469 a year, but the spending power of every dollar earned was shrinking.

The period from 1945 to 1965 proved to be the golden age for the nation's savings and loans. These institutions reaped an incredible harvest, supplying funds to build homes for a growing America. By 1965, the assets of the country's thrifts were fourteen times larger than when the boom started in 1945, but the lucrative housing market that had driven the U.S. economy forward for the past twenty years was losing steam. The postwar baby boom had ended, and as the nation's population growth leveled out, housing demand weakened. From 1950 to 1960, home prices in America had doubled. By 1965 the appreciation rate had slowed to 8 percent in five years as the average cost of a home stood at $13,600. Lending figures for First Savings reflected the slowdown in the real estate market. Loan demand declined for three straight years after reaching its peak for the decade in 1963. From 1964 to 1969, closings fell to an average of 199 loans per year with an average annual volume of $1,399,933.

In January 1965 the association received a letter from Wade Key of Home Federal in Palm Beach, Florida. Apparently the loan participations that First Savings had entered into with Home Federal did not sit well with regulators. Key's letter instructed First Savings "to repurchase the remaining four loan participations...to comply with the FHLB ruling." There is no mention in the institution's board minutes that First Savings had erred in the participation process or what the "FHLB ruling" involved, but apparently the FHLB found some irregularities on the part of Home Federal. The loan participations had been paid down substantially, and the amount sent to Home Federal did not seem to upset the directors as they repurchased the loans with little discussion.

A time and temperature sign was erected in February 1965 and was becoming quite popular as a Mebane landmark. The directors seized on this marketing opportunity by running a summer Sizzler Contest. The contest would award a $250 cash prize to the person who predicted the date the temperature on the sign would hit 95 degrees. Looking to increase deposit activity, the $250 prize would be doubled if the winner had an account with First Savings. The contest ended on July 15, and although the temperature never reached 95, George Lynch was declared the winner as he guessed June 23, the period's hottest day, which topped out at 91 degrees.

Across the street from First Savings, Carl McAdams was pumping gas at his Esso station for thirty-one cents a gallon. McAdams's Esso, like most stations of the day, was a full-service business with an attendant who pumped gas, checked the oil, and cleaned the windshield on vehicles at every visit. The world of self-service brought this ritual to an end. Ironically, McAdams's Esso was replaced in the 1970s by another popular Mebane institution and self-service center, Tommy's Mini Mart.

Downtown was still the hub for industry with White Furniture, the Mebane Company, and Dixie Yarn as its base. The Mebane Industrial Expansion Committee was formed with a mission to attract new commercial growth. It appeared that the efforts of the committee were bearing fruit when JFD Electronics, a Virginia company, considered Mebane for an industrial site. JFD eventually chose Graham over Mebane, citing poor water facilities as the reason for the decision. The town took action, passing a $280,000 water and sewer bond to upgrade facilities and extend water and sewer services.

As the town hoped to lure new employment opportunities, some of Mebane's established businesses were enjoying growth of their own. The Mebane Company completed a forty-thousand-square-foot addition while Dixie Yarn added eighteen thousand square feet to its existing building. Mr. and Mrs. Alton Rice moved Rice's Flour and Feed Company from its familiar location on Ruffin Street to the old Mebane Feed & Seed Plant on the corner of Highway 70 and Seventh Street. Kale Knitting Mills was purchased by Maro Industries of New York, and the plant changed its name to Roxy Hosiery Mills.

Money for a down payment had always been a challenge, particularly for first-time home buyers who had to overcome a steep 20 percent down payment to qualify for a loan. To clear this hurdle, First Savings extended mortgage loans that were additionally secured by savings accounts pledged on behalf of the borrower. These accounts were usually opened by a parent, relative, or even a builder who pledged the account as collateral. These accounts remained as collateral until the balance of the loan was paid down to a certain point or the property appreciated to a certain value. This method, although still available today, is seldom used but was a very popular alternative in the 1950s and 1960s when savings patterns were different.

Savings accounts, like mortgage loans, were of the plain-vanilla variety as consumers had few savings options from which to choose. Passbook accounts and a simple longer-term time account or bonus certificates were available. Interest rates on these accounts, which had been a model of consistency for over a decade, were changing. By September 1965, inflation pressures affected interest rates, and for the first time since the 1950s, savings rates increased from 4 percent to 4.25 percent.

Labor unions have never been popular in the South, yet attempts were made at this time to organize local industries. For over a year, White Furniture had been locked in contract negotiations with the Furniture Workers' Union of America. A strike had been averted in early 1965 when these negotiations broke down. White Furniture workers finally put an end to organizing efforts, rejecting union representation in the family-run business. A similar attempt was made to unionize Craftique Furniture, but its workers also declined efforts to unionize.

After three years of fund-raising, the football stadium at Eastern Alamance was dedicated on September 24, 1965. Permanent seating in the stadium was not fully completed in time for the first game so the athletic boosters brought in platforms to provide seats and temporary bleachers for fans. It was not the opening the school had hoped for its new stadium, as Eastern lost to Orange High School, 21-6.

The sleepy innocence found in the simplicity of small-town America made world issues seem a million miles away. By 1965 the war in Southeast Asia escalated as Operation Rolling Thunder began with full-scale bombing of North Vietnam.

The slow progress by U.S. forces and the lack of a clear strategy soon divided the nation's opinion on the conflict. Growing opposition to the war, coupled with the civil rights movement, defined the decade as the country continued its social revolution. War protests were common on college campuses as the student antiwar movement gained momentum. Civil rights demonstrations increased, and Dr. Martin Luther King Jr. led his famous march to Selma, Alabama. Fashion took a radical turn as well, much to the delight of male observers, as the miniskirt made its appearance and became a fashion staple.

Despite the ongoing shift in American culture, Mebane remained a small, conservative southern town somewhat removed from the chaos seen on the nightly news. Locals were more concerned about the disappearance of Betty's Snack Shack to make room for expansion of the post office. Betty's Snack Shack along with Dollar's Soda Shop had been Center Street landmarks since the 1940s. Although the popular trend of the day may have been longer hair, England West, Frederick Walker, and Tom Holt still gave crew cuts at their barber shop on Clay Street.

Tom Holt also helped many African Americans purchase their own homes in the Mebane area. Although the Civil Rights Act of 1964 had become law, the reality was that individual finances and covert racial factors often prevented many minorities from buying houses. Holt built modest homes, mostly in the West End area of Mebane, and many times personally pledged savings accounts at First Savings on behalf of buyers.

Mebane and Alamance County's roots ran deep in manufacturing and farming occupations. Many of the association's customers were of modest means regardless of race. Working-class folks may not have had a great deal of material possessions, but they were extremely loyal. Upon achieving the American Dream of owning their own home through a loan at First Savings, relationships were created that lasted for generations. This was particularly true of minorities, as they had fewer employment and financial options at the time. One minority customer of the association stated that First Savings had always "looked after the little guy," while banks had the appearance of catering to the wealthy.

During its first one hundred years, First Savings financed many local minority churches. Neal Smith recalled one such church in the West End area. "I was invited to the church and met with several of the church leaders, and they wanted to build a new church building. What impressed me was that there were probably ten people there who were willing to put their own personal homes up as collateral as well as pledge savings to obtain the loan for the church."

Local farmers who applied for loans were often unable to make regular payments because of the inconsistency of income. For example, earnings of tobacco farmers came during the fall market. For these folks, the association often modified their loans, accepting one payment for the entire year. This option was common with farmers during the 1950s and 1960s and is still available today.

Downtown was a busy place at noon as workers from White and the Mebane Company hustled to Warren's Drug and Carolina Drug, which had lunch counters. Doug Isaac recalls that Warren's Drug did a brisk business at lunch and that "the regulars would come in every day and order the same thing every day. It got so that the girls in the back [lunch counter] had their order ready and waiting on the table by the time they came in." Warren's was a teenage hangout after school, where milkshakes cost twenty-five cents.

In 1966 Fred Brady became the new football coach at Eastern Alamance. Brady was an ex-navy frogman, forerunner to the Navy SEAL, having served in World War II. Eastern Alamance was still forming its own identity, stepping from the shadows of Mebane and Haw River high schools. Like former coach Archie Walker, Brady built his own legacy at the school's new football stadium, a facility that would one day bear his name.

For the previous ten years, North Carolina had ranked first in the South for industrial growth and second in the nation for new business incorporations. Naturally Charlotte and cities in the Triangle and Triad were benefitting, but few businesses were moving to Alamance County. The Mebane Town Board, still miffed over losing one industry due to inadequate water facilities, joined with the Orange County commissioners to provide water and sewer services. Target areas of service were selected east of Mebane in western sections of Orange County. This joint effort would change Mebane's industrial profile by the 1970s. It wasn't long before the hard work and cooperation of the two governing bodies paid off. Piedmont Steel and Tubing committed to building on a site off Buckhorn Road once water and sewer connections were completed. As the town of Mebane and

Orange County scored a major victory, the Orange Alamance Water Corporation began running water lines from Back Creek in Haw River east to Efland.

As Mebane grew, so did the Mebane Home Telephone Company, which had over twenty-seven hundred phones in service. The 1960s was the era of the muscle car, and the fall ritual was for teenage boys to pack the showrooms of Amick Ford and Melville Chevrolet to get a glimpse of the new Mustangs and Camaros.

Interest rates on savings deposits increased a second time within a year, rising to 4.50 percent. Deposit insurance levels were raised to fifteen thousand dollars, reflecting a hint of inflation. An extended period of fluctuating interest rates started slowly in the mid-1960s and accelerated through the 1970s and into the early 1980s. The savings and loan industry had seen periods of unstable rates before, but these periods were usually short in duration and the industry adjusted. Inflation and rate swings that were on the horizon would have a detrimental effect on institutions and expose the true weakness of the savings and loan concept by the mid-1970s.

In prior decades Americans were content with the ritual of depositing their funds in a local savings institution and remaining loyal to that association. This loyalty was reinforced by a stable and regulated interest rate environment. As short-term savings rates began to rise, customers once loyal to their community institutions began moving their money around to chase higher returns. Deposits are a coveted commodity by all institutions, and competition from commercial banks accelerated.

Washington's reaction to this increasing competition for deposits is important to note here. The 1940s and 1950s had been an economic bonanza for the country and the financial industry. With the exception of fine-tuning some existing laws, Congress had left banking alone for the better part of thirty years. The 1960s would see changes in the economy and government regulation. Lawmakers grappled with the question of parity among institutions while ensuring fair competition. The overriding concern was how to deal with competition between banks and thrifts.

Congress went the route of regulating competition in 1966 with the Interest Rate Adjustment Act, allowing thrifts to pay more interest on savings deposits than banks. Regulation Q, part of the banking law passed in 1933, was extended to savings associations, limiting the interest rates that all insured financial institutions could pay on savings deposits. Regulators asserted that competition for deposits among banks and thrifts was driving interest rates higher. Placing a ceiling on interest rates for deposits at savings institutions would stop this rate escalation and reduce interest expense. Savings and loans were allowed to pay a slightly higher savings rate than banks, giving thrifts a competitive edge in attracting deposits. This edge held off competition from banks for a time, but as interest rates climbed in the 1970s, rate ceilings turned into a liability that threatened the entire industry.

The shift in rates that began in the 1960s and accelerated into the 1970s and beyond had an adverse affect on the savings and loan industry. As higher rates were paid on short-term deposits, these same funds were locked into long-term loans. Thus, short-term interest paid out to customers as an expense continued to rise while mortgage interest income was locked in at lower fixed rates for the long haul. As short rates began to rise, the spread between expenses and income began to narrow, and so did profits.

Rice's Flour and Feed Mill adjacent to White Furniture on Highway 70 had survived since 1917 with a long and storied history. F.H. Duncan closed the mill in 1963 and sold the facility to the Rices to relocate their thriving business. On May 5, 1966 the mill became the site of the second horrific fire to hit the town in six years. The Mebane Fire Department arrived quickly but could not prevent two nearby homes from being damaged. The location of the mill next to the furniture factory raised fears that the fire could spread to White's lumber yard. Fortunately, a southwest wind prevented what could have been an even worse disaster. Mebane has had its share of spectacular fires over the years, and the loss of the feed mill, like the warehouse fire, resulted in the disappearance of another part of the town's heritage. Undaunted the Rices rebuilt their business and by September erected a grain elevator.

On October 13, 1966, Sam M. Hupman Sr., a director of the association since 1928, passed away. His tenure spanned thirty-eight years. Hupman and A.B. Fitch were the only surviving directors who had witnessed the incredible transformation of the institution during the Depression and postwar boom. A resolution was passed reducing the number of board members from nine to eight following Hupman's death.

In November, the Mebane Merchants' Association gathered at the A&M Grill and planned the first Mebane Christmas Parade to be held at night. Hoping to cash in and help customers get a jump on the Christmas shopping season, downtown stores remained open after the parade. Still held on the first Friday night in December, the Mebane Christmas Parade remains one of the area's premier Christmas events.

By 1967 the population of the United States reached the 200 million mark. As the country grew, so did social unrest as Americans were deeply divided over the war in Vietnam. Large antiwar demonstrations were held in New York and Washington. The sex, drugs, and rock and roll subculture emerged, with its rallying cry to "tune in, turn on, drop out."

As tensions in the nation rose so did interest rates. This time it was mortgage rates, which hit a thirty-year high of 7 percent by late summer, further slowing the real estate market. This move was significant as mortgage rates had ranged from 5 percent to 6 percent for twenty years. Thrifts could do nothing but watch their spread or profit dwindle as savings institutions were limited to accepting deposits and granting home mortgage loans. Thrifts were prohibited from commercial or consumer transactions. But as the song says, "The times they are a-changin'."

Texas thrifts were the first to offer property development loans up to 50 percent of their net worth. This speculative and often risky lending was new territory for savings and loans. Seen as progressive, Texas was soon followed by most of the industry as thrifts struggled to improve their balance sheet. These steps were the first taken to modernize an industry that many thought was stuck in the past.

Mebane's industrial base grew as High Point–based Universal Textile Yarns opened a facility at the end of McPherson Drive in Mebane. The company eventually employed twelve hundred workers, joining textile giants Dixie Yarn and others as furniture and textiles remained Mebane's bread-and-butter.

In 1968 North Vietnam launched the Tet Offensive against targets in the south. Although it did not result in a military victory, the action convinced most Americans that the war could not be won under the present terms of engagement. The United States had lost over twenty thousand men in the conflict, and by spring, President Lyndon Johnson became its next casualty.

The Vietnam War stalled Johnson's domestic agenda, and although he pushed massive legislation through Congress, the Great Society he envisioned took a backseat to the conflict in Southeast Asia. The United States was trapped in an unconventional war where politics limited the military's ability to fight. Johnson could not possibly win the war under these conditions, and withdrawal would damage U.S. credibility around the world. In a prime-time speech, Johnson stunned the nation stating that he would not seek reelection in the fall of 1968.

On April 3, civil rights leader Dr. Martin Luther King Jr. was cut down by an assassin's bullet in Memphis, Tennessee. Cities teetering on the brink of racial violence exploded as riots erupted throughout the nation. James Earl Ray would later be convicted in King's death. Two months later, on June 5, presidential candidate Robert F. Kennedy was killed by assassin Sirhan Sirhan in Los Angeles. America's social unrest hit prime time as news cameras captured violent clashes between antiwar demonstrators and police at the Democratic National Convention in Chicago. The images were shown on live television throughout the country. Playing to the silent majority, Richard Nixon was elected president, defeating Hubert Humphrey in November.

As the world seemed to be changing at light speed, some things remained the same. One of the few things that had changed very little over the years was the simple process of mortgage lending. A customer completed an application, and most community institutions did an informal appraisal of the property. There were few verifications asked of the borrower, such as tax returns, and little paperwork to file. An attorney performed a title search, and the closing consisted of the customer signing a Note and Deed of Trust and a Closing Statement. Most real estate transactions could be processed within a week. The majority of home loans were originated by savings and loan associations, and mortgages were kept at that institution and not sold.

The securitization process of selling mortgage loans coupled with massive legislation transformed the real estate closing into the complicated process that most consumers know today. Neal Smith recalled that simple handshake transactions were done routinely during the 1950s and 1960s, and many times, home purchases rarely had written contracts between the buyer and seller. But the good old days ended with the 1968 passage of the Truth in Lending Act that created detailed disclosure requirements for the consumer. The law changed the regulatory climate and set the stage for a controlled business environment for all financial institutions in the years to come.

First Savings began the 1960s averaging $5,453 per home loan. By 1969 the average home loan stood at $8,608, reflecting increasing home values. In those days, savings associations were allowed to charge a prepayment penalty on loans that were paid off early. Most institutions chose not to do so. First Savings never charged any prepayment penalties, and for good reason. When customers refinanced or bought another home, they returned to their local savings and loan. Refinancing a home loan at that time had a completely different meaning compared to today's refinancing. The idea of a prepayment penalty could drive customers down the street to another institution. Although First Savings didn't go for prepayment fees, a ten-dollar appraisal fee was added on all new loans by 1969.

In 1969, First Philadelphia Bank started what would become a national staple in the banking industry by installing a "cash dispensing machine," and the forerunner of the ATM was born. Rates continued to move higher as Bonus Savings Accounts increased to 5.25 percent. The certificate required a hefty minimum fifteen-thousand-dollar deposit and matured in twelve months. The FSLIC raised deposit insurance to twenty thousand dollars, its second increase in just three years.

In the late 1960s, something unusual began happening in different markets across the country. Several Illinois savings and loans failed due to fraud and mismanagement. Some thrifts in Nevada that invested in speculative construction became insolvent when market conditions changed. Institutions also failed in California and other states, resulting mainly from the greed of management looking to turn quick profits. The savings and loan crisis was more than a decade away, but early symptoms were surfacing.

Since it first opened its doors in 1909, First Savings had struggled—as many institutions did—with liquidity and retained earnings. Maintaining sufficient cash to meet withdrawal obligations and to fund mortgage loans was a constant challenge. Money was always tight, and like most institutions the association borrowed funds as deposits never kept pace with lending activity. During the 1940s and 1950s having retained earnings was actually frowned upon by regulators given the cooperative nature of the industry at that time. First Savings' borrowing peaked at $750,000 in the early 1960s with most coming in the form of advances from the Federal Home Loan Bank. As the building boom waned in the mid-1960s and mortgage loans returned to manageable levels, local savings deposits adequately funded smaller loan demand and the association began to pay down its borrowed money. As this debt was reduced, the association's liquidity grew with excess cash invested in government bonds.

First Savings had not had a substantial surplus of funds since World War II, when it invested almost exclusively in war bonds. These investments provided some diversity of income to the institution without total reliance on mortgage loan interest as its only income source.

The pay down of borrowed money reduced expenses, and the undivided profits of the association began a slow but steady rise through the 1960s. As the 1950s ended the Association had one hundred thousand dollars in bonds and investments, but by the end of the 1960s that figure had grown to five hundred thousand dollars in bonds and investments. By December 1969 the Association had just seventy-five thousand dollars in borrowed money with assets over $7.5 million. The ability to go from three quarters of a million dollars in debt to half a million in income-producing investments over and above the loan portfolio was a significant achievement for the association, and the timing was crucial. First Savings was without a doubt in the best financial condition in its sixty years in operation, with an 8 percent reserve and minimal borrowed money.

Borrowing money is not necessarily a bad thing. Financial institutions wouldn't be in business if it was. Borrowing money for financial institutions is not only a good thing, but a very lucrative thing as all financial institutions live on borrowed money. Deposits are "borrowed" from the customer, just as are advances from the FHLB or other sources. Leveraging lower-cost money to make a higher return on loans or investments is the simple definition of a financial institution. In the 1960s, savings institutions and banks operated very differently compared to today. Mutual savings and loans borrowed short-term money (FHLB advances and deposits) and loaned these funds out in long-term, twenty-year mortgages. The problems with borrowing short and lending long are discussed in the next chapter as the rate environment beginning in the 1970s forever changed the industry. Banks, on the other hand, usually borrowed short-term money to make shorter-term loans or investments and were not a large player in the mortgage business during the 1960s.

Unlike most institutions, First Savings spent most of the decade getting out of debt while other banks and savings and loans borrowed funds and grew in assets.

This activity was a matter of choice. Following the crowd was something First Savings had done for most of its history. A pattern emerged during the 1960s and continues to the present as the association parted company with its fellow financial institutions. The consequences and rewards of this choice emerged in the 1980s.

From the association's perspective, First Savings had finally turned the corner. In its early days the business struggled to meet loan demand and felt its way through the good and bad times with borrowed funds and little retained earnings. With the steadily growing reserve now providing a cushion of funds, First Savings approached the future from a position of strength.

Regardless of size, an institution's reserve and liquid position are good barometers of that institution's strength. Regulations provided that an association create a 5 percent reserve requirement based on the amount of the institution's deposits. But the rules were about to change, and the century-old thrift industry would never be the same.

The looming savings and loan crisis of the 1980s had its beginnings many years earlier, with contributing factors coming from a variety of causes and events. By 1970 many of the pieces of this crisis were coming together, and the inflationary environment the country was about to enter would put the final nails in the coffin. As inflation continued to push interest rates higher, the once-lucrative profits for savings institutions continued to shrink.

Like the savings and loan industry, Mebane's identity was about to change. Interstate 85 was calling, and just as the railroad drew people and business to Mebane a century before, I-85 would do the same. Mebane began a transformation in the late 1960s and early 1970s from its traditional manufacturing base in the center of town to the interstate. This transition forever changed downtown and its once-vibrant business district.

The number of U.S. military forces in Vietnam peaked at 541,000 in 1969. Neil Armstrong was the first man to walk on the moon as Apollo 11's mission became the shining moment for NASA and the U.S. Space Program. In upstate New York 250,000 people gathered for the four-day Woodstock Music and Art Fair, and *Sesame Street* debuted on public television.

The 1960s had been an incredibly violent time for a country marked by war, social change, and the struggle for civil rights. Forty thousand U.S. soldiers had perished in the jungles of Vietnam, and the nation's value system was in a transformation unthinkable a decade earlier. But the 1960s had also been an incredible time of discovery. The moon landing in July 1969 captured the attention of the world, but a lesser-known event on October 29, 1969, had much greater impact. On that date, a computer in a lab at UCLA transmitted a word to another computer at the Stanford Research Institute in Palo Alto, California. The first word sent over what would become the Internet turned out to be "Lo," short for "Login." However, the computers crashed, and "Lo" was all that made it through the network. Quite an awkward start to a technology that would change mankind.

First Savings had entered the decade deeply divided, yet it survived and learned from a painful proxy fight. By 1969 the association was in the best financial position in its sixty-year history. After twenty-five years of unprecedented prosperity, the 1970s would again test the economic spirit of America, and bring about the beginning of the end of the savings and loan industry.

After eight years on Clay Street, First Savings built its current location at 206 W. Center Street in 1960. *Courtesy William Lynch Studios*

Shirley Oakley registers guests for prizes during the open house on December 2, 1960. *Courtesy William Lynch Studios*

Frances Terrell on the left and Neal Smith's wife, Sue Smith serve customers at the 1960 reception. *Courtesy William Lynch Studios*

A young girl accompanied by her parents opens her first savings account during the 1960s. *Courtesy Virginia Sellew*

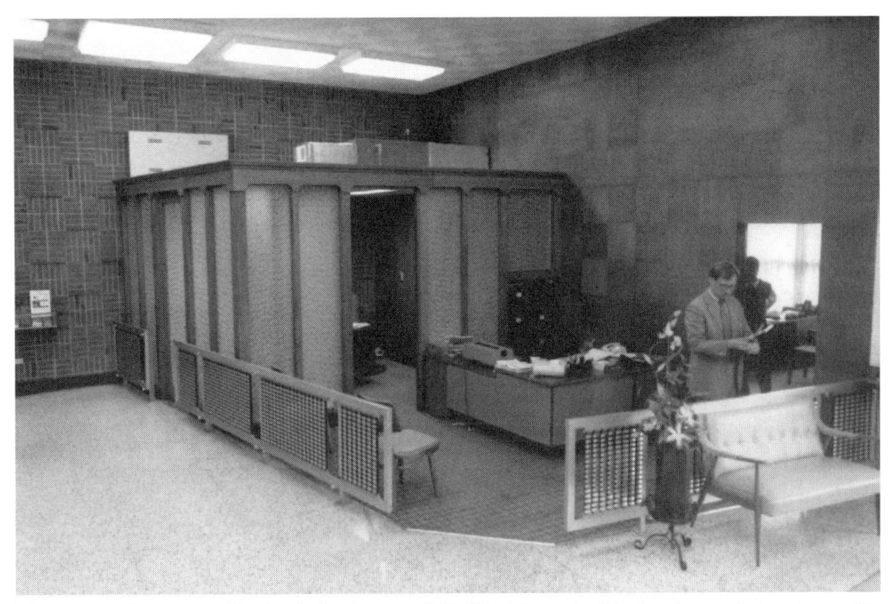

This photo shows an office built for director I.C. Clark in 1964. Notice the brick interior walls.

First Savings first time and temperature sign in 1965. *Courtesy William Lynch Studios*

In the 1990s a round clock and temperature sign replaced first generation of electric signs. *Courtesy William Lynch Studios*

A digital message board was erected in 2008. *Courtesy Mebane Enterprise*

CHAPTER SEVEN

On the Brink

1970–1979

WHAT A DIFFERENCE A DECADE MAKES. In 1960 the United States looked to the future with optimism and national patriotism was strong. But by 1970 the exact opposite was true. The 1960s had taken a profound toll on the American spirit, and the country was tired of the conflict in Southeast Asia that seemed to have no end in sight. The unthinkable was unfolding as the United States, with its massive military and economic power, lacked the strategy and most importantly the will to win the conflict.

The turbulent 1960s had been a solid decade for the U.S. economy, but that too was changing. Inflation had been virtually nonexistent during the 1950s, with a meager 2.04 percent rate that rose slightly during the 1960s to just 2.34 percent. Pressures from the war and social spending in the last half of the 1960s pushed inflation to its highest levels since the late 1940s, and by 1970 the annual inflation rate stood at 6.5 percent.

Home prices soared 85 percent during the 1960s, and by 1970 the average cost of a home stood at $23,000. Alamance County homes were affordable, averaging just below the national average at $22,500. That affordability was reflected in an ownership rate of 69.4 percent; the percentage of Alamance County residents who were home owners greatly outdistanced the national average of 58.9 percent. The average income of the American family soared 79 percent during the 1960s, beginning the decade at $11,419 a year. Over the next ten years, individual income could not keep pace with runaway inflation, changing the nation's economy.

The interest rate environment of January 1970 unfortunately set the tone for the decade as upward interest rate pressures sent First Savings rates higher. Passbook accounts hit 5 percent while a twenty-four-month savings certificate reached 6 percent. Higher deposit minimums remained common as six- and twelve-month certificates required a minimum of five thousand dollars while a twenty-four-month certificate called for a whopping ten-thousand-dollar minimum deposit, reinforcing the notion that financial institutions catered to the wealthy. The justification for higher deposit minimums was to attract larger accounts, something every institution desperately coveted.

Twenty years of low inflation coupled with the frugal American consumer borne out of the Depression had created a nation of savers. Although consumer spending exploded following World War II, Americans still comfortably added to personal savings. This frugality concerned local store owners during the Christmas shopping season as a local newspaper article stated Alamance County consumers were negatively affecting the economy by "holding back" $25 million in savings. The estimate from the Federal Reserve stated the average family in Alamance County made $10,500 a year, and of that, 7.8 percent of its income went into savings.

The consistent and stable economy that Americans had enjoyed for the previous two decades changed dramatically during the 1970s, testing consumers' ability to handle high energy prices, rampant inflation, and soaring unemployment. Coupled with consumer choices, these economic changes eroded the ability of most working Americans to save. The social upheaval of the 1960s and changes in American social values made a mark in the workplace as well. In 1960, 50 percent of women in Alamance County worked outside the home. By 1970, 66 percent of women were in the workforce.

First Savings entered the 1970s in excellent financial condition. Speaking at the February shareholders' meeting, President Neal Smith "emphasized the extra effort that had been taken by the association to create reserves to strengthen the association's position ... during these uncertain times." The reduction of borrowed money during the 1960s and the association's increased reserve could not have come at a better time, as First Savings was positioned to meet future economic cycles from a position of strength, something that had previously eluded the institution.

At the 1970 shareholders' meeting, Lee Settle was elected as the association's legal counsel, replacing T.C. Carter, who had been with the institution since 1915. It was common at that time for one attorney to handle most legal work for an institution, whereas today consumers have choices in attorneys. Carter had already relinquished most of the legal work to Settle during the late 1950s but remained the elected counsel. The 1970 meeting marked the end of an incredible fifty-five-year relationship between Carter and First Savings. Carter's expertise formed the legal foundation for the association from its earliest days through its coming of age as a savings and loan. Carter passed away in the 1970s, and Neal Smith described Carter as "always professional and the perfect southern gentleman."

Housing started off the decade on the wrong foot, and foreclosures were on the rise, with six scheduled for June alone. In all, First Savings instituted foreclosure proceedings eleven times in six months, reflecting a deteriorating local economy. Mortgage lending continued to fall as mortgage rates climbed. First Savings shifted its investments to the bond market, which was yielding a comfortable 8 percent.

Surprisingly, security procedures for most financial institutions were not a major priority, particularly in small towns. Associations had few or no policies in place, unlike their bank brethren in larger cities where risks were greater. The recently passed Bank Protection Act required an alarm system but not security cameras for savings institutions. The association would not install cameras until the 1990s. Small-town institutions often operate with a false sense of security when compared to banks in larger cities, a feeling reinforced by the fact that Mebane had never experienced a bank robbery. That unblemished streak ended in 2000.

After reaching the $8 million milestone in assets in 1970, First Savings entered a period of slow but steady growth. The association grew around $1 million a year in assets through the turbulent years to come. This slow-growth business approach seems somewhat unorthodox and contrary to American capitalism. The universal measure of success for a company is solid growth, signaling profitability and strength. That perception is true for stock-owned businesses, but growth for a mutually chartered savings and loan, although desirable, is not a prerequisite to success. For the first time in its history, First Savings was in a financial position that it could grow, but this strategy was never considered by the board as the association's market created over sixty years was stable and profitable. Any grand ambitions of rapid growth were virtually impossible unless branching to other communities was considered.

For better or worse, the association never built any branches, although a group of Caswell County customers had approached the board during the 1960s about opening an office in Yanceyville. The nature of the mutual savings and loan industry in 1970 may not have required an aggressive growth strategy, but First Savings found itself falling behind other savings associations in the county in asset size. The simple and unimpeded path that small-town thrifts had taken for the past twenty-five years was changing and would never be the same.

The North Carolina Zoological Society was looking for a one-thousand-acre site for a state zoo, and Mebane was on the short list. Although the zoo eventually built near Asheboro, Mebane's location in the center of the state was gaining broader attention. Situated on the Alamance-Orange County line, Mebane's potential for business and industrial development brought new opportunities, breaking the traditional molds of the past. The town's tremendous residential and industrial growth that shifted into high gear in the 2000s truly had its beginnings in the 1970s, with Mebane's migration to the interstate. One of the first steps taken in this march began in 1970 when the town annexed sixty-three acres along McPherson Drive and South Fifth and South Eighth streets.

Mebane's high hopes for industrial expansion had an inauspicious start. The Piedmont Steel and Tubing Company near Buckhorn Road was supposed to be the catalyst that drew more manufacturing to the city. After just two years in operation, the company closed, delivering a blow to Mebane's expansion efforts. The vacant plant soon attracted a permanent owner that launched Mebane into an industrial revolution.

Several local businesses were already looking to the future. Tommy Stevens cashed in on the growing popularity of convenience stores, opening Tommy's Mini Mart on the corner of Clay and Second streets, where PSNC Energy is today. James Rice relocated Rice's Jewelry from North Fourth Street to the familiar corner of Center and Fourth. James' Café moved from its original log cabin on Highway 70 east of town to North Second Street, where it operated for twenty-five years, and Vance Foust opened the Western Auto Store on Fourth Street.

Mebane's population now stood at 2,573 residents, an 8.8 percent increase during the 1960s. This growth brought with it changes to the town's image. The City Council and civic groups wanted to beautify the town, focusing on vacant homes, dilapidated buildings, and junk cars. The abandoned ice plant was deemed a hazard and torn down. The plant, located where Eighth Street meets East Washington Street and once owned by Southern Railway, was used to supply ice to refrigerate perishable items transported by rail. A clean appearance would attract customers to downtown, and the town then set its sights on the abandoned Southern Railway Depot.

Mrs. Audrey Garrett retired from Alexander Wilson Elementary after forty-three years in education. Garrett, who taught every grade except first, would be honored for her achievements some thirty years later when an elementary school bearing her name would be built in the Hawfields community. Construction delays pushed the opening of the new $1.4 million Woodlawn Middle School past the Christmas holidays. A departure from traditional schools, Woodlawn's design offered open classrooms employing a team teaching concept. It was also in 1970 when Stanford Junior High was dedicated in Orange County, and the $2 million school boasted a capacity of twelve hundred students.

The system of home financing changed when the Emergency Home Finance Act of 1970 created the Federal Home Loan Mortgage Corporation, known as Freddie Mac. Postwar American homes had been built largely on the financial strength of local institutions that relied on FHLB advances and local deposits to fund mortgage loans. However, this system of financing could no longer meet the nationwide loan demand. The industry was now looking beyond its own backyard. Freddie Mac and its counterpart, the Federal National Mortgage Association—Fannie Mae—revolutionized the mortgage industry by creating a secondary mortgage market and providing much-needed liquidity for lending institutions. This liquidity was created by purchasing and selling loan pools (bundles of loans) to investors. An institution, for example, in a hot real estate market and unable to raise funds through local deposits packaged mortgage loans and sold them to FHLMC or FNMA, a process referred to as securitization. This institution in turn received funds to continue generating loans. Likewise, an institution in a poor real estate environment might have excess funds or high liquidity that they could not lend due to depressed mortgage activity. This institution could invest excess liquidity by purchasing a package of loans through mortgage-backed securities and other instruments and receiving interest on its investment. This is a very simple explanation of the complex and sophisticated world of the secondary mortgage market. Fannie Mae, Freddie Mac, and the process of securitization transformed the mortgage industry, and home loans evolved into a commodity that was bought and sold based on its rate of return, quality of investment, risk, and other factors, just as a security or bond might be traded.

The demand for mortgage loans through securitization really took off in the 1980s when interest rates fell in the midst of the savings and loan crisis. Freddie Mac and Fannie Mae established themselves as primary mortgage funding sources. First Savings purchased Freddie Mac stock in 1971.

The Piedmont Steel and Tubing Plant had been vacant less than a year when rumors were confirmed that General Electric had purchased the facility. GE transferred its motor control division from Ohio and initially employed three hundred workers. At full capacity, GE projected that twelve hundred new jobs would come to Mebane. GE's announcement was huge, and the opening of the plant in 1972 sparked a new industrial beginning for Mebane. Other companies such as Webco, Panex, and Hancor opened at that time, and the addition of GE demonstrated that the local business environment was ripe for development with a strong workforce.

The significance here was not just job creation but the types of jobs that were on the way. GE and the plant's location on the interstate were a departure from the traditional North Carolina base in textiles, furniture, and tobacco, and the transition of the labor force in Mebane had begun. This new birth was due largely to the work of the Mebane Industrial Expansion Committee. Their efforts were honored when the committee received the North Carolina Governor's Award from Governor Bob Scott.

A parade of new industry soon followed, bringing with it jobs and people to Mebane. Until that point, most local industry had been homegrown with only a handful of businesses originating outside of North Carolina. These new companies came from different parts of the country and brought with them transplants. Mebane's culture began to shift as well, and by the turn of the twenty-first century,

Mebane, once steeped in southern tradition, became as diverse in its population as in its industry.

This commercial and business renaissance was met with open arms most of the time, but like anything else, development came with a price. The vacant depot on Fifth Street had stood watch over Mebane's main business and manufacturing district, an area that had changed very little in decades. The bulk of commercial activity that began in earnest in the 1970s accelerated development near Mebane Oaks Road and Highway 119 at I-85, forever changing the role of downtown Mebane.

And there was another problem. Thousands of towns across the country were feeling the effects of a new form of commercial real estate: shopping malls. Burlington's Holly Hill Mall had opened in 1969, and its effects were felt on the streets of every local city including Mebane. The Mebane Merchants Association fought back and considered turning downtown Mebane into a pedestrian mall. A feasibility study suggested blocking off Clay, Third, and Fourth streets to car traffic, but these plans were later scrapped due to the massive cost. One downtown Mebane landmark did change its name; the Mebane Company, founded in 1904, officially became Kingsdown.

Despite revitalization efforts, downtown Mebane—once a center of commercial activity—entered a period of decline beginning in the 1970s. Undaunted, Jesse Lewis, who had operated Jones' Department Store since 1940, opened Lewis' Department Store on Clay Street. Electrician Larry Wood Sr. felt the time was right to strike out on his own, and he opened Wood Electric. In 1977 Wood moved to the company's familiar location on South Eighth Street.

Another price of growth was increased traffic on city streets and a strain on water services. South Fifth Street residents were fighting a plan from the North Carolina Department of Transportation to widen Fifth Street from downtown to I-85. The sudden and rapid commercial and residential development prompted the town of Mebane and city of Graham to finalize plans for the expansion of Quaker Lake, including Backcreek Reservoir, which would have twenty-nine miles of shoreline.

First Savings was learning quickly that the business of making loans in the 1970s would be much different than times past. After a lackluster first quarter, loans picked up briefly in April 1971, but remained stymied most of the year. First Savings instituted foreclosure three times during 1971 as the economy stayed in the doldrums with inflation weighing in at 4.31 percent. Director A.B. Fitch, now in his nineties, reached the fifty-year milestone as a board member and was honored at a reception and presented with a lapel pin from the North Carolina Savings and Loan League.

Since the Depression, Greensboro had been home to a regional office of the Federal Home Loan Bank, greatly benefitting the state's savings and loan industry. The Bank offered classes and continuing education, and Neal Smith took full advantage of these courses over the years. The Federal Home Loan Bank Board announced the relocation of its regional offices from Greensboro to Atlanta, prompting opposition letters from the association and other lenders across the state. The Federal Home Loan Bank moved to Atlanta, where it remains today, serving as the Southeast Region headquarters.

As the first motor control starters came off the line at GE in early 1972, a spark of activity ignited Mebane. A shopping center was on its way to the corner of South Fifth and Washington streets, anchored by a Byrd's Food Store (Z-Bowl). Mobile home manufacturer Redman Industries from Dallas, Texas, built a plant in Mebane receiving 1,000 job applications for 125 positions. Universal Textiles was purchased by Dow Badische, and Mebane Packaging broke ground on its new facility near the interstate. The flurry of development brought new jobs and with it a changing of the guard, as established businesses bowed to the pressure of new consumer preferences. Jones' Department Store, an anchor downtown business, closed its doors after forty-one years of operation. As one Mebane icon closed its doors, another opened, as Jim Covington opened King Tire Service on Highway 70 east of town.

On the heels of the commercial activity came two large residential subdivision requests. Developer Bill Lester introduced Brookhollow with 195 home sites on the old Dogwood Golf Course property. This would be an upscale subdivision with homes priced between twenty-five thousand and forty thousand dollars. The second development planned for the 937-acre Cates Farm north of town came from Atlantis Corporation, headed by First Savings Director June Crumpler. Originally this development included 800 home sites and an eighteen-hole golf course. The ambitious plan never got off the ground and scaled back significantly to 124 building lots and 100 apartment units that would become Forest Ridge subdivision.

Enterprise reporter Steve Mills shared a story that reflects the real estate environment in Mebane during the early 1970s. Mills's father was part of the General Electric team that transferred to North Carolina, and these folks found out very quickly that Mebane was not a hot real estate destination. "There were several people that worked together, including my father, who came down to look for houses. At the time there just weren't any houses for sale. I think there were two houses on the market at the time and no apartments to rent. The property off Stagecoach Road which is now Laramie Drive was owned by the Huey family and contact was made with the Hueys and builder Garland Burgess. The Hueys wanted to develop this property and were willing to open the subdivision if they could get seven people to commit to buy houses in there." Seven families including the Millses agreed to purchase homes, and Laramie Drive became the town's newest subdivision.

Until this point, residential development for Mebane had been somewhat of a patchwork of homes in relatively small subdivisions. These new developments offered larger two-story houses and the latest in home construction style, called the split-level home. This popular multistoried plan separated bedrooms and living areas onto different floors. No doubt these new homes were tastefully decorated with the popular and endearing avocado green appliances, yellow plumbing fixtures, and of course, plush shag carpet.

The rise in commercial and residential development was somewhat overwhelming, and several Town Council members suggested discouraging new industrial development. This drew criticism from the Mebane Industrial Expansion Committee, which felt that its hard work was finally paying off. Although downtown was not the vibrant center of commerce it used to be, it was not going to buckle under without a fight. The old, vacant Mebane Theater was remodeled becoming the Welcome Finance building. A Chapel Hill company planned to bring a cable television franchise to Mebane, promising up to fifteen television channels to its customers.

The interchanges at I-85 in eastern Alamance County were slowly but surely changing. The Technical Institute of Alamance, opened in 1959, had outgrown its Vaughn Road Facility in Burlington. Governor Bob Scott donated forty-eight acres of prime real estate near I-85 on Jimmy Kerr Road that would later become its Graham Campus and is now known as Alamance Community College.

The Red Horse Restaurant opened in 1972 on Trollingwood Road at I-85. The twenty-four-hour-eatery was a favorite for truckers and could be seen easily from the highway with a distinctive large red horse on top of the building. Red Horse was known to host celebrities passing through as Merle Haggard, Loretta Lynn, and Dolly Parton were said to have eaten there. The Temptations and the Doobie Brothers also stopped in after concerts at the Greensboro Coliseum. The Red Horse is gone, but this location still caters to eighteen-wheelers as the Pilot Travel Center.

Although the war in Vietnam dragged on, U.S. troop strength had dropped to two hundred thousand. Concerns over inflation prompted the Nixon administration to implement a ninety-day wage freeze and a 10 percent surcharge on imported goods. Although there were questions about the state of the economy, Americans remained upbeat as mortgage rates stabilized and the Dow Jones Industrial Average reached the 1000 mark for the first time in history.

Several new companies that would shape American commerce made their debut in 1972, including Federal Express, which delivered a grand total of 186 packages on its first day, and a small California company named Intel, which introduced the microprocessor.

Five men with surveillance equipment were arrested after breaking into the Democratic National Headquarters at the Watergate Hotel Complex in Washington, igniting a scandal that rocked the nation. Despite the growing revelations in what would become known simply as Watergate, Richard Nixon was reelected, defeating Democratic challenger George McGovern in a landslide. Operation Linebacker II began just before Christmas, and for eleven days U.S. forces relentlessly bombed North Vietnamese targets in Hanoi and Haiphong. This offensive forced the Communists into intensive negotiations with Secretary of State Henry Kissinger to end the war.

The year 1973 seemed to be one in which the wheels of change were spinning out of control and events came fast. It was common for board members of mutual savings institutions to serve very long terms, and First Savings was no exception. At the end of 1972 the average term of service for a director had reached twenty-three years. The running joke was that when a person was hired by the association or joined the board of directors they were hired for life. Tragically three directors died within a six-month period in 1973, greatly altering the board and ending decades of consistency.

Since retiring from his dental practice, First Savings President and Director I.C. Clark had worked with Neal Smith on loan applications and closings. On January 4, 1973, the always punctual Clark was late for work and could not be reached by phone. Neal Smith drove to Clark's house on South Fifth Street, arriving the same time as Clark's son, Nelson, who had tried unsuccessfully to phone his father earlier that morning. They entered the home and found Clark sitting in his favorite chair, where he had apparently died the night before. The next day the board called a special meeting and named Dr. George M. Bullard vice president and chairman of the board. Neal Smith was named president, and Frances Terrell was appointed secretary of the corporation.

In his twenty years on the board, Clark saw the institution become a full-time business and prosper through the 1950s. He had endured the proxy fight of the early 1960s and was enjoying retirement, working some of the time and squirrel hunting when he had the chance. Big-game hunting was one of Clark's passions, and he often traveled to Canada on weeklong excursions. A prize moose head from one of his hunting trips was mounted and stood guard over First Savings' teller line until the building was remodeled in 1987.

The following day, January 6, another director honored six months earlier for his fifty years of service to the institution, A.B. Fitch, passed away. In the span of two days the association lost two close and longtime members of its family. At ninety-four and in failing health, Fitch was the institution's elder statesman, joining the board in 1922. In his fifty-year relationship, Fitch literally had witnessed every historical event of the association, with the exception of its birth in 1909. Placed in perspective, A.B. Fitch had already served ten years on the board of directors before President Neal Smith was born.

Fitch took his directorship seriously, placing the association above everything, including himself. Neal Smith recalled an incident that illustrates Fitch's level of dedication. "When the Fitch Riggs Lumber Company in Mebane was lost in fire in the 1940s, Fitch opened a lumber company in Carrboro. It was sometime in the 1960s that Mr. Fitch was working there and somehow injured his hand and had to be taken to the hospital. The injury was pretty bad and they were going to keep him overnight, and it so happened we had a directors' meeting scheduled for that night. I got a call at home later that day from Mr. Fitch's doctor saying that Mr. Fitch was determined to be at that meeting and for me to tell him it was okay for him to stay in the hospital and miss the meeting. That's the kind of man A.B. Fitch was."

On January 8, another called meeting was held, and local pharmacist Calvin Oakley and businessman Jack Phelps were appointed to the board. Phelps had close ties to First Savings, handling much of the insurance business of many customers as well as the institution. Having just stepped down as mayor, Phelps remained involved in the community and as a member of the Mebane Industrial Expansion Committee. Oakley was active in his church, community affairs, and civic organizations. The shareholders' meeting in February was a somber occasion as both Clark and Fitch were honored for their service to the institution.

Spring is typically the busiest time of the year for lending, and 1973 saw the strongest loan demand in over two years as Mebane was experiencing a small building boom fueled by construction at both Brookhollow and Forest Ridge. This springtime push underscored the importance Clark had in day-to-day operations, and the void left by his death was filled by Bill Griffith, who was hired as a loan officer.

For decades, competition among financial institutions in Alamance County had been somewhat low-key. Since savings and loans were essentially identical and offered the same basic products, the four thrifts in the area coexisted in a friendly business atmosphere as institutions carved out their base of customers. Graham Savings and Loan primarily served the city of Graham and the southern part of the county, while First Federal and Community Federal battled it out for Burlington and business in the western and northern sections of the county. First Savings secured a comfortable following in Mebane and went head to head with Hillsborough Savings and Loan for Hillsborough and rural Orange County customers. That was the good old days.

Many institutions expanded their consumer base through branching, and what had been quiet coexistence turned into heated competition. Wachovia opened a branch at the corner of Fifth and Washington streets in May after operating out of a modular building for several months. First Federal Savings and Loan purchased the old Apparel building directly across from Wachovia. The addition of these two financial institutions into the Mebane market altered competition and substantially reduced the slice of the deposit pie for all institutions.

After decades of familiarity, locals accepted change to Mebane's landscape as "progress," for the most part. The exception came with the demolition of the Mebane High School building in 1973. The town had purchased the property from the school system when Woodlawn Middle School was built. Watching the building come down was painful for those who had walked through its doors. When the building fell, a strong community symbol was gone, one that held a treasure of memories for generations. Only the gym, library, and a few classrooms remained and were renovated as a recreation center.

First Savings was still recovering from an emotional start to the year when Chairman of the Board Dr. G.M. Bullard died unexpectedly of a heart attack on June 7 at age fifty. Compared to the longevity of Clark and Fitch, Bullard's twelve years of service as a director had been relatively short, but his influence on First Savings was extraordinary. Bullard had joined the board at a time of controversy, during the proxy fight in the early 1960s. Given the uncertainty of the institution's future, Bullard could have turned the board nomination down in 1961. Instead, Bullard was instrumental in bringing stability and harmony back to the association at a time of hopeless division. Bullard served on the Alamance County School Board and was a strong supporter of Elon College. June Crumpler was appointed to the chairmanship, and Bill Griffith was added to the board and named vice president in November.

In 1973 the newly constructed World Trade Center towered above the New York skyline in lower Manhattan. Hostilities officially ended in Vietnam as a permanent cease fire was declared, and the war that had dominated the nation for a decade was finally over. Americans wanted to move forward and put this painful period of history behind them. Unfortunately a new and different crisis was looming that would change America's economy.

When the decade began, 24 percent of the oil consumed in the United States was imported, and that percentage continued to climb. By 1973 the United States had just 6 percent of the world's population but consumed one-third of the world's energy; moreover, a global oil crisis was emerging. During the 1930s the United

States produced 33 percent of the world's supply of oil. After World War II, oil production shifted to the vast reserves of Middle Eastern countries, and gradually the United States grew dependent on cheap foreign crude. That dependence was coming back to haunt the nation, and oil became a powerful economic weapon in the hands of countries hostile to the policies of the United States.

In 1974 a barrel of oil cost four dollars and a gallon of gasoline was thirty-eight cents. Oil prices quadrupled in one year when OPEC cut production, creating economic chaos and instability for the world's economy. This uncertainty quickly affected short-term interest rates, and First Savings began paying 6.75 percent on savings certificates. Although mortgage rates were soon to go higher, loan demand remained strong, boosted by local construction lending.

The Southern Railway depot was once a center of activity and critical to the growth of Mebane in its early years. Long abandoned, the aging building had fallen into disrepair and was considered by some an eyesore to a town struggling to attract shoppers downtown. The depot was torn down and replaced with the Mebane Town Square, complete with a fountain and gardens named in honor of longtime city employee Gilbert Scarlett.

Mebane was at a crossroads. Within two years, the town witnessed the disappearance of two of its most endearing and influential structures, which not only shaped the city's early economic development but touched the lives of everyone who grew up in Mebane. Although both were abandoned, the fact that the depot and Mebane High School disappeared said it all. Mebane was moving forward and letting go of its past.

General Electric had been open less than a year when rumors surfaced that another "big industry" was coming to Mebane. Firefighting equipment maker Walter Kidde Corporation confirmed it would build a plant on South Third Street Extension, and more diversity in manufacturing jobs was again on the way to North Carolina. Kidde hoped to employ five hundred workers and, like GE, fueled more industrial development. Coming at a time of a faltering economy, Kidde was a welcome addition as manufacturing was transforming from its base in textiles. Ironically, the world's largest textile maker, Burlington Industries, celebrated its fiftieth anniversary, praising the advantages, security, and longevity of a career in textiles.

As 1974 began, the nation was on the brink of another economic slide as OPEC flaunted its power by raising oil prices. Interest rates and inflation were climbing, and the Dow Jones Industrial Average, which briefly hit 1000 two years earlier, had fallen to 570. Postwar America had seen various economic trends and cycles, but for the most part the previous thirty-year period had been one of stability and prosperity. There had been recessions and inflationary periods, but they had been short in duration with steady and relatively predictable interest rates. That stability was disrupted when inflation hit 11 percent in 1974, affecting everything from consumer goods to housing. Energy had been something Americans took for granted, and frustrated consumers now had time to contemplate the economic impact of high fuel prices while waiting in line at service stations due to periodic gas shortages.

Despite the gloomy economic news, Mebane was thriving. The town of Mebane was growing as fast as the community itself, moving its offices to its current location on Washington Street (known then as East Center Street).

Jim Howington opened what would become Safeway Sprinkler in his garage on Jackson Street. The company moved to a former tobacco warehouse at the corner of Ruffin and North Third streets in the early 1980s. Another hometown business was born in 1974 when James and Mary Ellen Ball opened James Heating and Air.

On Wall Street, the Dreyfus Investment Fund offered the first money-market fund for small investors, and within six years over one hundred such funds sprang up. By offering higher interest rates, these accounts pulled away local funds, thus contributing to the growing deposit crisis facing traditional institutions. Saddled by the rate ceilings of Regulation Q, local institutions could do nothing but watch precious deposit money go out the door.

Hope for retaining local deposits was renewed when the Individual Retirement Account was created, opening new markets for much-needed long-term accounts.

Rates continued their climb, and by April 1975 First Savings' certificates of deposit were yielding 7.5 percent while mortgage rates reached 8.5 percent. Although the full effect of interest rate imbalances would not be felt for a few more years, there were signs that the industry was headed for trouble. The simple system that had served the savings and loan industry for a century was breaking down. The old saying, "Your greatest asset will someday become your greatest liability," was coming true for thrifts. The rapidly rising interest rate environment during the 1970s and into the early 1980s destroyed the simple investment strategy of borrowing short and lending long. Interest rate risk (the imbalance created when rates rise and fall with the potential for loss) had never been a concern. What had been prudent lending decisions made in a stable rate environment were coming back to haunt the industry as 6 percent long-term mortgage loans, approved with confidence in the 1960s, were suddenly underwater, yielding less income than institutions were paying out in interest costs for their deposits. Most institutions had no investment strategies in place and were unable to hedge any of the risk the escalating rate environment created.

The weaknesses in the savings and loan model sparked various studies and commissions to explore the problem. The Hunt Commission in 1972 and the FINE Study in 1973 recommended that savings and loans be replaced by savings banks and given broader commercial lending authority and product diversity. Despite these findings, lawmakers and regulators did basically nothing, hoping that the current economic pressures were temporary and interest rates would eventually return to stable levels. The government's failure to act by the mid-1970s was controversial and still draws mixed reviews. Some argue that if intervention had been brought about in the early stages of the escalating problem, much of the savings and loan crisis of the 1980s and its huge cost could have been avoided. Others argue that when government intervention and deregulation finally came, it only made matters worse.

In 1974, Sally Capps joined First Savings as a teller, bringing the number of full-time staff to seven. Director A.H. Jobe, now the longest-tenured member of the board, was honored for his forty years of service to the association. The first five years of the decade had been rocky, but the association averaged closing 173 loans a year, generating $2,201,666 in annual loan volume. The average loan extended by the association jumped from $8,666 in 1970 to $12,726 by 1974. Surprisingly, First Savings made its first-ever mortgage loan in the amount of $100,000 that same year.

The inflationary environment convinced the FDIC and FSLIC to raise deposit insurance levels to forty thousand dollars. The passage of the Real Estate

Settlement Procedures Act of 1974 and the Home Mortgage Disclosure Act in 1975 continued affecting the evolution of the mortgage loan transaction, and the days of simple mortgage loans were slowly but surely disappearing.

Televised Watergate hearings led by North Carolina Senator Sam Ervin brought the growing scandal into every living room in America. President Nixon resigned in August 1974, and Vice President Gerald Ford assumed the presidency and with it the daunting task of restoring the nation's confidence in its government.

Since World War II, the United States had been the envy of the world, setting the standard in everything from industrial ingenuity to military power. The postwar adage of "As GM goes, so goes the nation" reflected the might and stability of U.S. manufacturing. "Made in the USA" was the symbol of quality as the United States led the way and the rest of the world simply followed. By the mid-1970s, America's economic influence changed as Japan emerged as a driving global economic force. The Japanese took advantage of the energy crisis, solidifying their presence in the auto industry. General Motors, Ford, and Chrysler were caught totally unprepared as Toyota, Datsun (Nissan), and Honda flooded the U.S. market with small, fuel-efficient cars.

Housing prices had soared 82 percent in just five years to an average of $42,600 while incomes of Americans managed to climb just 26 percent during the same period to $11,800 a year. The nation's unemployment rate reached its highest level since the Great Depression at 8.9 percent, and inflation rose to 9.2 percent. The local economy was worse, as unemployment in Alamance County reached a staggering 16.6 percent, nearly twice the national average. Despite these uncertain times, Clyde Billings opened Mebane Hosiery Company, stating that twenty-eight of the thirty-four workers were jobless before the plant opened.

The Employment Security Commission stated that an influx of migrant workers, mostly from Mexico, working on tobacco farms in Orange County had "snowballed" to one hundred workers while there were an estimated twenty-five migrant laborers in Alamance County. The effects of migrant labor would dramatically change the American workforce over the next thirty years, particularly in home construction.

The slumping economy of the 1970s created a shift toward two-income families, creating a boom in the business of child care. Ten homes in Mebane registered to become daycare homes, joining several local churches and a few private day-care centers.

The economic downturn took its toll on First Savings as Neal Smith commented in a newspaper article that the association had "1324 home loans on the books and had plenty of money to lend." Smith went on to say that the previous year of "1974 will go down as one of the most challenging in the history of the savings and loan industry." The real challenges for the savings and loan industry were still ahead, and the tough times of 1974 were just the tip of the iceberg.

Delinquent loan payments are a fact of life for all lenders under the best of circumstances, but delinquencies intensify in uncertain economic times. First Savings employed various techniques to deal with this issue, including late notices and legal letters. Neal Smith became frustrated with one customer who previously had never missed a payment but suddenly stopped paying and failed to respond to repeated phone calls or letters. Smith drafted a rather stern letter stating foreclosure was imminent if the customer did not take action. Several days later the customer appeared at Smith's office explaining that he had been recovering in the hospital from a lengthy illness and that he appreciated the "get-well cards" that he received from First Savings.

Although lenders try to work with delinquent accounts, even the best of efforts sometimes fail. Neal Smith worked with one customer who was always on the delinquent list. After numerous failed attempts to contact the customer, Smith addressed an empty envelope and mailed it to the customer. Sure enough, a few days later the curious customer showed up at First Savings with the envelope in hand. Smith told him he was so frustrated that he didn't know what to send him so he just sent the empty envelope.

In its early years, First Savings made loans on homes lending up to 75 percent of the value of the property. As lending evolved, associations amortized mortgages over longer periods of time as well as lending a larger percentage of a property's value. First Savings followed suit, and by the mid-1970s was extending loans at 95 percent of the appraised value up to twenty-five years. Loans that were extended over an 80 percent loan to value were insured by private mortgage insurance. These high loan-to-value loans always seemed to have a high rate of delinquency, and the association dropped back to lending only 80 percent loans in the early 1980s.

By late spring 1975 mortgage loan demand caught fire and remained strong for the rest of the year, even though mortgage rates hit a record 9 percent. Despite an uneasy economy, First Savings' assets had nearly doubled in five years, approaching $13 million. Growth is nice, but without a doubt, the most striking number on the institution's financial statement was its reserve position, which had passed the $1 million mark for the first time.

Mebane was experiencing growing pains of its own, and the frustration and controversy that come with it. Despite heavy opposition, portions of Highway 119 North, Wilba Road, Charles Street, and Cates Road, all north of town, were annexed into the city. Town Council members and the developer of Forest Ridge had been feuding since the subdivision began, and things were getting worse. The council was "concerned and dismayed by the type of homes" being built in Forest Ridge. The developer shot back, stating the homes were excellent quality, met all building standards set by the town, and that the average cost of a house in the development should exceed thirty-five thousand dollars.

Frustrated parents of Woodlawn Middle School students met with school system officials about their disappointment with the unconventional and obviously controversial approach to school design with open classrooms. Parents complained that the high noise level and other problems prevented students from concentrating. Woodlawn eventually abandoned the open approach, and the school was remodeled.

For years, the stretch of Mebane Oaks Road from I-85 to South Fifth Street was a quiet half-mile strip of asphalt. This was about to change as a new shopping center anchored by a Winn Dixie grocery store was on the way. Downtown Mebane continued to lose shopper appeal as the Colonial Store, a cornerstone Clay Street business for fifty years, closed its doors.

North Carolina's road system is second to none, but some residents of the state aren't always pleased when development takes place in their own backyard. Orange County residents were outraged at a planned expansion of I-40 from Hillsborough to Raleigh, creating a four-lane interstate through rural farmland. The eventual construction not only made travel to Raleigh and points east easier but accelerated growth for Mebane and other communities.

Technology moved to a new level when nineteen-year-old Bill Gates and twenty-two-year-old Paul Allen started a computer software company called Microsoft. Sony introduced the first VCR, known as the Betamax, prompting threats of copyright lawsuits from television networks. The lucky owners of this new technology paid around fifteen hundred dollars for these first recorders to tape such shows as *All in the Family*, the number-one TV show in America. Technology improved office efficiency as fax machines and computer word processors were introduced. Two college dropouts, Steven Jobs and Stephen Wozniak, created Apple Computer, and the electronic age of banking arrived as ATMs grew in popularity.

Housing was demanding more from American consumers, who spent 24 percent of their monthly income on a house payment. Spending and saving habits of the nation were adjusting to an inflationary economy. One byproduct of this period was mortgage innovations; the days of the plain-vanilla mortgage loan were numbered. New lending options required less money for a down payment for a home. By 1976, 26.9 percent of houses were purchased with a down payment of 10 percent or less.

Signs of improvement in the nation's fickle economy emerged as mortgage rates dipped back to 8.5 percent and inflation for the year was cut in half to 5.75 percent. Americans had good reason to be positive, as elaborate bicentennial celebrations were planned for towns and cities across the country. Fireworks displays on the Mall in Washington and New York City drew tremendous crowds, and the events were broadcast to the nation.

Locally folks were not in a festive mood. In May 1976, troubled Dow Badische announced that its Mebane plant would close. At its peak, the producer of polyester yarn, formerly Universal Textiles, boasted a workforce of 1,200, and the plant's closing was devastating to an area already rocked by high unemployment. Burlington trucking giant Associated Transport, with roots back to the 1920s, filed for bankruptcy, sending another 275 workers to the unemployment line. But the big blow came when Western Electric moved its Burlington operations to Winston-Salem. Western had occupied the mammoth Fairchild Aircraft Plant on Graham-Hopedale Road since the 1940s, and was the foundation of Burlington's east side economy. The company's decision to leave accelerated Burlington's migration west in both residential and commercial development.

After operating as a one-man practice for twenty-five years, association attorney Lee Settle was joined by his son-in-law, Robert Steele. Steele worked closely with First Savings performing title work, and he eventually became the association's trustee in the 1980s.

On May 19, 1976, John M. McIntyre, whose powerful influence guided First Savings in its early years, passed away. Mr. Mac's leadership spanned four decades, from 1920 to 1961, and as secretary-treasurer and director he laid the foundation for the conservative institution that First Savings would become. The two-year proxy fight that ended in McIntyre's ouster in 1961 severed his ties with the association. Sadly, this relationship was never mended prior to his death and tends to overshadow his tremendous contribution to the institution's history.

The closest thing Mebane had to a fast-food restaurant in 1976 was Beef Burger, known more for its championship youth football teams than hamburgers. That changed when Hardee's opened beside the FCX on West Center Street.

Vietnam, Watergate, and a failing economy had dominated the news for the first half of the decade, and Americans were ready for a change. Georgia Democrat Jimmy Carter was elected president, defeating Gerald Ford in November. Hope abounds with the inauguration of a new administration, but when Carter took office in 1977 any expectations for an economic recovery in the near future quickly evaporated as inflation hit 11 percent for the year.

The nation's economic woes and rising rates didn't slow the momentum for First Savings, as 1977 was its strongest year in mortgage lending for the decade. First Savings set, at that time, an institution record for loan volume at $4,859,200 in 206 loan closings. This loan activity kept attorney Lee Settle busy, as he not only served as the association's attorney but ran the only law office in town. That changed in 1977 when Charles Davis and Bill Humbert opened Davis and Humbert Attorneys in the Welcome Finance building. Bill Humbert recalled the experience of visiting Lee Settle for the first time. "Charlie and I had been open for about a month. We had no business at the time and we thought the right thing to do was to pay a courtesy call on Lee. We went by his office and he made us wait for about ten minutes. When we finally got to see him he was pretty unfriendly and gruff and said he had seen attorneys come and go and that we hadn't shown him anything that would make him feel different about us. He leaned back in his chair at that point and busted out laughing." Obviously it was not the reception these two young attorneys were expecting from the veteran lawyer. As the years went by, their relationship mellowed, and Humbert described Settle as a real "treasure." Years later, when discussing this story, Settle admitted to Humbert that he couldn't recall that first meeting and his rather rude introduction, but stated that "it sounds like something I would have said."

Credit cards steadily made their way into more and more pocketbooks, although the popularity and interestingly the availability of this consumer staple was not as widespread as today. It was in 1977 that Bank Americard changed its name to Visa. Visa along with Mastercharge, soon to become MasterCard, became the major credit card issuers.

In February 1978 Bill Griffith resigned, and the association left the position of vice president vacant for the time being. Attorney Lee Settle had served as the association's legal counsel since 1970 and as a director for twenty years, but examiners brought Settle's dual role into question. Regulators saw this arrangement as a potential conflict of interest. Rather than fight the issue, Settle resigned as director but remained the institution's attorney. Settle's knowledge and expertise were invaluable to the institution, and his resignation as a director was a significant loss. Outside attorney E.T. Sanders was named as the association's trustee, replacing Settle.

Settle's resignation created the fourth vacancy on the board in five years, and in June 1978 Ned Gauldin was hired as vice president and appointed to the board. Gauldin began his banking career in his hometown of Fieldale, Virginia, in the 1940s. After serving in the navy in World War II and attending Elon College, Gauldin moved to Graham, taking a position with the Bank of Alamance. Gauldin came to Mebane when the bank opened a branch in First Savings and Loan's building on Clay Street in the early 1960s and had maintained a close relationship with the association. As a banker, Gauldin's financial experience varied greatly from traditional savings and loans, and this knowledge was invaluable as the industry was in the beginning stages of consolidation. The hiring of Gauldin still left one seat open on the board, but the board officially reduced its membership to seven in November.

The thrift industry muddled through the 1970s, but the problems embedded in the savings and loan concept of lending short-term deposits on long-term fixed-rate mortgages was deepening; the stage was being set for the next financial disaster. At that time, savings and loans had limited financial products and were restricted to making only home mortgages. The causes of the savings and loan crisis that became full-blown in the 1980s ranged from antiquated and restrictive laws and poor oversight to greed and deregulation of the industry. These factors and ten years of rising interest rates, an unstable economy, and runaway inflation contributed to the industry's downfall. At the time, the savings and loan crisis was the worst modern-day financial disaster since the Great Depression. However, this crisis would pale in comparison to what the financial industry would face in 2008. Both of these disastrous events would share many common denominators.

By 1978 the deteriorating situation facing the savings and loan industry had not garnered major headlines. Lawmakers and regulators were faced with a crisis that they were not prepared for and did not know how to solve. For the most part, government reacts to crisis situations rather than taking a proactive stance, and with the exception of a few committees and studies this was the approach taken on the savings and loan issue. Thrifts had survived for a century during periods of great economic stress, such as the Great Depression and two world wars. Yet the rate imbalances of the 1970s and the coming 1980s would prove far more detrimental. Institutional failures were increasing because of rate imbalances between long-term loans and short-term deposits. The case was building that massive thrift failures were a real possibility, which could cost the FSLIC and taxpayers billions of dollars.

The government's initial response came in the form of the Financial Institutions Regulatory and Interest Rate Control Act of 1978 (FIRIRCA), the first step toward deregulating the industry. The law removed some of the restrictions and regulations placed on savings and loans allowing land development loans, something that Texas institutions had been doing for a decade. Although intentions were good, the FIRIRCA was generally a weak statute and did little to stop the bleeding.

By allowing land development loans, the door opened for associations to take on new yet unfamiliar forms of business. Savings and loans were entering uncharted territory, with little knowledge or experience, at a time when the industry was precariously weak. Some institutions recognized this inadequacy and lured experienced bankers into the fold. Other struggling institutions, eager to turn the corner on their economic woes, implemented flawed policies and made hasty decisions resulting in fatal consequences. New powers and opportunities would be introduced to the industry in the decade to come, and many institutions would succeed within the framework of these new laws, setting the stage for broader legislation.

Unfortunately, the least prepared of all for the changes affecting the fragmented industry was the Federal Home Loan Bank Board, the savings and loan industry regulator. The FHLBB accompanied the rise of the savings and loan industry with its creation in the 1930s and would soon see its demise. In fairness, the FHLBB, like the associations it regulated, had no expertise in many of the changes sweeping the industry.

Inflation weighed in at 7.79 percent, and mortgage rates ended the year for the first time in double digits—10.35 percent—killing loan demand and ending the association's hot lending streak. As high as these mortgage loan rates appeared to disgruntled consumers in 1978, the worst was yet to come. Incredibly, mortgage loan interest rates would nearly double in a span of just five years. For decades, property appraisals for small institutions were subjectively handled by an internal loan committee. Escalating home prices forced many institutions, including First Savings, to begin using professional appraisers.

Change accelerated for the industry in 1979 as savings and loans were allowed to issue money-market certificates, which had been a cause for much of the deposit outflows from institutions. The most significant change occurred when certificates of deposits could be opened with just a five-hundred-dollar minimum deposit instead of ten thousand dollars, significantly increasing deposit inflows for community associations that catered to the working-class customer and modest saver.

Two of the association's longtime employees were honored at the February 1979 shareholders' meeting as Neal Smith and Frances Terrell received twenty-five-year service awards. First Savings had tried unsuccessfully to sell its former Clay Street location for over twenty years, renting the building most notably to the Bank of Alamance. The building was now once again vacant as Charlotte banking giant First Union bought out the Bank of Alamance and opened a new branch on the corner of Washington and Fourth streets, now the site of Capital Bank. First Savings' neighbor, Central Carolina Bank, now SunTrust, kept pace with the increasing competition, adding a two-thousand-square-foot addition to its existing facility.

Since its inception in 1909, First Savings, like most savings and loans in America, had remained a mutually chartered institution rather than a stock association. As the saving and loan crisis loomed, the distinct differences between mutual and stock-chartered associations, which had been little more than a footnote for decades, now provided an opportunity for struggling institutions and potential investors.

Stock-owned companies are the backbone of capitalism, paying stockholders returns for investing in a company. As a stock-held company profits, so do its stockholders. Larger stockholders have more voting rights and can control decisions and a company's direction. A mutually chartered association is owned equally by its members, regardless of the monetary investment each shareholder has in the company.

Most of the nation's mutual thrifts had been established years earlier with little initial capital. They grew very slowly as their local deposit base and loan demand expanded, gaining a conservative reputation and serving the working class. Conversely, stock associations attracted not only depositors but investors desiring rapid growth and high returns for their investment. These contrasting business styles resulted in varied business models and goals with different measures of success.

The negative effects of the 1970s' economy convinced many struggling mutual institutions to convert to a stock form of ownership. By doing so, these converting institutions could raise much-needed capital through the issuance of stock that could not be obtained under a mutual charter. As the industry faced shrinking net interest margins and little or no available capital, charter conversions made sense. With the weaknesses of the savings and loan model now exposed, mutual-to-stock conversions and mergers became commonplace in the 1980s and beyond. The temptation of capital infusion by converting to a stock association was just too great for some institutions to ignore. Once the stock conversion was complete, most institutions dumped the "savings and loan" label and became banks.

Stock institutions have exposure as well and can be bought and sold through mergers and acquisitions, an attractive feature to potential investors. As the looming crisis approached, the emerging phenomenon and trend toward stock conversions became a significant shift within the industry. Some associations were controlled and in some cases manipulated by groups of stockholders. The crisis would deepen with these abuses of power and personal greed.

Mutual associations, to be sure, were not insulated from manipulation, a scenario First Savings learned firsthand in the 1961 proxy battle. This fight was a classic example of how mutuality works where the wishes of a few cannot dictate to the majority. The savings and loan crisis brought out the worst in both stock and mutual associations as the fight for survival threw conventional wisdom, and in some cases wisdom itself, out the window.

The association's directors were curious about the process of mutual-to-stock conversion, and W.C. York, state regulator with the North Carolina Institutions Division, met with the board to discuss what a conversion would mean to First Savings. The meeting with York was essentially educational, as a mutual-to-stock conversion was never seriously considered.

Like the thrift industry, Mebane's identity was shifting as well, and the job diversity brought by GE, Kidde Corporation, and other companies during the 1970s was a sign of things to come. The auto industry came calling as GKN built a manufacturing facility south of town for its front-wheel-drive assembly operations, adding six hundred new jobs. Carolina Central Industrial Center (CCIC) opened on South Third Street Extension. Adjacent to Kidde Corporation on South Third Street, CCIC attracted Sandvik, MCR, and other companies. Electrical manufacturer A.O. Smith added its name to the growing list when the Wisconsin-based firm purchased the vacant Universal Textile–Dow Badische facility for the production of hot water heaters.

Although the homegrown businesses of Kingsdown and White Furniture remained the foundation for the local job market, the evolution of business and manufacturing was accelerating and positioning the town for the future. Sadly the closing of Dow Badische was an omen of what was in store for the textile industry in North Carolina. Cotton mills were as common as Baptist churches and sweet tea in the South, but the gradual decline of textiles over the next twenty years would redefine the southern workforce.

Out-of-control inflation and rising interest rates had plagued the nation's economy for more than a decade with no end in sight, despite the best efforts of the Federal Reserve. The events in the fall of 1979 were a turning point in this ongoing battle, forever altering the Fed's overall strategy against inflation. These decisions ultimately set a new course for the financial world, particularly the savings and loan industry. Through the 1970s, spiraling inflation remained a dominant force, permeating every aspect of the U.S. economy.

The straw that broke the camel's back occurred in September as OPEC again doubled the price of crude oil, signaling another round of rising prices and forcing the Federal Reserve to change its monetary policy. Through the entire decade, the Fed had fought a losing battle with inflation by raising the federal funds rate and flooding the financial system with huge cash infusions that only fueled the inflationary environment. On October 6, 1979, Fed Chairman Paul Volcker announced the Fed's monetary policy would now target and severely restrict the nation's money supply, a policy that would send interest rates through the roof. This decision meant that the Fed would no longer attempt to cushion the blow of economic shocks, such as rising oil prices, but would pursue a longer-term goal of price stability by controlled growth of the nation's money supply.

The cost of borrowing from the Fed skyrocketed, with the short-term federal funds rate reaching 11.2 percent by year's end, making it more expensive for financial institutions to borrow money. Reserve requirements for member banks were tightened. The already weak savings and loan industry that had struggled with rate imbalances for most of the decade knew that things would only get worse. As the Fed shifted gears in its fight against inflation, whispers became louder about the instability of the savings and loan industry. With rates sure to rise, only institutions with a strong reserve position could weather the storm.

The Fed's move sent shock waves through the weary industry. Institutions that were highly leveraged with large debt loads and little or no safety net knew they were in serious trouble. Regulations required associations to create a 5 percent reserve (which had been lowered from 6 percent during the 1950s) based on the amount of the institution's savings deposits. As associations struggled to meet these reserve requirements, newly chartered institutions were given ten years to reach this 5 percent benchmark. But as always, if the rules aren't working, change the rules. In the early 1970s, regulators had extended the period from ten to twenty-five years for an institution to create its 5 percent reserve, a feat that had been virtually impossible to accomplish in the turbulent economy. Essentially regulators were allowing some institutions to operate with little or no reserve, posing a threat to the safety and soundness of those institutions and the FSLIC insurance fund. Now the newly enacted Fed policy would cut the legs out from under these associations that had struggled along with little or no capital.

Although the association had amassed a 15 percent reserve, the board switched immediately to a defensive mode of operation. In November, several key changes were made to the association's lending policy, restricting loans to "home purchases, construction or home improvement." The loan-to-value ratio was reduced from 95 percent to 80 percent. As First Savings circled the wagons, mortgage loan rates hit 12 percent and the association placed more of its expanding liquidity of funds in the safety of the bond market.

The decade had been punctuated by war, political scandal, gas lines, discos, and a deteriorating economy. The independent spirit of Americans was pushed to the limit by foreign countries with mystifying names and cultures, rich with oil and wielding tremendous economic influence over the world's most powerful nation.

Despite the turbulence, the 1970s had been an incredible time of growth for First Savings. Assets and deposits climbed 139 percent during the decade and stood at $18,182,206 and $16,285,924, respectively. The association's safety net or reserve had climbed to 15 percent of total deposits at $1,718,096, nearly tripling since 1969. Mortgage loans had increased 128 percent during these ten years, reaching $15,463,260. But trouble was on the horizon. After crossing the $4 million mark in lending volume in both 1977 and 1978, loans fell sharply in 1979 as total loan volume reached just over $2.4 million, with just 111 loan closings for the year.

The composition of the board of directors of First Savings ended the decade much differently than when it began, as half its members had been replaced. Likewise, Mebane was a much different town by 1979. Mebane High School and the depot, symbols of its past, were gone. Gone, too, were hundreds of traditional jobs as plant closings and openings signaled a shift in manufacturing from its roots in textiles and furniture. Mebane again was on the brink of yet another transformation.

The financial world had ridden a post–World War II boom for over thirty-five years with few bumps or curves. After seventy years of existence First Savings was comfortable and almost insulated in its role as a small-town lender. But painful evolution was truly on its way. A transformation of the industry that lay ahead in the new decade changed the identity and purpose of savings and loans, while the differences between banks and thrifts, which had been clear and distinct for decades, disappeared. Likewise, so would many institutions themselves disappear, as 29 percent of the 4,363 savings and loans in existence in 1979 would vanish from the financial landscape through failure, merger, or acquisition. Even the term "savings and loan," common in the consumer vocabulary, would slowly be replaced by the word "bank," which would evolve into the generic term for all financial institutions. Savings and loans, known for their prudence and conservative style, were about to take center stage in what would become a three-ring circus in the political, financial, and media arenas, tarnishing their reputation and leaving the industry on the brink of extinction.

Uniforms were common for bank employees during the 1960s and 1970s. L–R Shelby Murphy, Carole Thomas, Sally Capps, Frances Terrell and Ann Sykes

Director A.B. Fitch celebrates his fiftieth anniversary with First Savings on July 27th, 1972. L–R Dr. George M. Bullard, June Crumpler, Neal Smith, John Henry James, Dr. I.C. Clark, A.H. Jobe, seated is A.B. Fitch. This was the last photo taken of this group of directors as Fitch, Clark and Bullard passed away the following year. *Courtesy William Lynch Studios*

Until the development of Brookhollow in 1972, Mebane's residential development had been a patchwork of small neighborhoods. Building trends moved away from ranch style with two story and split level design during the 1970s.

Eastern Alamance High School emerged from the shadows of Mebane High School by the 1970s with its own identity and bond with new generations of Mebanites.

General Electric's opening in 1972 sparked an industrial revolution and Mebane's industry migrated to the interstate.

Oakwood Street Extension attracted industry including AKG, Armstrong World Industries, and others to the east side of the city.

Relocation of industry from downtown created two industrial parks that attracted Sandvik, MCR and other companies to South Third Street Extension.

CHAPTER EIGHT

End of an Era

1980–1989

WHEN THE GLASS BALL DROPPED IN TIMES SQUARE at midnight on December 31, 1979, and the world said good-bye to the 1970s, Americans were anxious about the decade before them. The hope of every New Year's Eve is a new and fresh start. The expectation of better days ahead proved to be wishful thinking. As revelers nursed their hangovers and broke their resolutions of the new decade, like every year, nothing had really changed. Or had it? The Federal Reserve's new monetary policy was about to push interest rates to unimaginable levels, and although change was indeed on the way, it wasn't what hopeful consumers were expecting. In a short time a new banking era would emerge, and old traditions, like the 1970s, would become a thing of the past.

The new year ushered in the same questions. *How high can interest rates climb? Can inflation be contained? Will I still have a job at the end of the month?* But without a doubt the most burning question on the minds of Americans in 1980 was *Who shot J. R. Ewing?* The wounds suffered by the charismatic character of the hugely popular show *Dallas*, cleverly portrayed by actor Larry Hagman, were not fatal. Like J. R. Ewing, many wondered if survival for the savings and loan industry was possible as its condition had been downgraded to critical. The industry with a flawless reputation of financial conservatism would soon be rocked with scandals and thrust into unwanted limelight by the events of the 1980s.

By 1980 the steady drumbeat of inflation of the previous ten years was reflected in the cost Americans paid for virtually everything, altering spending and saving habits for a generation. Home prices had increased 226 percent during the 1970s and stood at an average of $76,400. During this same period the median household income rose 89 percent to an average of $17,710. The American Dream of owning a home was becoming less attainable. The cost of gasoline climbed 247 percent during the prior decade and stood at $1.25 a gallon. Although Americans had focused on rising interest rates, they were now more concerned with job security as rising unemployment had reached levels not seen since the Great Depression.

Although tough economic times continued for the country and Alamance County, Mebane's economy steamed ahead. In 1980 there were 1,086 houses in the town of Mebane, and its population had grown a modest 8 percent over the past decade. The local industrial revolution of the 1970s continued; influenced by foreign competition, it would bring changes over the next decade that no one ever dreamed possible.

A significant milestone in Mebane's manufacturing transition occurred in 1980 when Sandvik opened its plant in the Carolina Central Industrial Center. Sandvik joined Walter Kidde in transforming South Third Street Extension into Mebane's new industrial district. The facility was the toolmaker's third plant in the United States and its first in North Carolina. The move to Mebane proved successful as Sandvik expanded its operations in 2000 and again in 2009, adding jobs in the process. Sandvik proved to be as resilient as Mebane, becoming a foundation of the city's ever-diverse manufacturing sector.

First Savings closed just seven loans during the first two months of 1980, and the economy was the center of attention at the annual shareholders' meeting in February. President Neal Smith recalled the mood within the industry at that time as loan demand evaporated: "Everybody [lenders] had the same problem. Nobody was making loans, and what was frightening was that this was happening all across the country. Associations had tons of money on hand and paying dearly for it [interest on savings] and no place to put that money to work."

The Federal Reserve's assault on inflation pulled the plug on housing demand as mortgage rates reached 13 percent in February. Then two months later, without warning, mortgage interest rates skyrocketed to 18 percent, sending shivers of panic through nervous financial circles.

The collateral damage from the war on inflation was the rapid deterioration of savings and loans that struggled through the rate imbalances of the 1970s and were now faced with sudden and rapid interest rate shocks. During the previous forty-five years, 143 savings and loans had failed, but as earnings problems for the weakened industry intensified, 43 institutions became insolvent and 11 closed their doors in 1980 alone.

Ironically, fifty years earlier, panic had swept through the nation's financial sector at the start of the Great Depression, forcing Congress to overhaul the nation's banking system. Congress acted promptly, restoring the country's faith and trust in a system on the brink of collapse. By 1980 the financial needs of the nation were more sophisticated. Unfortunately, the country's fragmented financial system had not evolved to meet these needs. Banks and savings institutions were largely regulated by antiquated Depression-era laws. Savings and loans were operating much the same way they were in the 1940s, with virtually no ability to expand and offer competitive financial products.

Eighty-five percent of savings and loans were now losing money, and Congress passed a myriad of regulations in the early 1980s, consolidating the nation's financial system. These laws eliminated the distinctions and restrictions between banks and thrifts. In March 1980 the passage of the Depository Institutions Deregulation and Monetary Control Act expanded lending powers for thrifts, allowing speculation in development and construction loans. Deposit insurance levels were raised to one hundred thousand dollars. Savings associations could issue NOW (Negotiated Order of Withdrawal) Accounts to compete with checking accounts offered by banks. Broadening the appeal of the nation's thrifts would take time, and time was running out.

It is difficult to imagine in today's financial world a time when savings interest rates were restricted by federal regulation and limited by rate ceilings. Regulation Q, developed during the Great Depression as a defensive tool for institutions, prevented the open market from driving rates. Saddled with these interest rate restrictions, First Savings routinely advertised "Earn the Highest Interest Allowed by Regulation" in efforts to draw in deposits. Newspaper ads from all local institutions quoted the exact same interest rate for the exact same product. Regulation Q had become a liability. Eliminating interest rate ceilings and allowing markets to drive rates made sense, but the prospect of higher interest costs was the industry's worst nightmare.

First Savings faced the challenges of this new decade with the veteran staff of Neal Smith, Ned Gauldin, Francis Terrell, Shelby Murphy, Ann Sykes, and Carole Thomas. Contrary to the rest of the industry, First Savings had experienced little employee turnover in front-line teller positions that are invaluable to small institutions. Shelby Murphy began her twenty-second year in 1980 and was joined by Janice Wright, who came over from CCB. Murphy and Wright formed a consistent foundation of customer service in the early 1980s that carried well into the next century.

Banks and savings and loans were once shining examples of stability and longevity as employees developed lasting relationships that spanned generations. But as the financial industry changed, its workforce shifted in the opposite direction. Staff turnover, particularly in customer service positions, became a constant challenge. This trend continues today, further complicated by mergers and acquisitions.

Mortgage interest rates continued their roller-coaster ride as rates unexpectedly dropped in the summer as quickly as they had spiked during the spring. Remarkably, interest rates for home loans eased six percentage points to 12 percent, allowing lenders to temporarily regain their footing.

Amid the economic uncertainty, First Savings received some good news as the Saddlebrook Corporation published rankings according to net income for all 151 FSLIC-insured institutions in North Carolina. First Savings ranked eighth for the first quarter of 1980, bringing favorable recognition at a time when confidence in the industry was wavering. The association scored points again when the *National Thrift News* released the national rankings of the most profitable institutions based on size and resources. First Savings placed in the top 10 percent of the national survey, confirming the association's philosophy that an institution did not have to be huge to be successful.

With new lending options available, First Savings added commercial loans to its lending policy. To avoid potential risk, the association limited commercial lending to 50 percent of appraised value. This decision limited both risk and any potential customers in the process as First Savings made only one commercial loan the entire year.

A major source of revenue and customer criticism of financial institutions is fee income. Banks were notorious for charging fees, where thrifts, on the other hand, did not rely on fee income to any significant degree, due primarily to the limited product line and specialization of the thrift industry prior to deregulation. At that time, distinct differences in philosophies existed between banks and thrifts, and the few services that savings and loans offered had been largely viewed as complimentary. If savings institutions could have found ways to impose fees, they certainly would have, given the declining bottom line. Banks, with diverse services such as checking, consumer loans, and other financial products, justified accompanying fees. Although complimentary service has its place, First Savings succumbed to the temptation of fees by charging an eighty-five-dollar application fee on all mortgage loans beginning in September 1980.

The possibility of fee income was nice, but it would not save the thrift industry. Two areas that posed problems for savings associations were as old as the industry itself: maintaining adequate liquidity of funds and retaining local deposits. The Federal Home Loan Bank Board addressed these issues with two questionable and controversial rule changes. Since only 15 percent of the nation's thrifts were making money, the possibility was strong that failures could occur on a large scale. To forestall the growing insolvency, the FHLBB reduced the net worth requirements for savings and loans from 5 percent to 4 percent of its deposit base. This decision lowered the amount of money an association needed to have in reserve for contingencies. As the crisis worsened, the minimum requirement was reduced again to just 3 percent in 1982. The reasoning was that lower reserve standards would allow troubled associations time to recover and benefit from the new business opportunities that deregulation created. Unfortunately, lowering the regulatory minimum created the opposite effect, allowing associations to teeter on the brink of insolvency. Instead of buying time for associations to improve their financial situation, this approach hastened failure as institutions had virtually no significant capital to fall back on during the crisis.

The second questionable FHLBB decision was the removal of limits on the amounts of brokered deposits that savings and loans could hold on their books. Unlike local savings funds, brokered deposits could originate anywhere in the country as brokers pooled deposit funds from investors and searched the country for institutions paying the highest rates. Brokered deposits did supply the liquidity needs for many associations. But these deposits were by no means stable and could be moved quickly from one institution to another to earn a higher rate. Large blocks of funds, when withdrawn, posed significant liquidity problems for savings institutions.

Lower net worth requirements and allowing unlimited brokered deposits resulted in unintended and adverse consequences for the savings and loan industry. These actions by the FHLBB eventually drew criticism from lawmakers who questioned the regulator's competency. These changes would add millions to the eventual cost of the crisis.

The volatile interest rate environment gave rise to new and innovative mortgage products as home loans evolved with market conditions. The adjustable-rate mortgage (ARM) made its debut as an alternative to the high fixed-rate conventional mortgage loan. The standard conventional home loan had a fixed interest rate charged for a set number of years. The ARM usually had a lower initial rate than a conventional home loan, and the rate had the potential to rise or fall depending on market conditions.

An era came to an end in Mebane in November 1980 when Eastern Alamance High School football coach Fred Brady retired after seventeen seasons with the Eagles. The soft-spoken coach recorded ninety-eight wins during his tenure and touched the lives of many players and students who came through the doors of Eastern Alamance. Brady was well respected and known throughout the state for building a powerful and consistent football program. Everyone, with the exception of other local high school coaches, were saddened by his decision to step down. One former player whom Brady greatly influenced was John Kirby, a 1980 Eastern graduate, who, expressing his hopes for the future in a newspaper article, stated, "I would like to do something in sports, maybe coach or teach P.E." Kirby would do more than just realize his dream as twenty-six years later in the fall of 2006, Head Football Coach John Kirby would record his one hundredth win at Eastern Alamance, passing his coach and mentor, Fred Brady.

As Coach Brady finished his last season in style with a 9-1 record, another campaign ended as well. The presidential election of 1980 became a referendum on the nation's stagnant economy, pitting incumbent Democrat Jimmy Carter against Republican challenger Ronald Reagan. The slumping economy and political scandals of the 1970s had left Americans cynical about Washington. Reagan's landslide victory in November ushered in a new era that redefined the role of the federal government.

Reagan's inauguration speech on January 20, 1981, set the tone of his presidency. Stating that "Government is not the solution to our problem. Government is the problem," Reagan's crusade to reduce what he called "the intrusion of government" into the lives of Americans went against the tide and expectations of government set in place by Franklin Roosevelt's New Deal in the 1930s and Lyndon Johnson's Great Society of the 1960s. The shift to less federal interference and the promise of tax cuts resonated well with most consumers and was applauded by the business community. With federal jobs cut, oversight and supervision of the financial system diminished at a time when it was needed most.

The new administration's economic agenda, which became known as "Reaganomics," could not stop the tidal wave of rising interest rates as another spike sent the prime rate to a record 21.5 percent. Mortgage rates reached 21 percent, sending the country into a major recession. As spring approached, mortgage rates plummeted to 14 percent, creating a flurry of loan activity. Consumers who cared little about mortgage rates in the past found themselves following the volatile market intently. When a window of opportunity opened as it did in 1981, borrowers jumped in the market quickly, purchasing a home or refinancing their current high-rate mortgage. These occasional rate dips brought a surge in loan demand for First Savings, and April 1981 was the strongest lending period in six months, producing fifteen loan closings. The timing was perfect for the hiring of Janis Murray in March, filling the void left by Ann Sykes, who resigned in December.

The general consensus was that housing was the key to jump-start the economy, but few believed this was realistic with interest rates at their peak. Congress passed the Tax Reform Act of 1981, creating favorable tax incentives for real estate investment, development, and commercial construction. The bill ignited a building boom that drove the economy forward for the next five years.

Although the nation's economy struggled, the town of Mebane had a lot to cheer about in 1981 as the town celebrated its centennial. For most of its first one hundred years, Mebane's core manufacturing in furniture, mattress production, textiles, and tobacco took place in downtown's manufacturing district. The local industrial revolution that began during the 1970s impacted traditional industry, bringing more job diversity and expansion to the interstate. Drs. Steve Troutman and Michael Blankenship joined the southern movement, opening their new offices at the busy corner of Mebane Oaks Road and Fifth Street (present site of Walgreen's).

The interest rate environment of this inflationary time convinced regulators that double-digit interest rates were here to stay, and institutions were advised to position themselves for this environment in the future. The FHLBB encouraged associations to lock in certificates of deposit for as long as possible, minimizing the cost of funds when rates rose. Since certificate yields were hovering around 15 percent at the time, the thinking was that locking in such savings rates now would be prudent when interest rates climbed even higher. Neal Smith recalls a customer who apologized for transferring his money out of First Savings to a savings institution in Texas that offered a fixed 15 percent interest rate on savings for fifteen years. Smith advised his friend to take advantage of the opportunity since the money was FSLIC-insured. A few years later, that same customer contacted Smith, stating he had received his investment back when the Texas thrift failed.

First Savings steered clear of the questionable FHLBB recommendations, never offering longer-term savings plans. The association believed that tying up a high-cost liability for long periods could have dangerous consequences. Smith and Vice President Gauldin had issues with the long-term strategy of their regulator, and Smith stated that "the Federal Home Loan Bank was advocating things that just didn't make sense. They lowered the reserve requirements to 3 percent and wanted us to tie up [deposit] money for ten to fifteen years at high rates, and we could not figure out why. A lot of institutions that did what they recommended went broke." In fairness, the FHLBB implemented regulations they thought would prevent a major meltdown of the industry. Unfortunately, many of these recommendations backfired as the crisis worsened.

Not surprisingly, 1982 was the association's low point for loan volume for the entire decade as interest rates were at their peak. First Savings managed to close just eighty-one loans for the year totaling $1,624,900, its lowest loan volume since 1970. The average loan amount extended by the association exceeded $20,000 for the first time.

The once-powerful monopoly held by AT&T was broken after an eight-year antitrust lawsuit, dividing the communications giant into regional companies and allowing competition to drive long-distance service. The financial services industry was not far behind.

Despite the government's initial attempts to deal with the crisis, the savings and loan industry was firmly in the red, losing $4.6 billion in 1981 and $4.1 billion in 1982. In 1982, 415 savings and loans became insolvent and 73 associations failed, with others teetering on the brink of failure. The passage of the Garn–St. Germain Depository Institutions Act finalized deregulation of the savings and loan industry and thus changed the financial landscape.

Garn–St. Germain was an aggressive approach to the savings and loan problem, allowing thrifts into business reserved traditionally for banks. Savings and loans were now free to invest in consumer and commercial loans and speculative lending. The law further accelerated the phasing out of interest rate controls. These new powers combined with real estate incentives of the Tax Reform Act from 1981 fueled real estate speculation.

With the stroke of a pen, restrictions were gone, giving savings and loans virtually the same freedom as banks to pursue new ventures, services, and products. The lines that had clearly separated banks and thrifts began to disappear. But the reality was that the conservative thrift industry had changed very little in decades and maintained the reputation of moving forward with innovations at the speed of a glacier. Banks and thrifts competed for local deposits but rarely competed for loans, as both operated in different markets. Now the gloves were off. Financial institutions were free to go head-to-head in virtually every financial arena where banks overwhelmingly held the upper hand in a business they knew extremely well. In the past, savings institutions profited in a comfortable existence in home lending and savings accounts. This environment had existed with few competitive pressures, and taking on the banking industry at its own game would be not be easy.

Still the timing for these changes was perfect. Mortgage loan rates that began the year at 17.5 percent had moderated to 13.4 percent. The Dow Jones Industrial Average closed the year at 1046, beginning an incredible eighteen-year bull market. At a time when the financial sector attempted to redesign itself, the sluggish economy began a renaissance of its own. With real estate taking the lead, the recessionary cloud that had hovered over the nation lifted, and a new day dawned for the country's financial institutions.

It was 1983: decision time for First Savings and Loan as well as thousands of other thrifts across the country. John McIntyre, W.C. Weatherly, J.D. Taylor, and others who figured so prominently in the legacy of First Savings and Loan would hardly recognize an industry that was rapidly changing after years of predictability. First Savings was profitable in its current business form despite industry and economic turbulence, and few wanted to rock the boat. There was an ongoing debate within the association's board of directors of exactly how First Savings should approach this new financial frontier. One outspoken board member who was an advocate for new opportunities was Chairman June Crumpler.

A successful attorney and real estate developer, Crumpler was president of the Mebane Lumber Company. He knew the rewards and pitfalls of business risks and was willing to take them. Crumpler often pleaded his case during board meetings for new products and expanding financial services, leading to lengthy discussions. Crumpler followed these exchanges with a motion to bring these ideas to a vote. Time after time, Crumpler initiated a motion but could never convince anyone on the board to second his motion. This routine became somewhat amusing as Crumpler's desires for change and growth ran into a wall of ultra-conservatism. Crumpler took it all in stride, understanding what he was up against and that effecting change would be difficult. At one meeting an exasperated Crumpler, once again rebuffed after making a motion, turned to fellow director Jack Phelps and said, "Jack, I'll second your motion if you'll second mine!" to which the board erupted in laughter. The opportunities that Crumpler advocated were now available, but compared to its peers, First Savings was very small in assets and resources. Offering such products would mean expensive wholesale changes for the association. But no cost would be too great if it came down to survival.

In many respects, June Crumpler had a point, and like it or not, change was on the way and occurring at light speed. First Savings had faced a myriad of challenges during its history and had prospered through conservative management. Changing that style would be difficult. June Crumpler was the lone voice for change on a board that was not convinced that the new opportunities offered to savings institutions was the right path to follow. First Savings' competition, First

Federal Savings and Loan and Community Federal Savings and Loan, already offered diverse financial products, and Graham Savings and Hillsborough Savings would soon follow. Could First Savings afford the cost of keeping in line with its competition? More important, could First Savings afford not to?

President Neal Smith was approaching thirty years with the association and, like McIntyre and others, now had his own moment of decision. Smith admittedly was not a banker, and his entire career was firmly entrenched in the traditional savings and loan concept. Smith desired that First Savings remain a savings and loan, if that was still possible, in this ever-changing financial world. Smith's desire went against the conventional wisdom of the industry, and it appeared now that the risky move was not change, but staying the course.

Vice President Gauldin had decades of experience in the banking industry and agreed with Smith. Becoming a bank or introducing bank products was not the right path for the association, at least not at this point. Gauldin stated years later, "I didn't like what was going on with the banks and savings and loans, and I didn't think First Savings, as small as it was, had any business trying to compete with First Union or Wachovia. I'd been with the Bank of Alamance, and a small association like First Savings couldn't play with the big boys like First Union or Wachovia. Everything was happening so fast, you didn't want to do something stupid that would cost you down the road. Before we jumped in, we wanted to make sure there was water in the pool. If we had made a bunch of changes, First Savings would not be here today, 'cause we'd have gone under or been bought out."

Before changes were implemented, the association wanted to wait and see the long-term effects of this sweeping reform on the industry. One reason that First Savings did not embrace these new changes was the association's negative opinion of its regulator, the FHLBB. At a time of massive industry changes, the relationship between many savings and loans and their regulators became strained and frustrated.

Maybe it was distrust of the system that had built up over the years. Maybe it was holding on to the past, indecision, wisdom, or fear. Whatever the reason, First Savings was determined to stay on its familiar course as a community savings and loan. The association was not being forced to make quick decisions or policy changes to stay in business, as were so many associations on the brink of failure.

Still consequences accompany any choice. The path the association chose ultimately altered the institution, like it or not. Remaining a traditional savings and loan virtually sealed the association's future as a niche player in the local mortgage market where it had once ruled supreme. First Savings could honestly say it had financed nearly every home built in Mebane until the early 1970s. During its heyday, First Savings had seen assets grow an astonishing 450 percent during the steady 1950s and 200 percent during the home building of the 1960s and turbulent 1970s. But during the historic and pivotal 1980s, First Savings was able to grow just 65 percent in a ten-year period at a time when some aggressive associations grew that much in six months. First Savings had been the only local choice for home financing for decades, but now mortgages came in different packages from banks, mortgage brokers, and credit unions. One very crucial yet acceptable trade-off of remaining a thrift would be the institution's slow growth in exchange for safety and stability.

Industry consolidation ushered in a new and different banking environment. Regulatory incentives and liberal accounting rules encouraged mergers between financially strong associations and struggling institutions. A total of 184 supervised mergers occurred in 1982 as regulators forced associations to consolidate, and 215 thrifts voluntarily merged into other institutions. This activity appeased lawmakers as the industry appeared to be strengthening itself from within, temporarily quelling consumer and media concerns.

The fact that the industry was rapidly evolving did not seem to concern First Savings and Loan members, as just eleven members attended the February 1983 shareholders' meeting. The topic of conversation centered on the economy, interest rates, and the new changes coming to the industry. It would be the final meeting for longtime director A.H. Jobe.

On April 14, 1983, the last remaining link to the association's earliest days as the Mebane Home Builders Association was broken when A.H. Jobe passed away. First elected in 1934, Jobe served as a member of the board for forty-nine years and was an instrumental part of the association's transformation from a part-time venture to a full-time savings and loan. A.H. Jobe has the sole distinction of being the only director in the history of First Savings to serve during the struggles of the Great Depression and the golden years following World War II, and to witness the deregulation of the savings and loan industry. The loss of Jobe reduced the membership of the board to six, and the vacancy was not immediately filled.

Changes were occurring on boards of savings and loans across the country. A.H. Jobe and countless others who served on boards of the nation's savings and loans had experienced their share of challenges during their tenure, but their service had been a part of a totally different era. Until the volatile rate environment of the 1970s, savings and loans literally had enjoyed a wonderful life, no pun intended, with few hard choices to make in a seemingly foolproof financial system. The business concept of approving long-term home loans funded with short-term savings deposits had been a sure bet. Those predictable days were over. This new banking environment encouraged the formation of new thrift charters and mergers as well as a new breed of director and management. Ultra-conservative directors were replaced with progressive members who embraced change. Thrifts, once heavily invested in home mortgages, shifted their focus into every investment imaginable, including casinos, fast-food franchises, and ski resorts. In 1980, before deregulation, over 80 percent of savings and loan industry assets were invested in long-term mortgage loans. By 1983, that percentage had dropped to 65 percent and by 1986, just over 50 percent of thrift industry investments were placed in mortgage loans.

Less restrictions and oversight, liberal accounting, and speculative investing created the perfect combination to rally the forces of the industry's recovery. From 1980 to 1986, more than five hundred new savings and loan charters were issued. Investment fever pent up by high interest rates and restrictive regulation through the 1970s was unleashed and quickly became an epidemic. Savings and loans with their spotless reputation for safety and soundness were sowing their wild oats. The days of plain-vanilla home lending were replaced by the next big deal in commercial, construction, development, and speculation ventures.

Liberalized ownership rules for stock savings institutions encouraged start-up associations, and applications sailed through a scaled-down regulatory process. Many new associations were highly leveraged, generating fast returns as speculators entered the business looking for a quick profit. So many state-chartered institutions defected to liberal federal charters that state regulators were forced to loosen the reigns of supervision. Leading the charge was the state of California, whose Nolan Bill allowed state-chartered thrifts to invest 100 percent of their deposits in virtually "any kind of venture." Similar bills followed in the heavy growth states of Florida and Texas.

Savings institutions, designed to provide simple and conservative home loans, were diving headfirst into the unfamiliar territory of commercial ventures. The complicated mess that became the savings and loan crisis of the 1980s and early 1990s ironically came down to commercial development, something thrifts knew little about, as two-thirds of the troubled assets of thrift institutions during the crisis were tied to bad commercial loans.

Comparing the savings and loan crisis of the 1980s to the financial crisis of 2008 offers some interesting perspectives. The massive failures of the savings and loans, for the most part, affected the thrift industry. The failure of one institution in the 1980s did not pose a systemic risk to the entire financial system. This was not the case, however, with the financial crisis of 2008, as the failure of one large institution had the potential to create a domino effect, resulting in multiple failures.

Mebane expanded when the residential areas of Brookhollow subdivision, Cedar Lane south of town, and Stagecoach Road to the north were annexed. This move increased the size of the town by one-third, and although Mebane was indeed growing, not everyone was excited. Brookhollow residents bitterly opposed the annexation, resulting in a three-year court battle.

Things were spinning out of control in 1983, and Neal Smith recalls a "real sense of urgency at the time and almost a feeling of panic as associations felt they had to change in order to make it." It wasn't just troubled institutions that were merging, as opportunistic associations felt it was time to strengthen their market position. Burlington's First Federal Savings and Loan approached First Savings about a merger. In a letter to Neal Smith, First Federal's president, B.J. "Bobby" Gaydon, made a proposal with "printouts which provide a look at our Associations merged . . . [with] projections . . . through 1984." First Federal had evolved with the times and was now a full-service financial institution offering credit cards, ATM services, and other investment and lending products. Although First Savings passed on the proposal, a merger with First Federal would have undoubtedly solidified a large share of the Alamance County market.

Shortly after deregulation, red flags began to fly at the nation's savings and loan regulator. The Federal Home Loan Bank Board was having second thoughts about its liberal and questionable guidance to savings institutions in this transition period. True, the speculative practices of some fast-growing savings and loans proved profitable, but pitfalls remained.

Edwin Gray, the regulator's new chairman, changed course, attempting to correct a worsening dilemma. Gray pushed for stricter enforcement, but the savings and loan industry bitterly opposed stronger oversight. Convinced the path to success was now open, many institutions banded together, enlisting the support of well-connected developers and members of Congress. The FHLBB had lost control of a runaway train.

The rising tide of real estate development pulled the nation's economy off the floor, and a building boom, now firmly under way, breathed new life into the struggling savings and loan industry. The turnaround in the economy and real estate gave more ammunition to the thrift industry to claim that deregulation was working and to implore regulators to back off. The domino effect of building boosted construction-related businesses such as lumber, furniture, and home furnishings. Land values soared in areas where prices were depressed just a few years earlier.

Money and lots of it would be needed to fund the construction boom, and brokered deposits filled the gap. With rate ceilings now a thing of the past, the open market now set interest rates, and the FHLBB's earlier decision to allow unlimited brokered deposits was coming back to haunt it. Brokered funds provided much-needed liquidity, but this hot money could also be withdrawn from an institution, usually in large blocks, in search of higher returns. In attempts to keep these deposits, institutions extended longer deposit durations with high rates, locking in a long-term liability.

Empire Savings and Loan of Mesquite, Texas, made headlines in March 1984 when the $300 million thrift failed. Just three years earlier, Empire was a small-town thrift with assets of just $13 million. But like many associations in high-growth regions of the country, Empire became caught up in a building frenzy. At the time of its failure, a whopping 90 percent of Empire's liabilities were brokered deposits. For comparison, at the time of Empire's rise, First Savings was an $18 million institution. Although brokers frequently contacted First Savings wanting to place deposits, the association, with its high liquidity, never accepted them.

As real estate heated up, fast profits on loans from real estate development and speculation sparked bidding wars between banks and savings and loans. Appraisal values of potential projects often determined which institution received these contracts and the loan business of developers. The higher the appraisal, the higher the loan amount, pleasing both lender and developer. With so much riding on appraisals, collusion and corruption between savings and loans, appraisers, and developers created overstated values. A sudden or unexpected downturn in the real estate market would expose these institutions to huge losses. But the good times had finally returned to the beleaguered industry, and no one was looking back.

The failures of high-flying savings institutions made good press, but they were hardly representative of the thousands of savings and loans nationwide that were simply serving the needs of their local communities. Still, failed associations like Empire Savings were the ones featured on the nightly news, and this bad publicity eventually eroded public confidence in the savings and loan industry.

The high interest rate environment of the early 1980s severely affected home lending. From 1980 through 1984 First Savings averaged just ninety loan closings a year on an annual average loan volume of $2,136,400. Placed in perspective, ninety loan closings was consistent with the loan demand of the 1940s. By 1984 a corner was turned as mortgage rates and loan demand began to recover. With mortgage rates stable again, hovering around 13 percent, consumers with high interest-rate mortgages quickly refinanced, and those looking to buy a home jumped in the market.

With the nation's economy improving, so did President Reagan's popularity, and the Gipper was reelected for a second term in November. Inflation was no longer the demon that had tormented the country for more than a decade. Running at 13.5 percent when Reagan took office in 1980, inflation had stabilized near 5 percent, not only lifting Reagan's approval rating, but providing solid evidence that the Federal Reserve's monetary policy was working.

With the nation's economy on the mend, Americans were spending money again, and much of it was in the form of plastic. Although charge cards had been around for decades, they became entrenched in the minds of American consumers by the 1980s. Financial institutions, eager for income, jumped on board the credit card bandwagon.

Late fees on credit cards ran around five dollars until a Supreme Court ruling changed the way these fees were calculated, and late fees rose to thirty dollars.

Credit card interest rates were averaging between 12 and 14 percent, which made this a losing proposition for issuers as interest rates ran well above 15 percent. A solution was found in the liberal laws of two states that allowed virtually unlimited interest rates for companies which maintained offices in those states. As credit card companies moved operations to South Dakota and Delaware, the significance went virtually unnoticed. Within five years, credit card interest rates topped 25 percent. The economic recovery that took place during the 1980s would influence individual finances and spending habits of Americans for the remainder of the century. Armed with their credit cards, an improving economy, and pent-up demand, consumers went on a spending spree.

And spend they did. From videocassette recorders to Cabbage Patch Kids to immense satellite dishes, Americans flexed their purchasing power. The hottest-selling vehicle was the minivan, a huge improvement over the family station wagon of the 1960s. The popularity of the minivan pulled Chrysler back from the brink of bankruptcy and became a status symbol for middle-class families. But the must-have consumer item was the first generation of cellular telephones. One could make a lasting impression at any social occasion, chatting on a device the size of a small shoe box and with a service area of almost twenty miles.

On January 19, 1985, Chairman of the Board June A. Crumpler passed away. A member of the board since 1960 and chairman for twelve years, Crumpler's relationship with First Savings began in 1946 when he served as assistant attorney for the institution's counsel, T.C. Carter. Known for his progressive style, Crumpler added much-needed balance and discussion to the association's conservative board.

Crumpler enjoyed a good round of golf, often playing with attorney Lee Settle. While attending a savings and loan convention, Crumpler and Settle had a specific tee time one morning, and due to crowded play they were paired with two women. When asked later by their spouses if they enjoyed their golf game, Crumpler replied, "They teamed us up with a couple of old ladies, but it was fine." Later that evening, Crumpler, Settle, and their wives were at a restaurant waiting to be seated for dinner when who should walk in but the "old ladies," who just happened to be two very attractive women. Recognizing Crumpler and Settle, one woman said, "Well, if it isn't Junebug!" and gave Crumpler a hug. Once Crumpler and his party were seated after a few embarrassing moments and introductions,

June's wife Mitty remarked, "You know, it's amazing what a shower and a little makeup can do for an old lady."

At the January 31 board meeting, Director Jack Phelps was elected as chairman, and the vacancy left by Crumpler's passing reduced the board to just five members: Phelps, James, Oakley, Gauldin, and Smith. Although the association's bylaws required the board to have six members, First Savings operated with just five directors for nearly two years.

For more than a century, the state of North Carolina led the nation in textile production, with 40 percent of workers in the state tied to the industry. By the mid-1980s, the textile industry was in serious trouble as foreign imports forced consolidation and downsizing of U.S.-based companies. Even with attempts to improve the industry's efficiency, nearly 400,000 U.S. textile jobs had disappeared. In 1980 the United States imported 25 percent of its textile products, but by 1984 that percentage had climbed to 50 percent. Dan River closed its Mebane facility in 1983, and although Greensboro's Cone Mills shut down five of its plants, the Granite Plant in Haw River was going strong, running three shifts a day with 550 workers.

Furniture makers were feeling the heat of cheaper imports as well, and change was coming. Stephen White shocked everyone when he announced that White Furniture had received outside bids to buy the company. For 104 years, in good and bad times, White Furniture Company was a steady and unwavering presence in the town of Mebane. White and Kingsdown provided the city's manufacturing foundation, and for many of their employees, the only job they had ever known. White's workers were a familiar downtown sight at lunch or break time as they packed the green benches facing Highway 70 or congregated near the magnolia tree at the corner of Fifth and Center streets. For those people who had given their lives to the company or others who simply knew the unmistakable blare of White's whistle, the possibility of White Furniture Company being sold was frightening. By the 1980s only a fraction of the town's people actually worked in the historic building, but White still held part of the town's heart and soul within its walls.

In June, the transaction became official, and White Furniture Company was sold to Hickory White Furniture for $5.1 million. To quell any rumors, the new owners assured nervous workers that no major changes for the company were planned. But when fifty employees were laid off in September, fear and doubt replaced hope and security. The company whose unwavering presence was a comforting sign of strength and stability was no longer controlled by the White family and was now vulnerable. Plant closings had been a fact of life in the shaky economy of the last fifteen years, yet no one dared whisper that word about Mebane's oldest employer.

Growing interest in development south of town near I-85 alleviated some of the uncertainty regarding White Furniture. The two-mile stretch of interstate from Mebane Oaks Road west to Trollingwood Road was dotted with a few service stations, and the commercial development south of the city had been slow in coming. The only major addition had been the Arrowhead Restaurant and Motel at Mebane Oaks Road that was built in the early 1960s. Arrowhead Golf Course was now up for sale, and Carolina Central Industrial Park and Burlington's First Federal Savings and Loan were both interested buyers. CCIP had developed the business park on South Third Street Extension, home to MCR, Sandvik, and other companies. First Federal's interest, while surprising, was not uncommon, as new investment powers allowed thrifts to pursue new business endeavors. First Federal's offer was accepted, pending a zoning change from the city of Mebane. The Mebane Planning Board denied the request based on water and sewer concerns and the fear that an industrial park would "cause too much traffic on Mebane Oaks Road."

Buckhorn Road was just two miles east down I-85 and was somewhat less traveled than Mebane Oaks Road. That changed in 1985 when the Buckhorn Jockey Lot opened, creating the first of many weekend traffic jams. At the Trollingwood interchange and I-85, finishing touches were made on the twenty-four-hour truck stop, Fuel City.

As Mebane's southern expansion was in its infancy, downtown continued to lose customers to the convenience of shopping malls and strip centers. The Reliable Furniture Store still anchored Clay Street, but the hustle and bustle of the once-vibrant business district had all but disappeared. The Mebane Merchants Association changed its name to the Mebane Business Association (MBA), hoping to enhance its image. But despite the MBA's forty-two active members, downtown consumer traffic had given way to several vacant buildings.

Likewise, the real estate boom that sparked the nation's economic recovery and provided hope to struggling savings and loans was waning. Tax incentives, optimistic developers, and liberal lenders went unchecked for too long as regional economies faltered and states with high concentrations of development suddenly found themselves in overbuilt markets. Developers went bankrupt, and institutions that bet heavily on these commercial investments sank deeper into trouble when loans defaulted.

As institution failures accelerated, the FSLIC struggled to pay off depositors of failing savings and loans. This resulted in special assessments charged to safe and sound associations, and in March, First Savings was hit with an assessment of $6,846. No one likes to pay for someone else's mistake. Although the directors were outraged that profitable associations were being stuck with the bill for the mistakes of failing institutions, the reality was that this was the only option short of a federal bailout. First Savings paid into the FSLIC $49,559 in special assessments for the year.

Since the near-collapse of the banking industry in the 1930s, the government, through the creation of deposit insurance (the FDIC for banks and FSLIC for savings and loans), guaranteed the safety of a customer's deposit up to one hundred thousand dollars. Deposit insurance works basically the same as any insurance program; the more risk potential, the higher the premiums. Insured associations pay into the insurance fund each year a premium based on the strength and soundness of that institution as well as the condition of the industry in general. Depositors, except under extreme circumstances, have nothing to lose. The 1980s witnessed a period of institution failures on a level not seen since the Great Depression, but unlike the 1930s, depositors were protected. Bank runs that closed many institutions during the Depression were averted. But if the insurance fund itself became insolvent and failed, the government would be expected to cover the losses. As the FSLIC continued to deteriorate, and with more failures on the way, FHLBB Chairman Gray warned lawmakers on Capitol Hill that the insurance fund was broke and to recapitalize it would cost the government an estimated $20 billion. The FSLIC would indeed become insolvent in 1986.

The continued deterioration of the savings and loan industry baffled the general public. Everyone thought that the new and improved thrift industry created through deregulation, falling interest rates, and an improving economy would certainly resurrect the industry. Most consumers thought that deregulation had fixed the savings and loan problem, but by the mid-1980s, the problems with thrifts were clearly far from fixed, and perhaps deregulation had only exacerbated their troubles. The high cost of funds on deposit versus the low income from loans that plagued the industry for more than a decade never went away, and the damage was done regardless of new products and business options. Unfortunately, some associations were on life support and allowed to stay open and incur deeper losses.

By 1986 First Savings had assembled a solid staff experiencing very little turnover, with the exception of Carole Thomas who left in 1984. Shelby Murphy and Janice Wright handled the front-line teller duties and drive-through windows while Janice Murray assisted Neal Smith and Ned Gauldin with loan closings. Computer transactions had increased, and as operations became more sophisticated the association employed Holly Sims as a full-time bookkeeper in the fall of 1985.

From the 1920s to the early 1960s, John M. McIntyre had been given the name of "Mr. Mac" by many of First Savings' loyal customers. Neal Smith had served the customers of the association for over thirty years and had earned the trust of generations of customers who called him "Mr. Smith," while others simply referred to him as "Mr. Neal." In their early years, savings and loans were referred to as "building and loans," and one customer, who obviously misunderstood, came into the association wanting to speak with "Mr. Billy Malone."

NASA's Space Shuttle program had performed flawlessly since its first flight in 1981. The countdown to launches and space walks that captured the world's imagination twenty years earlier had disappeared, and the Shuttle's performance seemed as common and routine as airline flight. That routine was shattered on January 28, 1986, as the Space Shuttle *Challenger* exploded seconds after liftoff from the Kennedy Space Center. The loss of its seven crew members temporarily grounded NASA's Shuttle program and was an identifying moment for America's Generation Xers who were coming of age. Comfortable with technology, the Xers would become a driving force behind e-commerce and by century's end would alter conventional methods of financial services.

The other headline story in 1986 was falling interest rates, much to the delight of the American consumer and the financial industry. By year's end, mortgage loan rates dropped to their lowest level in eight years, returning to single digits at just over 9 percent, restoring confidence and stability to a wavering real estate market. Lending for First Savings improved 60 percent as the association experienced its best year since 1978, closing $4,088,500 in home loans.

New residential subdivisions sprang up from Mebane to Gibsonville as builders ventured back into speculative building. These new developments featured more two-story houses, replacing both the one-story ranch-style home that had been the mainstay of building dating back to the 1950s and the split-level house plan of the 1960s and 1970s. Open and informal living areas referred to as "great rooms" were common, and most plans had one- or two-car garages.

Another strip center next to Winn-Dixie on Mebane Oaks Road was gaining steam, but past efforts to develop this area had fallen through. Local residents opposed the development, stating they did not want fast-food restaurants invading their neighborhood. Mebane City Council members weren't sold on the idea either, fearing more development would have a devastating effect on struggling downtown businesses. Like it or not, development was coming, and Mebane's business district would soon find itself split between the traditions of the past and the wave of the future.

Mebane and the state of North Carolina were benefitting from the nation's economic recovery, as both were in a high-growth mode. The state was a popular area for retirees, second only to Florida as a retirement destination. Large businesses and international corporations were relocating to the state, driving the demand for housing. In contrast, real estate development nationwide continued to weaken, particularly in southwestern states. Markets that experienced high growth a few years earlier were now overbuilt. Banks and savings and loans were dealt another blow as the tax incentives that ignited the real estate boom in 1981 were severely restricted by the Tax Reform Act of 1986, further depressing commercial development. By the end of the year, 65 thrifts failed, but the worst was yet to come. Another 441 savings and loans were insolvent, and an additional 553 associations had just 2 percent tangible capital.

On December 16, 1986, First Savings and Loan lost a great friend when Chairman of the Board Jack Phelps passed away. First elected to the board in 1973 and chairman for only a year, Phelps's relationship with the association dated back to the 1950s. Always comfortable in public, Phelps had served as mayor of Mebane and was a successful businessman. He had a very affable personality and wit punctuated by a booming and unmistakable voice. "Jack was one of my closest friends, and we could share anything," said Neal Smith. "He was a joy to be around and a great man to have on your board. I still miss him." Phelps was remembered at the February 1987 shareholders' meeting with a resolution honoring his service to the institution.

The passing of Jack Phelps reduced the board membership to just four members. Two weeks later, on December 30, 1986, Calvin Oakley was elected chairman, and Dr. Steven E. Troutman and Dr. George M. Bullard Jr. were appointed to the vacancies left by June Crumpler and Jack Phelps. George M. Bullard Jr. has the distinction of following in his father's footsteps in both the medical profession and in serving as a member of the association's board. A Mebane native, Bullard joined the Aycock Mebane and Jones clinic upon graduating from East Carolina University Medical School and completing his residency in Newport News, Virginia. Troutman hailed from China Grove and was a graduate of the UNC School of Dentistry, with a successful dental practice for over thirteen years at the time of his appointment. Troutman and Dr. Mike Blankenship's building became a familiar Mebane business on the busy corner of Mebane Oaks Road and South Fifth Street until Walgreen's purchased the property in 2008.

The appointments of Bullard and Troutman signaled another generational shift in the composition of the board. At ages thirty-three and thirty-nine, respectively, Bullard and Troutman were the youngest members to be appointed to the board since Neal Smith in the 1950s.

In April 1987 attorney Robert F. Steele replaced E.T. Sanders as the association's trustee and legal counsel when Sanders lost his battle with cancer. E.T. "Curly" Sanders served as counsel for nearly a decade, replacing Lee Settle as trustee in the late 1970s. Known to speak his mind regardless of the situation or consequences, Sanders could rub people the wrong way. Lee Settle recalled an incident in court involving Sanders that apparently not only confirmed his outspoken nature but revealed that he had a temper to match. The story goes that Sanders was involved in a trial that became very emotional. During the proceedings, the opposing attorney supposedly said something disparaging about Mr. Sanders, and a shouting match between the two lawyers ensued. Sanders apparently had heard enough and lunged at the other attorney, punching him in the mouth. Sanders received a contempt of court warning after the attorneys were separated.

By 1987 it was clear that the American economy was back. The Dow closed above 2000 for the first time in its history. Alan Greenspan became chairman of the Federal Reserve, replacing Paul Volcker. The subdued and often inscrutable Greenspan became a legend during his twenty-year tenure as Fed chairman. The economy's prolonged period of expansion while maintaining low interest rates and inflation during Greenspan's tenure put him on the verge of sainthood. This image changed after his retirement from the Fed in 2006 when the first tremors of the financial crisis of 2008 surfaced. Some believed Greenspan's decisions at the Fed contributed to the financial crisis of the late 2000s.

The 1980s was the decade of the leveraged buyout, in which companies and conglomerates purchase other companies and each other. Businesses bought one another, often closing the competition down, and the money created for these deals usually came from Wall Street. One major investment bank that specialized in funding these takeovers was Drexel Burnham Lambert, offering junk bonds to finance hostile takeover bids. Drexel and investment bank Salomon Brothers were highly involved in the proliferation of collateralized debt obligations (CDOs), and collateralized mortgage obligations (CMOs). These complicated instruments bundled various assets, including risky subprime mortgages, with the idea of reducing risk while giving investors high returns. CDOs and CMOs would eventually contribute to the 2008 financial crisis as well.

First Savings struggled through the early 1980s with double-digit mortgage rates and poor loan demand, yet the association remained profitable. Falling interest rates made all the difference as the association followed the banner year of 1986 with its best lending year of the turbulent decade in 1987. First Savings closed 122 home loans, totaling $4,933,900, as rates continued to fall.

The good times may have returned to some associations, but for others, time was running out. Special assessments continued to be imposed on safe and profitable institutions, and First Savings was hit in May 1987 with its largest onetime amount to date of $37,995. The board was outraged, stating that the FSLIC assessment seemed incomprehensible and irresponsible. The board stated that the actions amounted to "confiscating" the association's profits, adding to more frustration with and mistrust of the regulator.

"Confiscation" seemed rather strong but certainly appropriate when the FHLBB required the association to adopt a resolution that "the Federal Home

Loan Bank of Atlanta be, and hereby is, authorized to charge any demand deposit account maintained with the 'Bank' by this institution for all amounts . . . due and payable by the institution to the FHLBB, to the FSLIC or to the Financing Corporation for any fees, charges or assessments, without notice to or further authorization from this institution."

Despite the savings and loan woes, the economy chugged along, fueled by consumer spending and a seller's market in home sales—until the fall, when panic hit Wall Street. On October 19, 1987, the Dow Jones Industrial Average experienced its largest one-day percentage loss in its history, losing 23 percent and closing at 1738. It took two years for the market to recover fully from the 507-point drop. The Crash of '87 ushered in another recession, pushing mortgage rates back to double digits, where they remained until 1991. Savings and loans on the brink of failure were pushed over the edge.

Texas savings and loans had been some of the most aggressive institutions during the 1980s boom and were hit hard when the commercial real estate market stumbled. By 1987, Texas thrifts accounted for 44 percent of the insolvent savings associations nationwide and 62 percent of total losses for the industry. The media smelled blood. As rumors spread of a government bailout in the works, the once-apathetic public became not only interested in the savings and loan scandal but outraged. Although much of the media focus was on Texas and California thrifts, the sensational stories and tales of impropriety rapidly changed the nation's perception of the savings and loan industry. The great majority of the nation's thrifts were managed quite conservatively but were guilty by association. These healthy thrifts had nothing to do with the massive failures but paid for it in both monetary assessments and a ruined reputation. Stories of the "savings and loan debacle" on the nightly news turned into a national soap opera. Every good scandal needs a central character with a dash of political intrigue, and by 1989 that figure emerged in Charles Keating.

This chapter of the story began in June 1987 when Edwin Gray completed his tenure as chairman of the FHLBB. The regulatory agency was already known for its questionable decisions and sometimes dangerous guidance. In fairness, Gray tried to tighten the screws on fast-growing savings associations engaged in risky investments and questionable lending policies. Thanks to Gray, liberal accounting practices that had prolonged the existence of some failing associations were phased out. Before leaving office, Gray was invited to a meeting in the office of U.S. Senator Dennis DeConcini. At the meeting were four other senators—John McCain, Alan Cranston, John Glenn, and Donald Riegle—who questioned Gray about the "appropriateness" of investigating Lincoln Savings and Loan in Irvine, California, managed by Charles Keating. All five senators had received sizable campaign contributions from Keating, and the meeting with Gray hoped to smooth over any potential problems. The scandal erupted with the failure of Lincoln Savings in 1989, costing taxpayers over $2 billion. The attempted influence of these senators became the epicenter of media attention, earning them the label of "the Keating Five." Deserving or not, Keating became the poster child for the savings and loan crisis and a example of greed and corruption as the plot thickened.

In Mebane, after serving just over a year on the board, Dr. George M. Bullard Jr. resigned on February 25, 1988, moving his medical practice to Newport News, Virginia. The seat was left vacant until May 26, and was then filled by Dr. David C. Jones, who began an eighteen-year tenure as director.

The street festival Arts Around the Square was an enormously popular event, attracting thousands to downtown Graham during the 1980s, and the Mebane Business Association, looking for ways to revitalize downtown, thought Mebane was ripe for a festival of its own. Coinciding with the flowering of dogwoods and azaleas, the town held its inaugural Dogwood Festival in April 1988. The celebration was an instant success, bringing thousands of people to the city's downtown business district along with a shot in the arm for local business owners. With events like the Dogwood Festival as a base, downtown Mebane began its economic revival.

More than a street festival was needed, though, to save the nation's troubled thrifts. In 1988 another 223 thrifts failed, as did 200 banks with combined assets of $35.7 billion. All efforts, quick fixes, and a determination to keep ailing associations open weren't working, and the savings and loan industry was on the brink of collapse. It was time to shoot the wounded and move on, but another year would pass before Congress had the nerve to pull the trigger.

Amid the scandals, good publicity was hard to find, but in August 1988, First Savings was named again in *National Thrift News* as "one of the High Performing Associations in the nation." First Savings had made the list several times before, but now the timing was perfect. Another endorsement came from the Sheshunoff Rating Service, which listed First Savings as "A+" in its publication *The Highest Rated Savings and Loans in America.* Until the 1980s, this type of recognition would have gone virtually unnoticed and left on the coffee table with other outdated magazines. Now everyone from local investors and customers to the national media viewed these ratings with close scrutiny.

As the savings and loan crisis escalated, the public's view of the industry deteriorated beyond repair. By the late 1980s it was a foregone conclusion that taxpayer money would be needed to bail out an industry that was now perceived as corrupt. At that time North Carolina was home to 137 conservatively operated savings and loans with assets of $20 billion, but they were stuck in a large barrel with some very bad apples. In fact, Tar Heel thrifts grew almost 10 percent in assets during 1988 due to a flight to quality amid the stock market meltdown in October 1987.

But positive stories didn't make national headlines; fraud and mismanagement did. The association's directors voiced this sentiment in the October board minutes, reflecting their frustration with the industry's sometimes dubious choices, stating, "If many of the failing savings and loans in this country had used a more 'unsophisticated' investment policy and operated in a 'simple nature' as the federal examiners have classified us, we would not be paying a special FSLIC assessment and have our reserves confiscated."

With government intervention on the way, a new day was dawning on the nation's financial industry. New regulations for savings and loans were phased in just ahead of massive reform. Regulators drew in the reins, and questionable internal policies and practices for savings and loans were scaled back. This new regulatory environment was already affecting the association. In April, the board was required to "adopt asset classification policies and procedures" and "policies for . . . appraisal procedures."

Questionable appraisal practices contributed to the failure of many savings and loans in the heavy speculative market of the Southwest. In any market, an appraisal can be the reason a real estate transaction succeeds or fails. An appraisal is simply an opinion of value, and often in transactions, if a property does not appraise for a certain price, borrowers, real estate agents, and even lenders might simply order another appraisal until the desired value is reached. This practice, together with collusion and arrangements with developers, led to a situation of overbuilt markets and failing projects. First Savings had employed the services of several different appraisers, but the wide range of values that resulted was troubling. The board recommended the exclusive use of J. Richard "Dick" Dodson as the association's appraiser.

By the late 1980s, good times had returned to Alamance County as the unemployment rate stood at a remarkable 2.7 percent while the state's average was just 3.4 percent. Nutrition Pak, GE, and GKN expanded operations locally, adding more jobs. The Employment Security Commission indicated that 49,993 people worked for the county's 2,393 small businesses. Manufacturing in America was still in a state of limbo, though. Mebane experienced this firsthand in 1988 when Redmond Industries closed its mobile home manufacturing facility, resulting in the loss of 90 local jobs, and Craftique Furniture Company was sold to Pulaski Furniture of Virginia. Craftique opened in 1948, becoming a Mebane tradition and producing high-quality furniture. With both White and Craftique no longer tied to Mebane, the level of anxiety was raised another notch as the future of furniture in Mebane appeared uncertain.

One of Mebane's oldest businesses disappeared in 1988 when the Eagle Oil Company that occupied the corner of Center and Third streets for decades closed its doors. The original building was upgraded later that year and became the home of Davis and Humbert Attorneys. The law firm opened its new location at the busy intersection after moving from its original office in the Welcome Finance building on Center Street.

First Savings completed a major renovation project of its own that year. The association was in need of a makeover as very little redecorating had taken place since an interior office space was added during the mid-1960s. After changes to the interior and exterior were completed, the association held an open house on October 13.

The nation's electorate agreed that the country was on the right track, and Vice President George H.W. Bush won the 1988 presidential race, riding the coattails of popular two-term president Ronald Reagan.

Before year's end, First Savings was hit with yet another special assessment for $26,000 to the shrinking FSLIC. Frustration with these assessments was soothed somewhat at the February 1989 shareholders' meeting as the conversation turned to First Savings' appearance in a *USA Today* article. The paper published the rankings of all savings and loans in the country based on each institution's net worth. First Savings came in at number 182 out of 3,046 thrifts, placing the association in the top 5 percent. This great news came at the peak of the savings and loan crisis and assured Mebane that First Savings was still the strong and safe institution it had been for eighty years.

Mebane was no longer a small town but a growing city. It's hard to pinpoint exactly when that happened, but there is no mistaking how it happened. Mebane officially changed its name to the "City of Mebane" in 1986, reflecting a more accurate description of its growth. Positioned between the Triangle and Triad, Mebane was enjoying a newfound popularity, proving the real estate axiom of "location, location, location." Raleigh was one of the fastest-growing cities in the country, and Mebane's close proximity to the Triangle brought house hunters to Alamance County looking for a slower pace. Raleigh's exploding growth affected outlying communities that had once been small North Carolina towns. The Wake County community of Cary had a population of just 7,600 in 1970 but was a thriving city of 40,000 by 1989. Cary subsequently became a growth phenomenon, reaching a population of 101,265 by 2004. Mebane and Hillsborough were within the Triangle's reach, and when the eleven-mile stretch of I-40 from Hillsborough to Durham opened in the fall of 1988, continued growth was assured.

Part of Mebane's growth was due to low taxes and real estate prices, but what was attracting more and more people was the small-town atmosphere. Maintaining that small-town charm would be a challenge as the town grew. The population nearly doubled from 2,300 in 1980 to an estimated 4,500 residents by 1988, and residential subdivisions seemed to be popping up everywhere. Canterwood, Burkewood, Sunset Ridge, Woodbridge, and Hunter's Run were the latest additions.

Land values were increasing, and it was no surprise that one of Mebane's largest landowners was the White family. In 1989 the White and Millender families placed several prime tracts of land for sale, and part of this land became Fair Oaks subdivision on South Third Street.

If future home owners found Alamance County attractive, long-distance truckers found the county downright irresistible. The Flying J Travel Center opened at

Jimmy Kerr Road and I-85, joining Fuel City and the Red Horse just down the road at the Trollingwood Road interchange as main truck stops along the soon to be widened I-85/I-40 interstate. The two interstates that merged in Greensboro to the west and Hillsborough to the east, running parallel through Alamance County, created a growing traffic problem. The heavily congested highway expanded to eight lanes by 1995, and Mebane was at the center of it all.

At the center of the savings and loan debacle stood Charles Keating for his role in the failure of Lincoln Savings and Loan, and the media closed in for the kill. Although the senators known as the Keating Five escaped virtually unharmed, Keating was found guilty of fraud, racketeering, and conspiracy and sentenced to ten years.

Keating turned out to be a very small figure in a much larger story. Charges were brought against other savings and loan managers as a new regulatory environment took shape and the freewheeling days of the 1980s came to an end. Three hundred and twenty-seven savings and loans failed in 1989, and all attempts over the previous ten years to keep the thrift industry going had failed as well. Somewhat anticlimactically, the final blow to the savings and loan industry came with the passage of the Financial Institutions Reform Recovery and Enforcement Act on August 9, 1989. Thrifts had been dying for a decade, and it was time to end the misery.

The legislation itself did not eliminate thrifts but initiated total financial reform, doing away with the FHLBB as the regulator of the savings and loan industry. A new regulatory agency, the Office of Thrift Supervision (OTS), born with a chip on its shoulder, was created to enforce new laws in a different financial era. The OTS was not about to make the same mistakes as its predecessor and took a hard line on enforcement. The freewheeling days of deregulation were replaced by restrictive legislation for an industry that most people felt had it coming. The Resolution Trust Corporation (RTC) was formed with the monumental task of resolving the nation's insolvent thrifts by 1995. The insolvent FSLIC was abolished, and the insurance funds of banks and savings associations were merged into the FDIC.

As the saying goes, it takes a lifetime to build a reputation and only one moment to destroy it. With financial reform under way, traditional thrifts distanced themselves from the tarnished savings and loan image as most became banks, whose reputation had mostly been spared during the crisis. The publicity generated by the savings and loan crisis thankfully did not have a significant effect on First Savings' credibility with its member base. First Savings knew its customers, and its customers knew First Savings. Cultivating new customers in a competitive market would be the real test in this new financial arena.

To be certain, the 1980s had been a huge challenge for the safest of financial institutions. Surprisingly, First Savings benefitted during the decade despite the turmoil, as assets increased 65 percent, reaching $29,906,475, but growth was slowing. Loans grew just 26 percent, with most of the volume generated in the last half of the decade as mortgage rates fell. Deposits, something that associations nationwide could not retain, grew an astounding 59 percent, well outpacing loan demand. The association channeled more funds into its securities portfolio, which grew 325 percent and diversified the institution's investment risk.

By far, the most powerful number that radiated from First Savings and Loan's financial statement was its net worth. Prospering during a decade when savings and loans were losing money and with many closing their doors, the association grew its reserve position an incredible 116 percent. With a reserve of $3,718,271, First Savings had more ammunition to support its argument of remaining true to the traditional savings and loan charter rather than making wholesale changes. But would its customer base support the association with so many financial options now on the market?

Just as the Berlin Wall, the most recognizable symbol of division and oppression, had disappeared, so too had the many differences that once separated financial institutions. When the 1980s began, 4,363 savings and loans faced an uncertain future, and by 1989 just 2,616 were left standing. Surviving thrifts had new rules, new restrictions, and a new regulator, as well as more competition and a public relations nightmare to contend with at the start of a new decade.

Through it all, First Savings made its decision to remain a community thrift in a new financial world where the focus was squarely on stockholders and the bottom line. Somewhere in the mix, the value created for stockholders replaced the value of the customer. Mutual institutions like First Savings, which were not controlled by stockholders, were disappearing as an era of takeovers, buyouts, mergers, and acquisitions changed the financial world and left some customers disillusioned.

Perhaps First Savings had more questions as the 1980s ended than when the decade began. *Would the negative image of the savings and loan name hurt business going forward? Does it matter to the customer if an institution is a bank or thrift? Does personal service count anymore, or is business strictly rate-driven?* The most important question of all, though, was *Could First Savings still survive as a traditional savings and loan?* For all practical purposes the simple days of the savings and loan were over. Or were they?

Center Street during the 1980s reveals the city in transition. The decline of downtown's business district can be seen as the windows above Roses are boarded up. *Courtesy Don Bolden*

Downtown's renaissance that began in the 1990s continues today.

First Savings lobby as it appeared in 1987 prior to renovations to both the interior and exterior of the building.

Former director I.C. Clark's prize moose stands guard over the teller line.

Storage space appears to be at a premium as Holly Sims and Frances Terrell shared this crowded office during the 1980s.

In some ways the vault hasn't changed that much over the years.

CHAPTER NINE

A New Beginning

1990–1999

AMERICANS ENTERED THE 1990S FULL OF OPTIMISM, and with good reason. The shaky economy of the previous twenty years had finally turned the corner, setting the stage for one of the most prosperous decades in the country's history. Two key numbers boosted consumer confidence; inflation weighed in at 5.4 percent, while unemployment fell to 5.3 percent. After a disastrous ten years of high interest rates and unemployment, it appeared that sanity had finally returned to the American economy. Another psychological barrier was broken when mortgage rates began the decade just inside single digits at 9.9 percent. Incredibly, the 10 percent interest rate that seemed like such a bargain in 1990 would seem outrageously high by the end of the decade, as mortgage rates fell to levels not seen in thirty years. Annual household income grew 64 percent during the 1980s, reaching $28,980 as 1990 began. The Dow Jones Industrial Average had rebounded nicely from its September 1987 crash, fully charged at 2753. Remarkably, the Dow would cross the 11,000 mark nine years later. America's economic engine was filled with a powerful mixture, and the only thing needed was for an eager consumer to step on the gas and start spending. And spend they did, as Americans were in a buying mood, with houses at the top of their shopping list.

Consumer confidence and falling interest rates put the housing industry back in business. Times had indeed changed, and America's financial system seemed to be on the right track after the embarrassing 1980s. Savings and loans no longer enjoyed their monopoly on home lending, as mortgages were now available through banks, mortgage brokers, credit unions, and a host of other financial outlets. Lower down-payment requirements were standard for home loans, and mortgage programs offered a host of interest rate structures, terms, and qualifications for the borrower.

The continued evolution of mortgage lending could be traced to many factors; the primary factor was the availability of money. The 1970s and 1980s saw record high interest rates, and money was expensive to borrow. Beginning in the 1990s and beyond, rates continued a free fall not only spurring the housing market but giving rise to the home refinancing phenomenon. Loan securitization hit full stride, moving home financing to a new level well beyond the simplicity of hometown lenders chasing local deposits. Borrowers from North Carolina might obtain a home loan from a lender in California and vice versa. The frenzy that mortgage lending reached during the 1990s was reminiscent of the credit environment of the late 1940s and 1950s. The difference in 1990 was how money was generated to meet this burgeoning loan demand. Just as home lending was reaching a grand scale, money to meet this nationwide loan demand had to be generated on sources equally as grand. With Freddie Mac (FHLMC) and Fannie Mae (FNMA) now controlling the majority of home lending through securitization, money poured into the mortgage market from a variety of sources, including Wall Street.

The special relationship between lender and borrower that had been the centerpiece of the savings and loan industry had virtually disappeared. Securitization changed the way borrowers paid their mortgage payments, which now were often sent to out-of-state lenders that owned their mortgage loan. For the lenders, selling mortgage loans was now common practice, and borrowers differed greatly from the golden years of the savings and loan industry. Most folks who bought homes in the 1940s and 1950s stayed in those houses longer, looking forward to the day the mortgage was paid off. Burning the mortgage signaled an end to long-term debt. By 1990 the mortgage landscape looked completely different as home owners relocated five times or more, and unlike their parents and grandparents, owning only one or two homes during a lifetime was a rarity.

Beginning in the 1990s and continuing until 2008, money to purchase a home became easier to obtain. A new and different generation of home buyers emerged as home ownership became more of an expectation than a dream. The once-elusive prize of buying a home, which past generations worked and saved for years to attain, was now within reach for most Americans. What had been known as the American Dream was becoming, much to the delight of the mortgage industry, the American Entitlement.

Expectations and reality, however, are two different things. While new lending products allowed more consumers to realize the dream of owning a home, others found it nearly impossible. The rapid appreciation of real estate values during the 1990s greatly outpaced the rise of consumer income. Even falling mortgage rates didn't help, as low- and moderate-income Americans were left out of the 1990s housing boom. By the end of the decade, affordable housing would become a major issue, once again altering mortgage lending and setting the stage for a financial catastrophe.

Although the supposedly improved financial world celebrated its new beginning, First Savings was reluctant to join the party. To be honest, First Savings had a hard time adjusting to the banking industry. Having thrived during the 1980s when many institutions failed was evidence enough that change was not a requirement for success and could pose its own risk. True to its character, First Savings shunned the conventional wisdom by continuing to retain the mortgages in-house rather than offering them for sale. This policy was just one example of the association's determination to remain a local savings and loan in the midst of a rapidly changing financial world. First Savings was placing all its eggs in one basket, staking its future on past successes. In a full-service banking world, the association offered just two products: mortgage loans and savings accounts. Resisting change to avoid risk was in itself a huge gamble, considering what happened to savings and loans in the 1980s.

The association did see one potential flaw in selling loans on the secondary market, and it had absolutely nothing to do with risk and everything to do with the customer. Selling mortgage loans transformed an otherwise easy transaction into a complicated ordeal that some folks found overwhelming. Loans originating in North Carolina could easily wind up in some other state, leaving customers disconnected with the original lender. With bad publicity surrounding savings and loans, the association was not about to take a chance of alienating its small but loyal customer base. The board felt that the risk of a dissatisfied customer far outweighed the interest rate risk of holding a long-term investment.

The association began the 1990s with its veteran staff of Frances Terrell, Shelby Murphy, Janice Wright, Holly Sims, Janis Murray, and Neal Smith. First Savings faced this new era of finance with a familiar board of directors, including John Henry James, Ned Gauldin, Steve Troutman, David Jones, Neal Smith, and Calvin Oakley.

The 1990s started with a borrowing boom that continued almost unabated for most of the decade. Although money for lenders was plentiful and available from a variety of sources, the coveted local deposit remained the lifeblood of small community institutions. Competition for these deposits tightened once again in the 1990s as the mutual fund emerged as a strong investment tool.

Mutual funds had been around since the 1920s, but their popularity exploded during the 1990s. In 1990, 3,081 mutual funds held $1 trillion in U.S. assets. When the decade ended, an incredible 8,171 mutual funds had mushroomed into existence, with total assets topping $7 trillion. Those investing in mutual funds were not disappointed, receiving an average 23.6 percent return as the stock market regularly hit new highs during the 1990s. As one observer put it, "The simple way to make money in the 1990s was to have a checkbook and a mutual fund." Star investment managers became financial celebrities, appearing in business magazines and on television talk shows. Manager Peter Lynch turned Fidelity Magellan into the largest mutual fund in the world by producing strong returns. Baby boomers saving for retirement and their children's college education poured money into mutual funds like never before. Community institutions once again were faced with deposit outflows as savings accounts seemed rather boring compared to the fast returns in the stock market.

Good times indeed had returned to the country and to Mebane, which was riding the crest of a real estate boom that began in the mid-1980s. The average price of a home in town had reached $60,600 by 1990. By any standard, Mebane real estate could be considered a steal, as the average price of a home nationwide stood at $149,800. The smaller towns in Alamance County took a backseat to West Burlington and Elon, particularly when it came to real estate. An agent from Vogler Realty observed that people new to the area were eager to look at homes in West Burlington, Gibsonville, and Elon, but stayed away from the eastern part of the county. By the early 1990s, that bias had changed. Mebane's growth had clearly shifted into the fast lane, due in part to the city's location and popularity with home buyers from the Triangle. Mebane's population grew an incredible 71 percent during the 1980s, with 4,754 residents by the decade's end. Alamance County managed a respectable 9 percent growth during this same time period, as its population reached 108,213 by 1990. Mebane's growth continued to concentrate on the south side of town, with the Board of Elections adding the South Melville precinct for the fall 1990 elections, and the surge of residents prompted a $1.3 million renovation to South Mebane Elementary School.

Mebane seemed to be growing in every respect with the exception of downtown, but that was about to change. The 1990s witnessed the revival of the once-vibrant business district that had struggled for the previous twenty years. In March 1990, Martinho's Restaurant opened, becoming an anchor business for Clay Street. Tommy's Mini Mart opened a new store on the corner of Center and Second streets, replacing McAdams Esso. Downtown's new beginning, however, would be painful as the area still relied heavily on support from White, Kingsdown, Influential Hosiery, Dixie Yarn, and other industries. Ninety-two workers at Influential Hosiery on North Fifth Street breathed a sigh of relief when Brown Wooten Mills purchased the struggling textile firm as the tremors of change in the textile industry continued. Just as First Savings was adjusting to the new financial world of the 1990s, downtown went through its own identity crisis. Manufacturing disappeared from the landscape, and with Clay and Center streets no longer a consumer destination, something had to change to bring back consumer dollars.

Mebane was growing faster than any other part of Alamance County, but some folks felt the city was slighted when Alamance Regional Medical Center planned its new hospital. The state-of-the-art facility was the consolidation of Alamance County and Alamance Memorial hospitals. The site on Huffman Mill Road southwest of Burlington and in the far western region of the county seemed an odd location as it was closer to Guilford County than to the county seat of Graham. The hospital's choice seemed to reinforce the perception that Alamance County revolved around the growth of West Burlington. The location drew sharp criticism from the Mebane City Council. Alamance Regional would more than redeem itself to the Mebane community in the decade to follow.

Perhaps the only sector of American life in the 1990s that was changing faster than the banking world was communication. The Internet was working its way into business applications, setting the stage for online banking. Cell phones evolved, and voice mail was a must for the office setting. Television was changing, as viewers had more choices than ever with the growing popularity of cable and satellite service. By 1990, 50 million homes had access to cable TV, having grown from just 17 million homes in 1980.

A popular motion picture of the day, *Field of Dreams*, featured the inspiration for the ubiquitous phrase, "If you build it, they will come." (The line is often misquoted. The actual quote from the movie is "If you build it, he will come.") The same could be said for the city of Mebane, as speculative building was occurring all across the city, from new residential subdivisions to commercial development. Many of Mebane's established companies followed suit as well. Royal Home Fashions added forty thousand square feet to its Oakwood Street Extension facility, creating 100 new jobs in drapery and curtain manufacturing. A.O. Smith doubled its workforce, adding 220 jobs to its electric motor operations.

Mebane learned a long time before that growth has a price. As in decades past, familiar landmarks disappeared in the wake of new development. One of the first to go was the old Melville Chevrolet building on Center Street, demolished for a parking lot at Central Carolina Bank. For decades, people who grew up in Mebane could return to discover that very little had changed in their hometown. Changes to the city's landscape that had been subtle and slow shifted gears in the 1990s and beyond, as development came fast and furious.

Ned Gauldin had spent the previous forty-two years of his life in banking and felt it was time to spend more time on the golf course with his wife Mabel. On May 23, 1990, Director and Vice President Gauldin celebrated his sixty-fifth birthday, and he retired from First Savings in June. The team of Ned Gauldin and Neal Smith had set a remarkable standard since 1978. Under their leadership First Savings had prospered during a time of incredible change. Gauldin's retirement, however, forced the association to think about management succession for the first time. Neal Smith was fifty-eight years old, and although he wasn't going anywhere, Gauldin's departure left him with both the day-to-day operation responsibilities as well as the closing of mortgage loans, which topped $4.9 million in 1990, a record at the time.

Smith's oldest son Rick had spent the last five years as a real estate agent for Vogler Realty, and like most agents he was enjoying the success of a strong seller's market. This experience proved valuable, and the board offered Rick Smith the position of vice president on August 15, 1990. The opportunity for father and son to work together is something many folks never get to experience. Neal Smith cautioned his son that coming to work at First Savings offered no guarantees as "the savings and loan business is not what it used to be."

The elder Smith was right. A year had passed since the government tried to fix the failing savings and loan industry once and for all, but the situation was still shaky. The laws passed in 1989 and subsequent years ended the days of deregulation, and the industry entered a period of consolidation and strict oversight. These laws, however, did not end the savings and loan crisis, which would take the better part of the 1990s to clean up. In 1990, 223 more savings and loans failed, and the Resolution Trust Corporation, created to resolve the crisis, had 313 troubled institutions on its list.

Savings and loans had endured the wrath of lawmakers, the media, and consumers for more than a decade, but not only the thrifts were in trouble. The nation's mutual savings banks had problems of their own. Between 1990 and 1992, 842 banks went under, and financial institutions of all kinds were finding the path to this new era of banking very difficult.

After joining the association, Rick Smith was initiated into the loan committee's weekly property inspections. Each Wednesday, Smith, his father Neal Smith, Calvin Oakley, John Henry James, and Ned Gauldin piled into Neal's car and took off to look at property. What was interesting and gained more meaning over time was the atmosphere of these outings. Neal Smith would pop in a tape of 1940s music for the listening pleasure of this group of men from the Greatest Generation. Smith drove rather slowly, enjoying the time with his friends. There was never a rush to get back to the office, and no one had a cell phone. These outings offered quite a contrast to the fast-paced real estate environment that Rick Smith had left to come to First Savings, but the younger Smith came to cherish these trips. These Wednesday rituals were always amusing, as Calvin Oakley and Ned Gauldin kept everyone entertained with jokes and stories.

These outings were more social than business, reflecting the values of these men. Other bankers would no doubt find these trips old-fashioned and a total waste of time. The loan committee seemed stuck in the 1950s, oblivious to the fact that the entire banking world had changed around them. As time went on, these relaxed trips and the committee's casual attitude made sense to its newest member. These men were not mainstream lenders — not by a long shot. Moreover, they didn't want to be. They didn't know what interest rate futures were or what LIBOR was, and furthermore they didn't care. What they did know, they knew very well: the value of relationships and small-town lending. Most of the time when the committee drove by a home that was under consideration for a loan, they always knew the family and someone would share a story or encounter he had in the past. The years of knowledge and experience that each of these men had on a personal level with the association's customers was priceless.

These men were in some ways representative of what First Savings and Loan itself had become in the midst of the changes and consolidation in the banking industry. First Savings was out on its own, detached from the mainstream banking world. It sounds naive, but these directors were comfortable with the association's profitable and safe niche as a home lender that viewed business from a personal standpoint, something most institutions had been proud of years before the big profits came calling.

Away from Mebane in August 1990, America's role in the Middle East changed as Iraq invaded its southern neighbor, Kuwait. President George H.W. Bush assembled an international coalition led by U.S. forces to deliver an ultimatum to Iraqi dictator Saddam Hussein: withdraw the Iraqi forces or face military consequences. As the United States prepared for the possibility of armed conflict, the price of oil doubled from seventeen dollars a barrel in July to more than thirty-four dollars by October.

In January 1991, Iraqi forces remained defiantly in Kuwait, and Bush made good on his promise by launching round-the-clock air strikes on Iraqi positions. By February the ground war began, lasting just four days as U.S. forces quickly overwhelmed the Iraqi army. The Gulf War was just the tip of the iceberg, and U.S. involvement in the Middle East intensified during the 2000s.

The victory gave President Bush a 90 percent approval rating. As Republicans planned for a repeat win of the White House in 1992, few Democrats thought they had a realistic chance at winning. One virtually unknown candidate contemplating a presidential run was former Arkansas governor Bill Clinton.

Something special that began at Eastern Alamance High School in November 1990 ended in a state championship at the Dean Smith Center in March. Coach Tal Jobe's Eagles led by Tyrone Satterfield, Derek Mann, and Mikey Bynum defeated T.C. Roberson High School for the Men's State 3-A basketball title. Championship fever hit Duke University as well, as Mike Krzyzewski's Blue Devils defeated Kansas for the Men's NCAA basketball title after flirting with the Final Four for several years. The Blue Devils repeated as National Champions in 1992, continuing their dominance through the 1990s.

The religion of basketball in North Carolina and the rivalries between the Tar Heel, Blue Devil, Demon Deacon, and Wolfpack fans are legendary and are taken very seriously. These rivalries last all year but heat up at ACC Tournament time. The staff of First Savings fell victim every year to tournament fever, decorating the offices with pennants of ACC schools and other memorabilia. Naturally a television was in place to watch the games, and staff came to work in their favorite team's school colors, which tended toward a light shade of blue.

For the Mebane community, orange and white seemed to be the favorite colors. From the widening of I-85/I-40 to the clearing of land for commercial ventures, orange and white road construction barrels were common sights around Mebane through the 1990s. Work began on Brookhollow Plaza at Fifth Street and Holmes Road, a development that included a Food Lion grocery store, Subway Restaurant, Domino's Pizza, Piedmont Veterinary Hospital, and a Revco (CVS) drugstore. The commercial development that accelerated on both Highway 119 South and Mebane Oaks Road were significant, as until that time most of the growth in this area had been primarily industrial and residential in nature.

Mebane had once been a sleepy southern town but was now wide awake, and all this building and development was a lot for the small town to comprehend. For most of the twentieth century, when people talked about growth around Mebane they were referring to their tobacco fields or vegetable gardens. During the 1920s, the town borrowed funds for water and sewer service. But like most small southern towns, Mebane drifted along until World War II. By the early 1990s, growth was accelerating at a pace few could imagine, and the city of Mebane had to change as well.

Two key elements were added to the city, beginning in 1991, as Mebane planned for the future. The Graham-Mebane reservoir at Quaker Lake was completed, securing the community's future water supply and creating the possibility for water recreation and prime home sites around the lake. A significant milestone in the city's history occurred when plans were announced for the Mebane Arts and Community Center on a twenty-acre site off South Third Street.

A gala celebration marked the opening of the Arts Center on April 29, 1995, complete with a catered dinner and dancing. An art gallery welcomed visitors to the twenty-six-thousand-square-foot center, and among the first items placed on display was a painting by local artist Jill Troutman. The large multipurpose arena soon hosted various sports and civic events. Originally there were four athletic fields on the grounds, with a centrally located concession stand and press box. In 1994 First Savings made its largest onetime contribution of twenty-five thousand dollars to the city toward the construction of the baseball fields. The Arts Center quickly became a hub of activity, and new traditions began that summer with the first Mebane Fourth of July Music Festival. The festival, like others that followed, was a day of activities with bands, softball, volleyball, food, and of course, fireworks.

The Arts Center became an immediate town treasure, home to numerous events, from high school graduations and proms to citywide celebrations—a position once held by Mebane High School. Family recreation was a common bond that many shared, and children's sports became a community and family priority. The completion of the Arts Center in 1995 was the first brick in the foundation of change as the city embarked on numerous building projects that continued well into the next decade.

As these amenities became a foundation for Mebane's future, part of the town's historic past was stumbling. Hickory White announced the closing of the Hillsborough plant of White Furniture. The furniture maker's workforce had dwindled to just 215 since being purchased in 1985, and now 70 more jobs would be lost under consolidation.

Melville Furniture, which had operated on East Washington Street since 1969, closed its doors when the company was bought by Bush Industries of Greensboro. Like many businesses, Melville was the victim of a buyout from a stronger competitor that in the end put the company out of business, sending 45 workers to the unemployment line. Manufacturing was clearly changing throughout small towns as industries that had been solid foundations of communities for decades continued to disappear.

Since the mid-1960s, First Savings held its monthly board meetings at 12 noon on the last Thursday of the month at the A&M Grill. But lunchtime at the Grill was a busy place, and conducting a private meeting became increasingly difficult. By the early 1990s the association moved the meeting to another popular lunch spot: the Arrowhead Restaurant on Mebane Oaks Road.

On June 14, 1991, Director John Henry James passed away after several years of failing health. James originally joined the board during the controversial proxy fight in 1960 and for thirty-one years provided strong guidance and leadership at a time when the savings and loan industry was in jeopardy. Ironically, James stood on the other side of the aisle as part of the Shareholders' Group opposing the direction and vision of First Savings' management. When the proxy fight ended in 1962, James was again elected to the board, becoming one of the association's strongest supporters. At the board of directors' meeting on June 27, 1991, a resolution was passed honoring James's service, and Vice President Rick Smith was appointed to the board.

Charlotte-based North Carolina National Bank (NCNB) had become bored with being the "best bank in the neighborhood," having much loftier aspirations. NCNB was now one of the largest banks in the country, achieving that position by acquiring other banks. The bank's colorful CEO Hugh McColl Jr. had taken the bank from a $60 billion institution in 1988 to $118 billion giant in just three years. NCNB's "neighborhood" grew larger when the bank acquired Atlanta-based C&S/Sovran Corporation in 1991 and the company changed its name to NationsBank. The bank eventually acquired and took the name of San Francisco's Bank of America in 1998.

The rise of megabanks hit full stride during the 1990s, and NationsBank (Bank of America) led the charge. Between 1985 and 2003, more than seventy-four hundred mergers and acquisitions took place, and more were on the way. Although community banks constituted 94 percent of all banks in the nation, they controlled only 13.5 percent of banking assets. The top twenty-five banks, with thousands of branches spanning coast to coast, continued to grow through acquisition and merger, and they controlled nearly 60 percent of all banking assets at this time.

As large banks gobbled up the smaller competition, the safety of these banking giants became a concern. While some argued that the failure of one of these giant banks could place the nation's entire financial system in jeopardy, most observers were convinced that these mega-institutions were well diversified over a broad area of investments and thus posed very little threat. This "too-big to-fail" argument gave large institutions the ammunition they needed for continued growth, pleasing stockholders. Two financial entities that were included in this too-big-to-fail mentality were the Federal Home Loan Mortgage Corporation (Freddie Mac) and the Federal National Mortgage Association (Fannie Mae). Fannie and Freddie were the foundation of the mortgage market, and with housing recovering and interest rates falling, most observers felt that it was virtually impossible for these mortgage giants to fail. In 2008 the impossible would happen.

One very unpleasant result of this new era of banking change was the seemingly endless regulations that followed the savings and loan crisis. For decades, associations operated independently and set up internal controls accordingly. In all honesty, these internal procedures were sometimes enforced, occasionally ignored, and other times forgotten. Those days were gone. Free markets are the key to capitalism, yet the events of the 1980s and later in the 2000s convinced lawmakers that the price of unbridled freedom was too high. When deregulation and poor decisions led to the near failure of the entire savings and loan industry and a taxpayer bailout, the government stepped in with heavy regulation.

At the time, First Savings was a state-chartered association with two regulators. The Office of Thrift Supervision (OTS) served as its federal regulator while the State of North Carolina Savings Institutions Division was its state regulator. From a small-town thrift's perspective, the FHLBB examination process in past years had been constructive and informative. Most small associations viewed these two- to three-week examination periods as a time of inconvenience more than anything else, but a necessary part of doing business. The FHLBB—OTS's predecessor—had been blasted for mishandling the savings and loan crisis, so OTS took a different approach to examinations.

The OTS arrived with guns drawn in October 1991 for its first examination of First Savings, and it didn't take long for the fireworks to begin. OTS was sure that First Savings had problems, and the examiners were bound and determined to find them. Policies and procedures that had served First Savings well for decades came under fire as examiners scrutinized everything from investments to home loans. Although the examination yielded no violations, the three-week ordeal felt like three months, and the issues seemed petty in nature. Adding fuel to the fire was the fact that First Savings, like other healthy associations, had over the past several years been hit with one monetary assessment after another. The association felt that it had been paying for the mistakes of other failed thrifts and was in no mood for petty criticism. The examination experience created resentment and mistrust between First Savings and its new regulator that would take several years to repair.

The reality was that the OTS was also under a microscope by both the press and lawmakers, and unfortunately the new thrift regulator chose intimidation to restore the broken industry. Over time, this confrontational style subsided as the OTS learned to trust savings and loans; likewise, thrifts gained confidence in its new regulator. What started out on the wrong foot in this first examination would eventually turn into a long and beneficial relationship.

Mebane lost a real treasure in October 1991 when Milton McDade passed away. Owner of McDade's Appliance, which operated for years on Clay Street, McDade's true passion was the Mebane community and its history. He possessed a wealth of knowledge of the town's legacy, and McDade's memorabilia would provide the foundation for the Mebane Historical Museum.

Two local figures were not only making history in 1991 but preserving it as well. With fiddle and banjo in hand, Joe and Odell Thompson kept alive traditional African folk music that had passed down through generations. Joe Thompson first picked up a fiddle at age five, learning the craft from his father. The Thompsons were known throughout the country, playing for audiences from Washington state and Massachusetts to Carnegie Hall in New York, and they received the North Carolina Folk Heritage Award from the North Carolina Arts Council. Tragically, Odell Thompson was struck and killed by a car in 1994. Determined to preserve his musical heritage and the memory of his late cousin, Joe Thompson continued to perform well into the next decade.

In early 1992, mortgage rates dipped to a fifteen-year low at 8 percent, and the drop was a prelude of things to come. Confident that rates were in single digits seemingly to stay, customers jumped into the housing market while others rushed to refinance their higher-rate mortgages. For the first time in its history, First Savings closed over $10 million in mortgage loans. The association had set itself apart from other institutions by closing loans quickly, usually within two weeks of application. The sudden deluge of loan applications was somewhat overwhelming, making this once-solid promise hard to keep. Janis Murray worked with both Neal and Rick Smith in handling loan closings, and it was becoming clear that another position was needed to meet the increased demand for loans. Ann Allison filled that position in March, bringing the number of full-time employees to seven. The timing was perfect as First Savings extended thirty-six loans totaling $2,186,000 in April, its largest lending month ever at the time.

Financial institutions, like most businesses in small towns, are asked and expected to donate to various community activities. Throughout its history First Savings has supported local projects ranging from school fund-raisers to church activities. In 1992 the association donated five thousand dollars each to South Mebane Elementary and E.M. Yoder Elementary to upgrade computer equipment. This side of mutual associations is rarely publicized, unlike with their stock institution brethren. Make no mistake, stock institutions give substantially to community endeavors, usually with a great deal of press coverage. Some institutions with vast resources that dwarf those of smaller mutual associations are often reluctant to give monetary donations to small-town projects due to stockholder pressure.

Savings associations were feeling the pressure from a variety of sources and not just stockholders. The sensational stories of management malfeasance that surfaced as the cleanup of the industry continued had savings associations nationwide running as fast as they could from the name "savings and loan." Several local thrifts that had served their communities with distinction for decades decided it was time for a name and charter change. Hillsborough Savings and Loan became Hillsborough Savings Bank in 1992. In the late 1980s, Burlington's First Federal Savings and Loan became Financial First Federal Savings Bank, and Graham Savings and Loan was now Graham Savings Bank. These name changes not only separated these institutions from the negative connotation of a savings and loan but reflected the changes within these institutions as they offered bank products and commercial accounts.

Throughout their histories, savings banks and savings and loans served somewhat separate functions. Savings banks fostered the idea of thrift and personal savings while savings and loans promoted home ownership. The savings and loan crisis of the 1980s changed all that, and the savings bank charter became the choice of most converting savings and loans. The switch made sense as these institutions could pursue more business opportunities as banks while shedding the "savings and loan" label.

Trade organizations took on new names, reflecting their ever-changing membership. The North Carolina Savings and Loan League became the North Carolina Alliance of Community Financial Institutions as more of its members were now banks. The North Carolina Alliance merged with and assumed the name of the North Carolina Bankers Association later in the decade, giving its membership one representative voice on financial issues.

In the summer of 1991, Cone Mills had celebrated its one-hundred-year anniversary with much fanfare at its Granite Finishing Plant in Haw River. But there were no cheers or laughter in the spring of 1992 as Cone announced a major restructuring of the company, sending 280 of its 380 employees at Granite to the unemployment line. For sixty years, Granite had been a major component of the textile giant, but as the popularity of corduroy declined, so did company profits. The Haw River operation alone had reportedly lost $50 million in the previous four years. With only 100 jobs left, folks knew it was just a matter of time before the huge facility on the banks of the Haw River would sit idle. Adding insult to injury, the new Haw River bypass opened, connecting Highway 70 directly to North Church Street in Burlington, completely rerouting traffic from the small mill town. Haw River, a town once alive with textile production and notorious for daily traffic jams, stood virtually empty.

The devastating effects of plant closures were occurring in once-vibrant communities all across the country, but the impact was magnified in small towns where life revolved around one or two large industries. North Carolina's base in textiles was declining, and a severe economic recession in 1992 placed the industry in jeopardy. The Alamance County Chamber of Commerce reported that 13,378 residents, 13 percent of the county's population, were employed in the textile industry. Towns like Mebane and Haw River held their breath and wondered about jobs in the future if textiles and furniture, the very fabric of North Carolina's manufacturing, were in trouble.

Many southern states thought the answer to the ailing manufacturing job market and the trauma of plant closures could be found along a stretch of I-85 near Spartanburg, South Carolina. In 1992 automaker BMW chose this site for its North American assembly plant. It seemed rather strange for automobile plants to be constructed in former tobacco and cotton fields when industrial cities like Detroit came to mind as the center for automobile manufacturing.

Automakers had migrated to rural areas such as Marysville, Ohio, and Smyrna, Tennessee, during the 1980s, and some felt that the automobile industry might be one solution for states rocked by rising unemployment. Automobile plants were certainly attractive, but even more appealing was the myriad of other jobs that these plants brought with them. Fifty-two auto-related companies followed BMW and located in the Spartanburg area. With this type of job potential and with traditional manufacturing on the ropes, states lined up to offer lucrative incentives to the now-coveted auto industry.

North Carolina made its pitch to the auto industry in August 1992 when Governor Jim Martin unveiled the state's aggressive marketing plan at a press conference at GKN in Mebane. The plan hit the ground running as automotive component maker Bosch purchased the Arrowhead Golf Course after considering sites in Graham and Greensboro. The Bosch announcement sent rumors flying that the company would build a large manufacturing facility and employ two thousand workers.

But something else was happening on South Third Street Extension and Lake Latham and Trollingwood roads that really fed the rumor mill. Options were quietly being offered to local residents who owned tracts of land in the area, and no one seemed to know who the buyer was. The agents securing the options were tight-lipped, but the attractive prices offered to owners of everything from small tracts to large parcels said someone big was looking at Mebane.

The Mebane Auction Gallery, off Highway 70 east of town, opened for its first sale in 1992 in the large building behind Huey's Restaurant. With Jon Lambert taking his familiar position behind the microphone, this popular business became a Friday tradition for antiques collectors.

Another Friday night tradition in the fall is high school football. Whether it was the 1952 Mebane Tigers or the 1992 Eastern Eagles, this autumn ritual was a huge social event that brought out the entire town eager to see its local warriors take the field. Eastern Alamance High School named its football field the Fred Brady Athletic Complex, honoring the longtime coaching and sports legend at a halftime ceremony on September 11, 1992. New head coach John Kirby found the complex quite comfortable, guiding the Eagles to an undefeated regular season that year. Football seems to be a passion in Mebane that starts at an early age. Local recreation teams sponsored by Biff Burger gained a winning reputation beginning in the 1970s and continuing in the 1980s. Foust Fuels followed that successful tradition and in 1992 won the Midget Football State Parks and Recreation Championship, defeating Lee County 20-12.

Physician and First Savings Director Dr. David Jones left the Mebane Medical Center and joined Kernodle Clinic in 1992. This move coincided with the announcement that the Burlington medical practice would open a facility on Mebane Oaks Road, an area that was gaining more attention as commercial development snowballed in the early 1990s. Leading the charge were fast-food chains Bojangles and McDonald's as well as Waffle House, while Burger King and KFC joined the parade on Highway 119 South. Wachovia Bank, which had operated in its familiar Fifth Street location since 1972, opened a new branch at the intersection of Fifth and Mebane Oaks Road.

As these new businesses opened, a seller's market for residential real estate was in full bloom. Bradford Place, adjacent to Brookhollow, offered upscale home sites, and Webster's Grove in the Haw Fields area had one-acre lots going for $16,500.

Mebane's future looked brighter than ever when the sad news came in November 1992 that White Furniture would close its doors. The announcement was like a death in the family for people who grew up in Mebane, particularly those who had worked at the factory. Although Hickory White's announcement was hard to take, it wasn't a total surprise. The company had been struggling, but locals were hopeful that the former cornerstone of Mebane's economy could somehow survive. Some knew it was coming while others were stunned. Management blamed the plant's demise on the recession of the time and foreign competition, but ultimately the company became a victim of living in the past. Dedicated to quality, White operated for decades with antiquated equipment, taking pride in a proven method, but that formula did not always work in a changed environment where production and speed drove success. When Hickory White purchased the company in 1985, some upgrades were made on some of the older machinery, but it still wasn't enough.

This account is by no means a criticism of White Furniture—far from it. White and First Savings had a lot more in common than being founded by the same family. Although furniture manufacturing and banking are completely different, White and First Savings both strongly believed that the future of their companies were rooted in the successful traditions of the past. The outcomes of choices often take years to emerge, yet both businesses found out that what had worked successfully in the past held no future guarantees.

Many of the workers at White, like those laid off at Granite Finishing in Haw River, had given their lives to these companies and had to start all over again. Seeing folks out of work was bad enough, but perhaps the hardest things to accept were the realizations that nothing in this world is ever constant and that a very important part of Mebane's heritage was gone forever. In February 1993 a small chest of drawers rolled off the assembly line at White Furniture Company, the last piece the furniture maker would ever produce. The furniture was presented to the city of Mebane by Hickory White at a short ceremony and accepted by Mayor Glendel Stephenson. White officially closed on February 15, and the large brown building once full of activity sat silent—a monument to Mebane's industrial age.

Like White, Kingsdown was one of the city's most recognizable businesses and an economic cornerstone since 1904. Many wondered about that company's future now that White was closing. White Furniture tried to hold on to its past successes using older technology and making very little investment in an ever-changing marketplace. In contrast, Kingsdown invested for the long haul, adjusting to market conditions and a global economy and becoming an industry leader and innovator. The company, however, did eventually do away with the familiar whistle that sounded during the workday.

The high approval rating that President George H.W. Bush enjoyed following the Gulf War eroded along with the U.S. economy. The unemployment rate that began the decade at 5.3 percent had climbed to 7.5 percent by 1992, and mortgage loan interest rates topped the psychological 10 percent mark. The second term in the White House that seemed like a sure thing for Bush a year earlier was now very much in doubt. As the presidential race tightened, North Carolina became a key state. President Bush made a campaign stop in Burlington as part of a statewide train tour, while Democratic challenger Bill Clinton and running mate Al Gore attended a rally in Graham. Americans tend to vote their pocketbooks, and as the economy continued to falter, so did Bush's reelection chances.

Although the nation hit a recession in 1991, North Carolina and Mebane seemed recession-proof as both remained in a strong growth mode, managing to avoid any major economic damage. First Savings ended its strongest year on record, dodging the fallout that continued to rain down in the aftermath of the savings and loan crisis. Three years had passed since Congress had revamped the financial services industry, and although most institutions were shying away from the "savings and loan" label, First Savings found success by embracing it.

For most institutions, however, the timing seemed right for change. Acquisitions and mergers were commonplace, and new banking charters were springing up. Like countless times before, First Savings discounted conventional wisdom and headed in the opposite direction. For eighty-three years, First Savings and Loan had been the primary mortgage lender for Mebane and the surrounding community. With competition from banks, credit unions, and mortgage brokers, prospective home buyers were lured away from conventional lenders. The 1990s saw the slow erosion of the association's once-dominant market share as First Savings became a small fish in an ever-expanding pond.

The talk at the association's annual shareholders' meeting in February 1993 centered around an article recently featured in the *Raleigh News and Observer*. The article ranked the state's financial institutions by using the institution's capital reserve as the yardstick for determining safety and soundness. First Savings ranked twelfth out of ninety-nine savings and loans in the state and was the highest-ranking institution in the area. The paper cited that North Carolina banks and thrifts had remained conservative during the trying times of the 1980s and were very safe, with just nine savings and loans listed as having below-average capital.

On March 27, 1993, "Miss" Frances Terrell passed away after a brief illness. Mrs. Terrell had worked as the association's bookkeeper for most of her career and served as corporate secretary. Miss Frances was the association's last remaining link to its days as the Mebane Home Builders Association, and her passing ended a forty-nine-year relationship with First Savings. An infectious smile and wonderful sense of humor endeared her to staff and customers alike. A resolution honoring the life and service of Mrs. Frances Terrell was entered into the board minutes of April 29. Janis Murray was appointed as the association's corporate secretary upon Mrs. Terrell's death.

The city of Mebane had to consider itself fairly lucky when it came to the subject of traffic compared to other growing communities and small towns. There were the occasional backups when White's was changing shifts, but those days were obviously over. The increasing traffic jams now resulted from more and more people traveling on Mebane's two-lane roads. Highway 70 and South Fifth Street were always the main culprits for traffic congestion, and the city's southern expansion now added South Third to the list of clogged arteries. Traffic through downtown was a growing concern, with the flow from Highway 119 that ran north to south through the heart of the city. Large tractor trailers struggled to make the turn in front of First Savings from Highway 70 onto Highway 119, slowing traffic at this busy corner. With Mebane and its traffic growing at such a rapid pace, the City Council set into motion plans to ease the problem. The council sent a recommendation, known as the Highway 119 Thoroughfare Plan, to the North Carolina Department of Transportation. The proposal would reroute Highway 119 from White Level Road north of the city, around the west side of Mebane, and connect to South Fifth Street near Brookhollow Plaza. This route, known as the Highway 119 Bypass, would later become a source of heated debate around town.

The summer driving season of 1993 saw the price of gasoline ease to $1.08 a gallon by Memorial Day, and more and more drivers were climbing behind the wheel of hot-selling sport utility vehicles. The SUV was selling faster than the popular minivan that captivated car buyers in the 1980s. The Ford Explorer, Chevy Blazer, and Jeep Cherokee led the way, and almost every automaker was introducing new and different SUV styles into this growing market. The latest company adding the SUV to its product line was luxury car maker Mercedes-Benz. The German automaker was looking for an American site for an auto plant and concentrated its search in the southern United States.

North Carolina was campaigning hard to attract the auto industry, and the state found itself in the running for the Mercedes plant. Speculation grew that the optioned property around South Third Street Extension was an industrial mega-site that the state was promoting to Mercedes. The state estimated that an auto plant could create fifteen hundred jobs and bring in $20 million in tax revenues. With traditional manufacturing in transition across the South, capturing Mercedes was a once-in-a-lifetime shot, and every state knew it. North Carolina and other states offered up everything from tax incentives and training programs to sway Mercedes' decision. The battle was on, and it became a high-stakes poker game.

Small talk at the clubhouse at Arrowhead and breakfast at the A&M Grill centered around the prospects of Mercedes coming to town and the changes it might bring. A lot of information and stories that floated around seemed to be based on rumor; nothing seemed certain. Most folks reasoned that it made sense that Mebane had to be the site Mercedes was considering. A year earlier, automotive component company Bosch had purchased the Arrowhead Golf Course, and Governor Martin had made it a point to announce North Carolina's recruiting efforts from Mebane's GKN plant. Headline stories were common on the nightly news as reporters and news trucks invaded the city.

Although the possibility of an auto plant created tremendous excitement, not everyone shared in the euphoria as the subject drew mixed opinions. Mercedes-Benz's reputation as a luxury car maker influenced some folks. As one local put it, "This ain't just a car company. It's Mercedes." Some were happy about the employment possibilities and the boost it would bring for Mebane and the state. Others were concerned that a super-employer would completely change the town and its identity. Both arguments held some truth. Ironically, not so long before, Mebane was dominated by not one but two large employers, White's Furniture and Kingsdown. Many were crossing their fingers that it could happen again. No matter how one felt about Mercedes, one thing was certain. Change was again coming to Mebane even if Mercedes did not.

Anticipation grew throughout the summer as the waiting continued. Mercedes finally broke its silence, stating that an announcement of its site choice would be made at a news conference on September 30. Then a story leaked to the national press, and the *Washington Post* and *New York Times* both quoted sources close to the selection process saying that Mebane had been chosen for the Mercedes site. The media frenzy that surrounded the story turned up another notch. But in this poker game, all the cards had not been played. The state of Alabama raised the ante yet again, and this time the bet was too high for North Carolina. When Alabama offered incentives topping $280 million, North Carolina folded.

Some thought Mercedes was coming to Mebane and that it was a done deal. The announcement that the plant was to be built in Vance, Alabama, blindsided everyone. The reaction of local folks ranged from shock to relief to disappointment and anger. One upset Mebane native said, "Who wants to buy a Mercedes built by some guy in Alabama named Bubba anyway?" Still another local resident, believing the high unemployment situation in Alabama was worse than North Carolina, remarked, "We have more options here. Alabama needed Mercedes. We didn't." But one Mebanite summed up what many folks were thinking but weren't saying: "No one likes to lose. Mercedes was the big one, and we let it get away."

Regardless of the reactions, most people felt Mebane would somehow come out better in the long haul, and local and state officials put the best possible spin on the situation. Mebane had received more media coverage and business exposure than anyone ever dreamed possible. Before Mercedes, no one outside North Carolina knew much if anything about the city of Mebane. After Mercedes, Mebane was on everyone's radar screen. It just might play out that Mebane held a winning hand after all.

Although local news crews and satellite trucks had disappeared from the streets of Mebane, excitement about the town's future had not. Local talk turned to the plans of a Raleigh company to build the largest residential development in Mebane's history. The development of 750 home sites on 654 acres complete with an eighteen-hole golf course would be located just north of the city and a departure from the accelerating expansion south of town. The upscale subdivision that would become Mill Creek offered building lots priced between forty-five and fifty-five thousand dollars, with some homes priced over two hundred thousand dollars. Some questioned whether a high-end development like this could be successful in a small town. These concerns quickly vanished when sixty names were on a waiting list for building lots.

Mill Creek was an example of how residential development was changing in North Carolina. Tract builders were touted as the wave of the future and had concentrated their efforts for years in high-growth states such as California and Florida. Mill Creek was highly restrictive in that prospective buyers were required to build from certain floor plans and use approved builders. The city of Cary and other Triangle towns experienced firsthand the impact of tract builders. Now Mebane had officially joined the party, and tract development dominated new construction, placing competitive pressure on small builders.

After years of complacency, downtown Mebane began to stir once again. Farm Bureau Insurance completed its new office building in November 1993 at the corner of Ruffin and Fourth streets. One strong incentive for businesses to consider downtown was that commercial real estate prices were a bargain compared to the high-dollar figures for new construction or rent south of town. Some small towns that crept toward the interstate had been able to hold on to vibrant downtown business districts. Local merchants hoped the success that towns like Hillsborough and Graham experienced would repeat itself in Mebane.

The Mebane Home Telephone Company became Mebtel Communications in 1993, reflecting the constant change in communications. The seventy-year-old company remained in the Hupman family, as it had been since Sam Hupman Sr. first purchased the operation in 1922. His grandsons, Bob and Mac Hupman, now ran the company and planned renovations to the offices on South Seventh Street to go with the new name.

In January 1994 Gail Jordan joined the association as comptroller, replacing Holly Sims, who left the institution a year earlier. Jordan came with a strong financial background that began with Northwestern Bank in 1968 and took her to both First Federal Savings and Loan and Wachovia. Jordan's savings and loan experience was invaluable, and a rarity in this new era of banking.

Lonnie Dickie had been a part-time employee of the association for more than thirty years as custodian. Dickie celebrated his ninetieth birthday in January 1994 and remarkably still performed his duties for the association. Much to his surprise, the association's staff held a party in his honor, complete with a birthday cake. Standing six feet six inches tall, Dickie was quiet and reserved with a soft-spoken voice. One hot summer day, Dickie came into the association's office and the conversation naturally turned to the sweltering heat. In his typical soft voice, Dickie complained, "It sure is hot outside, but the humanity out there is terrible!" At times Mr. Dickie's innocent mispronunciations revealed the unfortunate truth.

The cleanup following the savings and loan crisis dragged on, severely impacting the few remaining thrifts that stuck it out. Ironically, First Savings enjoyed some of its most profitable times during this period. Through the first five years of the 1990s, First Savings averaged 132 loan closings a year with a volume of $7,329,600 in home loans. The always coveted and local savings deposits grew 14 percent during this time, easily funding the institution's loan demand.

The banking world continued its transition as well. In 1994, laws were passed allowing interstate banking and branching, opening the door for mergers and acquisitions on a grand scale. First Savings never desired to become a big institution, and by the mid-1990s it was getting its wish. The association was growing thanks to its loyal customer base, but nothing compared to stock institutions. Burlington's Community Federal Savings and Loan officially became Community Federal Savings Bank, and First Savings now had the sole distinction of being the only savings and loan in Alamance and Orange counties. But did that really matter in this new financial age? Besides, did anyone really care? At the time, Rick Smith was working with a person on a loan application who asked, "What exactly is a savings and loan?" The question was a sign of the times.

To say that Mebane was a popular destination for home owners and businesses in 1994 was an understatement, as ceremonial groundbreakings for new businesses seemed to be a weekly occurrence. From medical offices to dance studios and restaurants, new and diverse businesses had discovered Mebane thanks to the "Mercedes effect."

First South Bank (RBC Centura) held its grand opening on April 19, 1994, joining Wachovia at the intersection of South Fifth Street and Mebane Oaks Road. The Burlington-based institution that first opened in 1988 is a good example of how community banking was evolving, as many local banks had disappeared through mergers and acquisitions. Familiar institutions that generations of customers had known on a personal basis were now controlled and operated by larger banks in other cities. Customers accustomed to quick and instant financial decisions from their local banks were now at the mercy of strangers elsewhere. The formation of First South was timely for its customers and stockholders. Its success reinforced the notion that small local community banks could indeed thrive in an environment of change.

Kingsdown and White Furniture had been the industrial bond that held the town of Mebane together for a century. Most everyone who grew up in Mebane had someone in the family who was connected in some way to these companies. Neal Smith's father and brother both worked for many years at Kingsdown. The shock of the White closing had been hard enough for the town to absorb, but now Kingsdown was fighting off an attempted buyout. Eastern Sleep Products of Richmond, Virginia, made a public attempt to purchase stock from the major shareholders in the ninety-year-old Mebane institution. If successful, Eastern Sleep could force Kingsdown to sell or merge. Standing in the way of this takeover bid was Kingsdown's board of directors, which held 70 percent of the company's total stock. After a few frustrating months, Eastern Sleep abandoned its efforts as the company was unable to purchase any stock from the existing Kingsdown stockholders.

The leveraged buyouts and takeovers that garnered headlines in the 1980s and 1990s affected all areas of commerce, but perhaps no sector was more affected than the banking industry. The process of a financial merger or acquisition was complicated enough, but even more so for mutual savings and loans. Before entering the merger arena, mutual associations had to convert to a stock association with the blessings of regulators and the institution's depositors. Once the conversion was complete, stock could be issued; regulations allowed management, directors, and depositors to receive stock at a discounted price, with the remainder of the stock offered to the general public. Institutions large and small with strong capital positions became caught up in the merger and acquisition sweepstakes. This complicated process was not without controversy, as investors, depositors, management, and acquiring parties locked horns over who should benefit from potential mergers.

Graham Savings and Loan found out the hard way. Central Carolina Bank acquired the local thrift in October 1993, but legal action brought by a few Graham Savings depositors blocked the completion of the deal. The complaint focused on the compensation that Graham Savings' management received from CCB, and the soap opera played out in the local papers. The board and management of Graham Savings had done nothing improper and acted well within the regulations. Hundreds of conversion-acquisitions similar to that of Graham Savings had occurred since the 1980s. The depositors' actions raised questions regarding who should profit in an acquisition or merger and to what degree.

Finally an agreement was reached in which the former depositors of Graham Savings received additional compensation.

The dwindling number of mutual associations, like First Savings, were particularly interesting to investors who saw an opportunity. The crisis of the 1980s convinced most industry analysts that all mutual institutions would eventually convert to stock associations. Investor/depositors who opened accounts with mutual institutions by a certain date in the conversion process could purchase future stock at a discount. Professional investors opened accounts in mutual savings institutions nationwide in hopes that those institutions would eventually convert. If that occurred, investors had a built-in gain in the stock.

First Savings attracted investors from Maine to California wanting to open savings accounts. Since the association was flush with cash, the funds were promptly sent back to those individuals. Interested institutions approached First Savings wanting to merge, mostly institutions that did not have a presence in Mebane or others that were short on capital. Some simply saw First Savings as a dying breed of institution and wanted to be first in line for the association's assets. The association's board remained steadfast in its desire to remain a savings and loan as long as the community supported the institution in its current form. Although First Savings received some interest from would-be acquirers, the larger institutions gained the serious attention in the merger game, as First Savings was viewed as just too small an institution.

The conversion-merger process was new to mutual savings and loans. This segment of the banking community had remained virtually unchanged for a century until the 1980s. Management of local associations made a comfortable living but were never going to get rich at a savings and loan. The conversion-merger process changed that. Directors and management in some instances received large compensation packages when a merger took place. The financial rewards and speculation opportunities were all legal, but troubling to regulators who saw these compensation agreements as undeserved windfalls. Aging board members of longtime mutual associations, faced with an unknown and different financial landscape, saw a chance to cash out and went the route of stock conversion while professional investors circled above, waiting their turn.

In September, auto parts maker Bosch announced it was selling the Arrowhead

Golf Course after purchasing the property two years earlier, and the chances of North Carolina attracting an auto plant appeared to be fading. The golf course itself remained open for golfers while others contemplated its future. The exposure from recruiting Mercedes continued to pay dividends as 3-C Alliance announced in 1994 that it would construct a multimillion-dollar battery plant in the Carolina Central Industrial Center. The company broke ground in January 1995, promising to bring 650 jobs producing rechargeable batteries for cell phones, camcorders, and other consumer electronics.

School buildings are another valued type of construction in small towns, and for generations Mebane High School occupied such a sentimental spot for local residents. Early generations felt the same way about Woodlawn School, which had stood proudly on Mebane Rogers Road for eighty-three years. Built in 1911 the original one-room schoolhouse was the home to grades one through eleven for local children until the school closed in 1933. To those in the Woodlawn community, the building was much more than a schoolhouse, serving as a symbol of community pride and hosting events such as reunions, club meetings, picnics, and even weddings. The storied structure was showing its age, and sagging floors, peeling paint, and a leaking roof made its use almost impossible. Individuals, civic groups, and local businesses, including First Savings, opened their pocketbooks in a fund-raising effort to restore part of the community's past.

Interest rates continued to fall, and like all mortgage lenders, First Savings was enjoying the ride. Loan data from that time reveal that the success of the institution was due largely to loyal customers who refinanced and kept their loans with the association. Such repeat business is significant for this time in the association's history. The mortgage industry continued to change throughout the decade, as did Mebane's demographics. The trends would inevitably alter the fortunes of First Savings well into the next decade as once-loyal customers left for greener pastures.

Strong loan demand, a solid deposit base, and low cost of funds created the perfect mix for lucrative income as First Savings experienced record net profits during the 1990s. This success allowed the institution to follow up its donation to the Mebane Arts Center by giving fifty-seven hundred dollars to Eastern Alamance High School for computer equipment and forty-three hundred dollars to Woodlawn Middle School's science department. Unfortunately, this benevolent spirit was about to come to an end. The change had nothing to do with the institution's philosophy and everything to do with the federal government.

The Resolution Trust Corporation (RTC), responsible for the cleanup of the savings and loan crisis, completed its work in 1995. Between 1989 and 1995 the RTC closed or resolved 747 thrifts with assets of $394 billion. Figures that seemed obscene at that time would pale in comparison to the next financial crisis, which was still a decade away. Much of the money to pay for the savings and loan crisis was taken from healthy institutions in the form of assessments, and First Savings was notified by the FDIC that the association could be assessed as much as $250,000 during the coming year of 1996. The possibility of such a large assessment outraged the association's directors, putting a damper on the institution's benevolent giving. During this time, E.M. Yoder and South Mebane elementary schools submitted requests for donations for new computer equipment. Under normal circumstances the association would have strongly considered these requests, but with such a large assessment looming the directors reluctantly declined. The situation frustrated the association's directors, who could do absolutely nothing to stop it. Put in perspective, an assessment of $250,000 was more than the net income of First Savings for the first six months of 1995.

As First Savings and other institutions were paying for one financial crisis, the seeds of another, more costly one were being sown. In 1995 Fannie Mae (FNMA) and Freddie Mac (FHLMC) began receiving affordable housing credit from the government for purchasing mortgage-backed securities from lenders, which included loans to low-income borrowers. Many of the loans in these mortgage-backed securities were imbedded with risky subprime mortgages. Since Fannie Mae and Freddie Mac were willing to buy subprime mortgages from lenders, loan originations of poor quality—subprime loans—jumped 25 percent per year between 1994 and 2003.

Even while the seeds of systemic weakness were sown, symbols of strength still endured—temporarily anyway. For more than a century, a large magnolia tree had graced the corner of Fifth Street and Highway 70, part of the original White family property next to the furniture company. The house had long since disappeared but the tree remained, and generations of Mebane children and adults had come to identify the tree as an important piece of the town's heritage. For years, workers from White Furniture took breaks and had lunch near the tree, and children had played in its huge branches. The land where the magnolia stood was one of Mebane's busiest intersections, the site for a proposed new Rite Aid Pharmacy (Kerr Drug), but the tree was in the way. Folks had seen the old depot and Mebane High School disappear, and the stately tree would suffer the same fate. Some Mebane residents protested and Rite Aid did its best, listening to local concerns and even going so far as to design the store to retain the tree. Such is life in a small town that childhood memories of something as simple as a tree could evoke such passion in its citizens. In the end, the beloved magnolia tree, like so many other Mebane landmarks, lost its battle with progress.

People who mentioned "progress" in Mebane during the 1990s probably were speaking of the businesses relocating in droves to the new business district south of town. But Mebane's changing demographics pumped life back into downtown as well. The *Mebane Enterprise* did a feature on downtown's revival titled "Downtown Mebane: A Ghost Town to Boomtown." The latest business willing to take a chance on downtown was the Mebane Sports Center at the corner of Clay and Third streets. Across from the Sports Center, Food Deals opened in the old Melville Chevrolet building, and Hawkins Realty moved to an office on Fourth Street. There were few restaurants downtown besides Martinho's, with the exception of Just Pizza and Morazi's, which offered free home delivery.

A turning point for downtown came in 1995 when Alison Goforth (Brewbaker) opened Gifts of Distinction on Clay Street, selling specialty items including Beanie Babies, which were hugely popular. Gifts of Distinction is gone now, but Goforth's business was a unique departure from the traditional downtown retail stores and set the tone for downtown's transition in years to come.

Every town has its heroes, and Mebane is no different. Most people who attain the status of hero never set out to do so. Some are labeled a hero by answering the call to serve their country, while others simply perform a job they love and in the process change and save lives. Police officers and firefighters are highly regarded in small towns, as these public servants are neighbors, friends, and coworkers. When it comes time to take care of business, these first responders are no longer just the person next door. Most folks slow down when they see a police cruiser go by, and what little boy has not been captivated by the flashing red lights and loud siren of a passing fire truck? Thank God some of these children are seduced by this excitement when they become adults.

The summer of 1995 brought record rainfall to the area, transforming tranquil streams into raging rivers. Low-lying streets and roads quickly became impassable and dangerous to motorists. On August 27, 1995, thirty-four-year-old Gregg Hinson, a Mebane volunteer firefighter, responded to an emergency call, as he had always done since joining the department in 1991. The call summoned Hinson and his fellow firefighters north of town to Stagg Creek, which flowed under Highway 119. Hinson's truck arrived at the scene to find a motorist trapped in a car that was in danger of being swept away. Attached to a safety line, Hinson entered the floodwaters, successfully freeing the driver. But suddenly the swift current shifted, pulling Hinson and two other firefighters into the rushing stream. Workers on the bank labored frantically, pulling two of the firefighters to safety, but Hinson remained submerged for several minutes. Gregg Hinson gave his life to save a total stranger. He was a firefighter, the guy next door, husband, father, coworker, and hero.

Longtime educator Iris Abernathy retired in 1995, completing fifty years in education and serving as an inspiration to generations of former students who attended her science and biology classes. Abernathy began teaching at Mebane High School in 1945 and continued at Eastern Alamance when the school opened in 1962. She influenced decades of students from Mebane, including Neal and Rick Smith. In 1972 she and her husband Bill moved to Florida, where she continued teaching, ending her career at Auburndale High School.

Natural forces influenced daily life in Mebane as well. Sixteen inches of snow fell on the city in January 1996, closing schools and businesses for days and sending locals scrambling to the grocery store for bread and milk. The chill in the air served as a contrast to Mebane's hot real estate market. The city was experiencing historic growth, and the sheer number of potential homesites in the works was astounding. On the north side of town, Mill Creek had 750 homesites planned for the community, while Beaver Creek subdivision off Stagecoach Road added another 90 building lots. The core of Mebane's growth still remained to the south, with the addition of Holly Ridge, Indian Head, and Briarwood subdivisions. Two large apartment projects were also planned, offering more housing choices.

A rapid rise in home prices reflected the demand for Mebane real estate. In 1994 the average sale price of a home in Mebane was $96,848. In just two years' time, the average sale price had jumped 25 percent and stood at $121,035. Mebane took the lead in Alamance County in the number of homes sold and total real estate volume sold, according to the Alamance County Multiple Listing Service. The city's residential expansion prompted building projects for South Mebane and E.M. Yoder elementary schools, as well as improvements to Eastern Alamance High School.

But what did Mebane have that made the city so appealing to newcomers? The list seemed endless, and the usual reply to this question was its location, with Raleigh-Durham to the east and Greensboro to the west. The low tax rate and affordable real estate prices were also drawing cards. But then came the numerous intangibles that only a small town can provide. One couple experienced this phenomenon firsthand when they were looking to relocate to North Carolina. Tired of living through routinely harsh winters and paying high taxes, the couple headed south from New York and were literally driving through the state looking for a place "that felt like home." The two exited I-85 on a whim at Mebane Oaks Road and drove into town on Fifth Street in mid-April when the dogwoods and azaleas were at their peak. Before the couple reached the railroad tracks at Center Street, they knew their search was over. One thing led to another, and First Savings made these folks a loan to purchase a home. What is striking about this couple and others is the visible excitement they had about coming to North Carolina and Mebane. The pity is that some Mebanites who have lived in the city their entire lives seem oblivious to the beauty around them and sometimes forget just how lucky they really are.

Mebane's incredible growth prompted a letter to the *Mebane Enterprise* in April 1996 from Mayor Glendel Stephenson, contrasting the town when he arrived in 1963 to 1996. Stephenson mentioned many businesses that were the foundation of the city in the 1960s including Rose's Department Store, the Colonial Store, Riggs' Shoe Store, Young's Jewelry, Malone Crawford Clothing Store, Tyson Malone Hardware, Carolina Drug, Jeffrey's Texaco, and others. Most of the longtime businesses in Stephenson's letter had long since closed, and in their place was a new generation of businesses and industry that was reshaping Mebane's future. Stephenson ended his article with thoughts of Mebane's rapid growth and the guarantee that "You ain't seen nothing yet." Stephenson himself thought it was time to move on, retiring from CCB in December 1996 after forty-three years in banking.

Stephenson and other council members grabbed their worn-out shovels in 1996 for yet another groundbreaking, this one for the Mebane Medical Park on Mebane Oaks Road, which would become home to Kernodle Clinic and Alamance Eye Center. Kernodle Clinic's decision to come to Mebane was largely due to the lobbying efforts of First Savings and Loan Director Dr. David Jones. Mebane attracted another Burlington medical group when Dr. Charles Scott and the staff of Mebane Pediatrics opened on South Fifth Street across from Brookhollow.

Like the city it served, First Savings was enjoying one of its best decades, and by the mid-1990s it was no doubt that the association had adjusted quite well to the new banking world. The association crossed the $40 million mark in assets in 1996, after reaching $30 million in assets when the decade began. Loan demand continued strong, and First Savings closed over $8 million a year in mortgage loans in both 1996 and 1997. More than 20 percent of the loans extended by the association were construction loans, reflecting Mebane's growth.

On March 18, 1996, First Savings' attorney and trustee Robert F. Steele submitted his resignation and was replaced by a longtime friend of the association, Lee W. Settle. Settle had served First Savings in both these capacities in years past, and the directors unanimously approved his return to the association. At age seventy-seven most folks have dropped their landing gear and slowed down somewhat, but not Lee Settle. Age was of no consequence, and Settle kept the work hours and daily schedule of attorneys half his age.

In 1996 Armstrong World Industries dedicated its new Mebane facility on Oakwood Street Extension, and the long awaited 3-C Battery plant opened as industry focused on areas east and south of the city. With these dedications came the announcement that Brown Wooten Mills would close its Mebane textile operation. Most folks employed there knew the end was coming, and the majority of the ninety-two employees had already found a job prior to the plant's closing as jobs were plentiful.

Mebane's growth and expansion reflected a nation enjoying a vibrant and seemingly unstoppable economy that was clicking on all cylinders. Inflation fell below

3 percent, and unemployment stood at 5.4 percent. Mortgage interest rates held steady in the 7 percent range, and if folks weren't buying a home, they were certainly refinancing mortgage loans taken out just a few years earlier. The Dow Jones Industrial Average blew through the 4000- and 5000-point levels in 1995, and topped 6000 before the end of 1996. The Dow was certainly hot, but the story in the U.S. stock market was the incredible performance of the National Association of Securities Dealers Automated Quotient or NASDAQ Composite Index. Loaded with technology stocks, the NASDAQ opened the decade at 459. By 1995 the index had passed the 1000 mark for the first time and was on its way to closing over 4000 by the end of the decade. The double-digit returns of the NASDAQ and other stock indexes naturally pleased investors, but had some experts worried, including Federal Reserve Chairman Alan Greenspan. The rapid rise in the stock market prompted Greenspan's comments that investors and Wall Street were caught up in "irrational exuberance." Usually when Alan Greenspan spoke the world stopped to listen, but this time the Fed chairman's opinion had no effect; markets continued to set new records. The good economic times easily assured President Bill Clinton a second term in the White House in November 1996.

Although Americans were enjoying unprecedented prosperity, consumers were piling up personal debt at an alarming rate. In 1994 consumer credit topped the $1 trillion mark for the first time. It would take less than ten years for consumer debt to reach $2 trillion. Many reasons explain this massive debt, including the rising costs of health care and higher education costs as baby boomers were sending their children off to college. By the 1990s, a shift had also taken place in the use of credit cards that changed the buying habits of the nation. The credit card had gone from being a simple charge card to an all-purpose consumer loan.

From 1993 to 1997 credit card debt doubled to $422 billion, and the American household in 1997 was carrying an average outstanding balance of seven thousand dollars. The effects of the growing debt problem were revealed when more Americans (1.6 million) filed for bankruptcy in 1997 than graduated from college. Bankruptcies hit previous highs in 1980 and 1992 amid recessionary periods, but this trend was disturbing considering the good economic times of the 1990s. Whatever the causes, bankruptcy was becoming a first option of choice for the financially strapped, rather than the last resort that it used to be.

Not only was the attitude toward debt changing, so was the issue of saving. As Americans racked up large credit card debt, the ability or willingness to save money became less important. The Greatest Generation had set the standard for saving money and was less likely to incur large debt balances, but that was changing, too, as many senior citizens resorted to living on credit cards to meet financial obligations. As late as the 1980s, Americans were still saving between 5 and 10 percent of their incomes. That percentage began a downward trend during the 1990s, eventually reaching a negative rate in 2005 as Americans spent more than they made in income.

One contradiction to this trend was that many Americans, particularly the baby boomers, saw themselves as investors rather than savers. Lured by the high returns of the stock market and instantaneous information from the Internet, the day trader emerged as investment firms catered to the individual investor. With the click of a mouse, investors bought and sold securities, making or losing thousands of dollars in a day.

As money left Main Street for Wall Street, community institutions once again struggled with deposit outflows, placing community institutions in a quandary. First Savings and smaller institutions attracted savers, and despite the allure of the stock market, retirees were the bread and butter of community institutions, desiring the safety of FDIC-insured accounts.

Whether they were investors or savers, the profile of the local depositor had changed for all institutions over the years, but more so for small-town associations. In the early 1960s First Savings had nearly four thousand "members" or depositors — not bad for a town with a population at that time of two thousand. However, much had changed by the mid-1990s as White's Furniture had closed, and with Mebane's manufacturing base relocating from downtown, the blue-collar savers who were regulars to the association disappeared as well.

Mebane attracted a bed-and-breakfast in July 1996, as the Mebane House Inn opened for business. Once part of a large plantation, the Mebane House had a rich history dating back to 1853. Nestled in a grove of hardwood trees off South Fifth Street, the large two-story home was built by Dr. Benjamin Franklin Mebane, who practiced medicine in a small cottage near the main house. The original home and acreage stayed in the Mebane family until the 1940s, when most of the land was sold off for development. The Mebane House's opening occurred at an opportune time. The inn came to the rescue of Mebanites in September 1996 when Hurricane Fran hit North Carolina, cutting power to many local homes and businesses. The bed-and-breakfast had its power restored quickly as the inn was on the same power grid as the police department and was able to provide shelter and ice to local residents.

A disaster of a different kind hit First Savings that fall as the FDIC assessed the association $191,733 for the continued cleanup of the savings and loan crisis. Although the assessment was not unexpected, board members remained frustrated as responsible associations, which played by the rules, continued to see their profits given back to the government. Despite the assessment taking a huge bite out of revenue, First Savings felt obligated to fund community projects. It was impossible to know if and when another assessment would occur, and First Savings returned to local giving, donating five thousand dollars to Woodlawn Middle School's technology program.

In January 1997 Cone Mills confirmed what everyone knew was coming and closed the Granite Finishing Plant in Haw River. One worker stated, "If you grew up in Haw River, you were expected to work at the mill at one time or another." Since 1930, Granite had been the largest producer of corduroy in the world and the foundation of the town, donating to schools, parks, the civic center, and even the police and fire departments.

As Haw River dealt with the Granite Finishing trauma, the city of Mebane expanded once again through annexation. The city grew fifty-eight acres when property from South Mebane Elementary School on South Third Street to the entrance of the Mebane Arts Center at Corregidor Drive was annexed. Some citizens welcomed growth, while others felt that change was coming too fast and that the city was in danger of losing its small-town identity. One of these changes was the proposed Highway 119 Bypass around the west side of town. The plans drew opposition primarily from those in the Woodlawn and West End communities who argued that the road would pass through established neighborhoods and the town's watershed area, and disturb historical landmarks. Those favoring the road believed the bypass would relieve traffic congestion downtown and open development north of the city. Heated discussions took place at Eastern Alamance

High School and at several Mebane City Council meetings. The proposed bypass remained an ongoing issue for the remainder of the decade.

Another topic that stirs emotions for growing cities in the southern Bible Belt is the question of liquor by the drink. A&M Grill and Huey's Restaurant were two of Mebane's oldest and most popular dining spots, and both were in Orange County where liquor by the drink was legal. The Grill and Huey's each completed extensive renovations during the 1990s that included a full-service bar. Other restaurants in the Alamance County side of Mebane pressured the city for a referendum on the subject, arguing that liquor by the drink would bring more upscale businesses to the area. Mebane voters rejected mixed drinks in 1977 but passed the measure in May 1998.

A mixed drink was not the only thing for sale in the late 1990s. From banks to businesses, the investment environment of the 1990s represented a time of buying and selling. Kerr Drug purchased Rite Aid, Revco became CVS Pharmacy, and Byrd's Foods became Lowes Foods. Two sales included businesses that were Mebane fixtures. Pulaski Furniture sold Craftique Furniture to investors Craig Shoemaker and Larry and John Erwin, who stated the furniture company was once again a "family-run business." Mebtel, formerly the Mebane Home Telephone Company and a family-run business, was sold to Madison River.

These changes were quite overwhelming, but what caught everybody by surprise was 3-C Alliance's sudden announcement that it would close its doors after just one year of operation. There were great expectations when the high-tech company chose Mebane. Instead 152 people were let go before the business fully got off the ground.

Calvin Oakley celebrated his seventy-seventh birthday on September 23, 1997, and retired from the association's board of directors. Oakley joined the board in 1973 and became chairman in December 1986. The association's CPA, Bobby J. Massey, was appointed to the board to replace Oakley as a director. Massey brought a wealth of experience, having worked many years with numerous financial institutions. Oakley was elected as director emeritus, the first time the association had given that honor to a retiring director since Paisley Nelson in 1958.

The financial news of 1998 centered on the resilience of the stock market, which seemed to set new records almost daily. The other story was the refinancing boom in the mortgage industry. But one 1998 event would have implications for the mortgage and housing industries well into the next decade. The 1990s offered a vast array of investment instruments, and one that gained popularity was the hedge fund. Some hedge funds used complicated strategies, various investment theories, and models designed to reduce risk for their investors. Long Term Capital Management (LTCM) was one very successful hedge fund, producing spectacular returns since opening in 1993 and attracting numerous investors, including many of the nation's major financial institutions. When Russia defaulted on its debts in 1998, worldwide financial markets unraveled. The theories that LTCM had used so successfully failed, and the company was on the verge of bankruptcy.

In a surprising and controversial move, Alan Greenspan and the Federal Reserve came to the rescue, bailing out the floundering fund. The Fed's justification for a taxpayer bailout was that if LTCM was allowed to fail, a serious financial crisis would emerge and banks that invested with the fund could be taken down in a domino effect. This decision by the Federal Reserve in 1998 was significant, setting a precedent with far-reaching consequences when another, more serious crisis threatened the nation's financial system in 2008.

The year 1998 turned out to be the institution's best lending year in its one-hundred-year history as the association closed $15.7 million in mortgage loans. This was an incredible accomplishment, but even more lurked inside these numbers. Of these loans, 77 percent were refinancing loans made to existing customers. What is striking about the lending data from 1998 was the decline in construction and purchase loans, two segments of the market that First Savings dominated during the 1950s and 1960s. Construction loans that had composed 20 percent of the association's lending two years earlier accounted for only 13 percent of loans in 1998. Although Mebane was a prime real estate destination, home purchase loans accounted for just 10 percent of the association's lending that year. Increased competition and the vast array of new lending products were negatively impacting the association.

Competition itself no longer came from a handful of banks or mortgage lenders. The Office of Thrift Supervision reported that 181 different lending entities generated mortgage loans in the Mebane area in 1998. The refinancing and building boom of the late 1990s brought lenders out of the woodwork from all over the country as online mortgage sites, credit unions, and mortgage brokers pressured traditional lenders.

Like the banking industry, consolidation of American manufacturing had been the storyline over the previous ten years. Towns like Mebane and Haw River had learned the hard way that no company was safe. By the mid-1990s and well into the next decade, U.S. companies continued their exodus to other countries. In March 1998 General Electric moved 200 jobs from Mebane to Monterrey, Mexico. GE's Mebane plant employed 939 workers at the time of the move, and that number continued to fall.

Ironically, as jobs moved south of the border, a book about the demise of White Furniture was released. *Closing: The Life and Death of an American Factory*, written by Cathy Davidson with photographs by Bill Bamburger, chronicled the last days of the company through moving individual stories and spectacular pictures.

As traditional manufacturing seemed determined to leave, other forms moved in. Synthon Pharmaceuticals announced in April 1998 that the company would locate its North American headquarters just south of Mebane, bringing one hundred high-paying jobs. The plans included research and development labs along with corporate offices on a 132-acre campus south of the city. But there was a catch. The site needed $1.2 million in sewer improvements as the property on Old Hillsborough Road was not in the Mebane city limits. The nearby Hebron community opposed the company's move to the neighborhood, and a firestorm erupted when the city of Mebane took steps to annex the property.

Strip centers became more plentiful, with Cambridge Square on South Fifth Street and Mebane Oaks Shopping Center (now Mebane Oaks Village) joining Brookhollow Shopping Center. Deerfield Commons (Kingsdown Commons) was completed, bringing with it hotels and restaurants to Highway 119 South.

The commercial environment on I-85 and downtown seemed polar opposites. A new business seemed to open somewhere along the interstate corridor every day while downtown's revival was slow in coming. Business owners found out quickly that operating a small business downtown was not for the faint of heart. There were just as many business closings on Clay and Center streets as success stories, and downtown fought hard to redefine itself. Another company shutting its doors was Western Auto, which closed after twenty-eight years on Fourth Street. Across from Western Auto, the once-prominent Jones' Department Store sat vacant and was used for storage, while the old Colonial Store on the corner of Fifth and Clay streets also sat empty. After forty-two years of treating patients, the Mebane Medical Center on Fifth Street closed when Dr. William Aycock passed away in 1997 and Dr. G.Y. Mebane retired. One successful downtown business established in 1998 was Walker Insurance, which opened on Clay Street.

Downtown received a much-needed boost in 1999 when the Five Star Center opened. For more than a year, the 100 block of Center Street between Fourth and Fifth streets underwent extensive renovations. This stretch of Center Street had been home to Rose's 5 and 10 Cent Store, Carolina Drug Store, the White Hotel, and many others—the backbone of Mebane's early retail days. Five Star's investment was significant and came at a time when downtown needed direction. Everyone hoped that Five Star's willingness to take a chance on downtown's business district would lure other investors to follow suit.

City services expanded with commercial and residential growth. After nearly two years of construction, Fire Station Number One opened its doors, all eight of them. The station was built on city-owned property on North First Street and was formerly the site of the public works department.

The late 1990s was a time of change for the association as well. Originally chartered as a state savings and loan in the 1940s, First Savings was not only supervised by the Institutions Division of the state of North Carolina, but also regulated by the Office of Thrift Supervision. Being subject to two regulators was becoming not only redundant but expensive. The fees to the state and OTS in 1997 alone amounted to twenty-five thousand dollars, and it was time to move on. The association adopted a federal mutual charter on February 18, 1999, and the Office of Thrift Supervision became its sole regulator.

Financial institutions had enjoyed an incredible decade of profits and growth, and by 1999 it seemed the sky was the limit. The association's new financial beginning came at the same time as the consolidation of banks large and small, as well as the rise of giants such as Citicorp (Citigroup) and Bank of America. Laws allowed interstate branching, and although banks' products and services were more diverse than ever, some thought one regulation was holding the industry back. The Glass-Steagall Act of 1933 was a direct result of the 1929 stock market crash and prohibited the banking industry from engaging in certain types of activities. The law separated Wall Street investment banks from the commercial banking sector, reducing risk in the system. With business and consumer needs constantly changing, Glass-Steagall was repealed with the passage of the Gramm-Leach-Bliley Financial Modernization Act (GLBA), and the door flew open for institutions to offer everything from insurance to brokerage services. Commercial lenders could underwrite and trade instruments such as mortgage-backed securities and collateralized debt obligations. With the hurdle of Glass-Steagall out of the way, banks were poised to reach even greater heights. Ten years later, the passage of GLBA would be another in the long list of factors many believed contributed to the financial crisis of 2008.

The disappointment of the 3-C Alliance Plant closing was short-lived, as the Liggett Group announced it would move its cigarette manufacturing from Durham to the former battery plant. Liggett's role in the tobacco legacy of North Carolina had lasted over a century, but like other manufacturing sectors, tobacco companies had been hit by downsizing, and the modern facility in Mebane served Liggett's purposes. For decades, travelers through the cities of Durham and Winston-Salem could catch the distinctive aroma of tobacco. In a few years that familiar scent would be found drifting through the air again in Mebane as the tobacco industry had been revived.

Ironically, as Liggett opened its doors, the Piedmont Tobacco Warehouse closed its doors as cuts in federal tobacco quotas forced Alamance County's last remaining warehouse out of business. Home to many tobacco auctions, the warehouse had been a major part of Mebane's economy, but its impact on the city by the turn of the twenty-first century was minor. During its heyday, the fall ritual brought a flurry of activity to downtown each September. The warehouse had survived the toughest of times, even a devastating fire in the early 1960s, but it could not escape the shifting economy of the new century.

Two longtime Mebane manufacturing plants fell victim to acquisition in 1999 as R.L. Stowe purchased Dixie Yarn and Mebane Packaging was bought by Westaco (Meadwestvaco). Dixie Yarn had been Mebane's textile stalwart as other companies had long since closed. Although the plant was still in operation under a new owner, the future of textiles was obviously bleak. Mebane Packaging, on the other hand, had been a success story, and its purchase by a larger company was a sign of the times as another homegrown business was now under the control of a new owner. As these local businesses changed course, Kingsdown unveiled a new research and development center on Fourth Street, demonstrating its ability to adapt to an ever-changing market.

The end of the twentieth century was quickly approaching, bringing with it plenty of predictions. Some thought the runaway stock market would continue its remarkable run, including the chairman of one of the state's largest banks. Speaking at a conference of the North Carolina Bankers Association, the optimistic chairman proclaimed that the Dow Jones Industrial Average would reach 25,000. However, in his own "irrational exuberance," the chairman failed to mention that it might be two or three centuries down the road. Others were sure that the end of the decade would surely mean the end of the world. But what frightened people more than the destruction of mankind itself was the slight possibility that computers might not work on January 1, 2000. The Y2K scare created a lot of hype and concern that the world's computers would fail to function when the date changed from 1999 to 2000. Financial institutions were required to implement detailed programs, procedures, and contingency plans to address the Y2K issue. Businesses large and small, including First Savings, upgraded or replaced computer systems.

First Savings celebrated its ninetieth birthday on November 4 and 5 with a two-day open house and reception. The movie *Titanic* was popular at the time, and the association's staff dressed in period costumes of that era. This delighted customers, many of whom stopped by to take pictures.

The anniversary was not only a time of celebration but also a time of reflection. When the decade began, First Savings entered this new banking world wondering if there was still room for a small-town savings and loan. Although its role had diminished, the association had some of its best years in the 1990s. Assets grew 59 percent and stood at $47,351,964, while mortgage loans increased 62 percent, reaching $31,361,655 despite increasing competition. Deposits grew 52 percent, reaching $39,349,948, a remarkable feat considering that the association was competing with the gains of a bullish stock market. The association's reserve position, a measure of its strength and safety, grew 109 percent and stood at $7,758,828. The fact that the Mebane community supported the association when banks ruled the financial world was a strong vote of confidence. First Savings had indeed changed in the past ninety years, but its core values had not.

In many ways Mebane was a completely different city than it was ten years earlier, as it too struggled with its identity. Growing and holding on to its small-town image was proving to be a challenge, and the contrast between its storied past and promising future was readily visible. Stately downtown buildings erected at the turn of the last century were joined by new modern structures, such as the Mebane Arts Center and the fire station. Still some things were the same, as older, iconic buildings like White Furniture remained. A shiny Mercedes could be seen on Mebane streets followed closely by a riding lawnmower, which was still an accepted form of transportation. The Mebane Christmas Parade and Dogwood Festival were bigger than ever, and so was the town. The city's population grew 53 percent during the 1990s and stood at 7,284. That figure only scratched the surface, as other communities outside the city such as Woodlawn and Hawfields were growing almost as fast.

Mebane's foundation of economic strength at the beginning of the twentieth century had all but disappeared as the century ended. Furniture, textiles, and tobacco, though important, were no longer the center of employment for the city. The whistles at White Furniture and Kingsdown had fallen silent for very different reasons. Mebane had become a diverse place to live and work, and a destination for new industry and businesses that continued to shape its future. Historic downtown was on its way back, and the rally would hit full stride in the decade to come.

Mebane firmly established itself as a prime location for home owners after years of playing second fiddle to other sections of the county. The Alamance County Multiple Listing Service reported that the average sales price for a home in Mebane rose 136 percent during the decade, standing at $142,072 by 1999. Mebane was the fastest-growing city in Alamance County, with more total home sales than any other city in the county from 1995 to 1999. The city was a commercial and residential destination, with all the ingredients for continued growth and prosperity.

The financial system's new beginning saw the industry shape and reshape itself as the 1990s weeded out weak institutions through mergers and acquisitions while creating megabanks. The Internet became a force in the nation's commerce as transactional Web sites, online bill pay, and other uses by the financial industry became mainstream.

One sector of the financial industry that evolved at a rapid pace was mortgage lending. Once an exclusive product of savings and loans, mortgage lending had become an economy unto itself through a variety of originators as the century drew to a close. The influence of government-sponsored enterprises, Wall Street, and a booming real estate market stabilized the business of mortgage loans and interest rates. Influences would increase in the decade to follow, turning what was once a safe and secure investment into a risky and speculative commodity.

The U.S. economy enjoyed a decade of unprecedented prosperity, giving no hint of trouble ahead with the exception of a subtle rise in interest rates. Wall Street opened its doors to the small investor during the 1990s, and the rewards had been nothing short of spectacular. The NASDAQ closed 1999 at 4069 after opening ten years earlier at 459. The incredible run of the NASDAQ was partly due to technology spending during the last half of the decade, as businesses prepared for Y2K. Soon after the new decade began, technology stocks lost their luster and became less of a market driver. Still, the consumer-driven economy seemed to have no end in sight, and experts were convinced the new decade would see more of the same. Happy investors were partying "like it was 1999," and the remarkable returns in the stock market left them hungry for more. No one knew it, but the party was winding down.

Mill Creek was an upscale subdivision that began construction in the early 1990s with a golf course and was the largest development north of the city.

Completed in 1995, the Mebane Arts and Community Center became the focal point for recreation and community activities. A position once held for generations by Mebane High School.

Fire Station Number One was completed in 1999 on North First Street. Mebane's fire department had operated with just one station since the 1920s.

Known as "The Judge", attorney Lee Settle's relationship with First Savings spanned more than half a century. *Courtesy Judy Settle*

White Furniture closed during the 1990s as Mebane's commercial identity evolved. This treasured structure remains a monument to a different time in Mebane's history.

The staff dressed in period costumes celebrate First Savings 90th birthday. L-R Janice Wright, Rick Smith, Shelby Murphy, Janis Murray, Neal Smith and Gail Jordan

CHAPTER TEN

Back to the Future

2000–2009

THE 2000S BEGAN IN HUMAN TRAGEDY and ended in mortgage chaos. Sandwiched in between was an economic roller coaster in stark contrast to the joy ride of the 1990s. First Savings entered the new century on top of its game, coming off the most profitable decade in its history. The same could be said for every mortgage lender, as 67.4 percent of Americans owned their own homes. But it wasn't enough. Mortgage lending was about to change once again, and this time the consequences would be catastrophic.

Fueled by housing, low interest rates, and consumer spending, the widespread prosperity and growth of the 1990s had been a textbook example of the virtues of capitalism. Economic expectations for the new century were riding high. Few would have predicted that before the 2000s were over, the government would initiate the largest relief package in history to keep its financial system from failing. Over the ten years from 2000 to 2010, housing and mortgage lending went from the penthouse to the outhouse, leaving everyone scratching their heads as to why. To understand the essence of the mortgage debacle of the late 2000s, one must go back to the 1980s.

One of the top films of 1987 was Oliver Stone's *Wall Street*, starring Michael Douglas as a ruthless corporate raider. Set amid the real-life hostile takeovers of the 1980s, the film featured a scene in which Douglas's character, Gordon Gekko, lectures on the virtues of greed. "The point is, ladies and gentlemen, that greed, for a lack of a better word, is good. Greed is right. Greed works. Greed clarifies, cuts through, and captures the essence of the evolutionary spirit. Greed, in all of its forms, greed for life, for money, for love, for knowledge has marked the upward surge of mankind." Greed was no doubt the "evolutionary spirit" and catalyst that drove mortgage lending during the 2000s to the point of national and worldwide crisis.

Fireworks and lavish celebrations welcomed in the twenty-first century with a bang that was repeated in every time zone around the world. It is unclear whether the global fanfare on January 1, 2000, was from the excitement of the new century or from relief that the world's computers did not shut down, as the Y2K scare suggested. The much-anticipated Y2K problem was much to do about nothing, coming and going with few problems.

The New Year's celebrations that took place in Times Square could just as easily have been held on Wall Street, as the markets were on an incredible roll. Most economic indicators supported the idea that the bull market would continue, as the ingredients fueling the nation's economic engine in the 1990s were still in place. Inflation weighed in at just 2.6 percent, interest rates were stable, and employment remained strong. But how in the world could the U.S. economy top the incredible prosperity of the 1990s? Unfortunately Americans found out very painfully that it couldn't.

First Savings and Loan wondered, too, how the association could top the success it had experienced over the previous ten years. Like the stock market, First Savings found that it couldn't keep the momentum going either, as an out-of-control mortgage lending environment emerged during the 2000s, taking a heavy toll on community lenders. The U.S. stock market and housing sectors that ran so strong in the 1990s both stumbled during the 2000s. In a strange twist, mortgage lending would bring Wall Street to its knees by the end of the decade, ultimately biting the hand that fed it.

By 2000, most customers assumed that all financial institutions were the same, and that most were banks or credit unions. First Savings was one of a handful of institutions that still referred to themselves as "savings and loans," as most thrifts had converted to savings banks. Any leftover suspicion from the savings and loan crisis that had followed thrifts through the early 1990s had disappeared. Interestingly, First Savings was now viewed as somewhat of a curiosity by real estate agents, lenders, and a new generation of customers who didn't know what a savings and loan was and didn't truly care. Throughout the late 1990s and early 2000s, First Savings advertised, "If you like what savings and loans once did, you'll love what we still do." That comforting slogan appealed to the retiree base but did little to foster new business.

From commercial endeavors to home loans, mortgage lending had mushroomed into big business during the boom times of the 1990s as more banking and nonbanking entities found mortgage lending an attractive investment. With favorable rates and lending products available, customers were courted on television and online as Internet commerce took hold. With the click of a mouse, consumers could research rates and apply for loans online with a lender on the other side of the country, never setting foot inside an institution.

Although changes were coming quickly in the financial world, the fact that First Savings made it through the transition years of the 1990s provided further ammunition for the board to stay its conservative course. First Savings began the decade with its veteran staff of Janice Wright, Janis Murray, Gail Jordan, and Rick Smith, while Shelby Murphy and Neal Smith began their sixth decade with the association. At the February shareholders' meeting, the incumbent board of Neal Smith, Rick Smith, Ned Gauldin, Bobby Massey, David Jones, Steve Troutman, and Director Emeritus Calvin Oakley were once again reelected. By decade's end, the makeup of the association's staff would be much different, as four new staff members joined First Savings, replacing longtime employees whose storied careers came to an end.

As Wall Street and First Savings hoped to maintain momentum in the new decade, the city of Mebane had no doubt about its own continued success. The only possible question the Mebane community had was *Where are all these people coming from?* Houses were in such demand that the average home in Mebane sold for an incredible 103 percent of its asking price in 2000, according to the Alamance County Multiple Listing Service. The selling price of a house in Mebane reached $150,348 by 2000, reflecting a 21 percent increase in just three years. The average home loan amount extended by First Savings in 2000 was $85,695, and it increased to $130,566 by 2004. Mebane's diversity in both industry and population meant higher-income loan applicants. In 1998 just 3 percent of First Savings' loan applicants made above $100,000 a year. By 2000 that percentage had climbed to 21 percent.

The commercial expansion south of town continued, and banks led the charge. First South (now RBC Centura) and Wachovia (now Wells Fargo) were joined by the State Employees Credit Union, which opened a branch in the Mebane Oaks Market Place. Fidelity Bank completed its new branch in a prime spot at the Brookhollow Shopping Center. The proximity of these branches to the interstate and growing subdivisions attracted new customers and also made them a target.

On January 6, 2000, First South Bank became the first financial institution in Mebane's history to experience a robbery. Bank branches near interstate highways are convenient but vulnerable, as robbers can hit these locations and be miles away in a short time. No one was hurt in the incident, and the suspects were later apprehended. Law enforcement determined that the individuals who hit First South were responsible for a string of bank robberies from Virginia to South Carolina. Later that same year, First South's next-door neighbor, Wachovia, was also robbed.

Another January snowstorm dumped fourteen inches of snow on the Mebane area, closing schools for eleven days. Local sledders found the packed powder conditions perfect on the steep-banked hills surrounding the field at Eastern Alamance's football stadium, and snowmen dotted lawns across town.

Orange Truss Company's president Clyde Belangia found the Mebane economic climate perfect and moved his longtime Orange County business to West Holt Street. Orange Truss produced building trusses for residential and commercial construction and once supplied woodwork for the sleep products that Kingsdown made.

Orange Truss and other companies connected to the housing industry enjoyed a booming business. Mill Ridge was the latest subdivision to open off North Second and North Third streets, offering eleven-hundred-square-foot homes priced between $95,000 and $120,000.

The stock market wasted no time picking up where it left off, as the Dow quickly topped 11,700 for the first time while the NASDAQ cruised to the 4300 level with no problem. It looked like a repeat performance of the 1990s until suddenly the bottom fell out and by March the Dow was off 16 percent from its January high. The unstoppable NASDAQ briefly cracked the 5000 mark that spring, driven by the hot sectors of technology and communications, dot-com companies, and computer stocks.

Evolving technology carried markets to record highs in the 1990s, and the expectation was that the NASDAQ would continue its torrid pace. That wishful thinking went out the window when the tech bubble burst and the markets began to slide. By October the Dow was down 38 percent, and the carnage on the NASDAQ had just begun. Hopeful investors, certain that a rally was just around the corner, held on, spurred by the confidence of double-digit returns over the previous ten years. That rally never came. The drop in the NASDAQ was slow and painful, bottoming out two years later at 1139. The NASDAQ advertised itself at that time as the "stock market for the next hundred years." One frustrated investor who obviously lost money in the market described the index as "the stock market for the next fifteen minutes."

On May 11, 2000, Director Emeritus Calvin S. Oakley passed away after several years of declining health. While Oakley had been part of the First Savings family since the early 1970s, in all honesty Oakley was a friend to everyone and never met a stranger. Before retiring, Oakley had cracked jokes while filling prescriptions behind the pharmacy counter at Warren's Drug Store for generations. Involved in every conceivable civic group, Oakley loved Mebane as much he did his alma mater, the University of North Carolina at Chapel Hill. His nonstop sense of humor never seemed to phase his wife, Christine, always the prim and proper southern lady who managed to remain above her husband's harmless mischief. The life of the party, Oakley carried on his typical foolishness with anyone who would listen, often admitting that he had "married above his raising."

Another favorite Oakley saying was, "If it ain't broke, don't fix it," when referring to First Savings' successful conservative strategy. By 2000, First Savings found its niche market, which was not only a good fit for the association but for Mebane. This philosophy presented a polar opposite to an innovative financial system eager to shed a perceived old-fashioned stuffiness. The evolving banking industry appeared to be adopting another popular saying of the day, "If it ain't broke, break it," which is exactly what happened in 2008.

Straight-line winds hit the area on May 24, 2000, knocking down trees and cutting power to thousands of residents for days. The sudden storm caught everyone off guard, resulting in $1.3 million in property damage to 112 homes and businesses. The storm hit just before the association's monthly board meeting. Three directors managed to make it past downed trees to the association's office for an abbreviated session.

Jill Thornton (later Auditori) purchased the old Jones' Department Store at the corner of Fourth and Clay streets in May 2000, and in doing so sparked a revival of downtown's business district. After months of remodeling, Solgarden opened in December, offering unique gifts and crafts. Following on the heels of the Five Star Center and the success of Gifts of Distinction, Solgarden convinced other small business owners that downtown still had viable business potential, but with a twist. Solgarden and Gifts of Distinction were niche businesses, not the traditional retail stores that had once thrived on Clay and Center streets. Joy Albright, Thornton's mother and owner of Clay Street Printing, watched downtown struggle to get back on its feet. Her print shop was now a cornerstone downtown business. Only a few folks remembered that First Savings and Loan once occupied Albright's building in the 1950s.

As the former Jones' Department Store found new life, so did four of Mebane's older businesses locations. John Hawkins and Mickey Tripp opened Hawkins Tripp Realty (now Coldwell Banker/Howard Perry and Walston) in the former Mebane Medical Arts Building on Fifth Street. Dr. Greg Barker opened Mebane Eye Care on East Center Street in a building that once belonged to chiropractor Dr. Arnold Garren. Discount Furniture Connection moved into Winn-Dixie's former store on Mebane Oaks Road, as the grocery chain became the anchor for Mebane Oaks Marketplace.

Coaxing customers back to Clay Street took patience and creativity as the new century brought with it a different business world with changing consumer preferences and strong competition. Clay Street Afterwork was introduced, featuring live band performances on Friday nights through the summer months. Folks brought lawn chairs to a blocked-off Clay Street and spent evenings dancing to a variety of musical talent while catching up with friends.

As downtown began to stir once again, part of its past faded away when the Reliable Furniture Store closed in December, ending an incredible eighty-one-year run. First Savings and Loan's John McIntyre had founded the business in 1919, selling appliances and furniture to generations of Mebanites who were now saddened by the news. Reliable was a window into the town's past, when downtown was in its heyday. Owners Richard and Bobby Langley were ready to retire, and facing the competition of big-box stores had become a huge challenge. First Savings' personal connection to Reliable ran deep, as the association operated in the store from the 1920s until the early 1950s. Some of the association's old papers dating back to 1914 were found in the store's safe and were used in documenting this history.

Sixty-five workers lost their jobs when Ridgeville Inc. on Crawford Street closed. Originally founded in 1975 as Mebane Hosiery, the company suffered the same fate as Dixie Yarn, Brown Wooten, and hundreds of other textile mills across North Carolina as foreign imports were killing the industry.

The new century seemed to be ushering in changes everywhere, and First Savings was no exception. The 2000s would see more changes in the institution's personnel than in any ten-year period in its history. The influx of new people began when Jamie Park joined the association's staff on July 3, 2000, replacing Ann Allison, who left in August 1999. Park worked with Rick Smith on loan closings as Neal Smith had turned this part of the operation over to his son. Park came well-prepared, having worked for seven years in the real estate department of Davis and Humbert Attorneys.

As Park became the newest staff member, the association honored two of its veteran employees at the July 26 board meeting when Janis Murray and Janice Wright received service awards for twenty and thirty-five years, respectively.

Mebane's population growth resulted in one of the most anticipated events of the year, the opening of Hawfields Middle School and Audrey W. Garrett Elementary School. Built on an eighty-three-acre campus south of Mebane in the Hawfields community, the newest addition to the Alamance-Burlington School System was nothing short of spectacular. More than seven hundred people turned out for a glimpse of the modern facility at a dedication ceremony on July 23. Mrs. Audrey Garrett, who began her teaching career in Mebane in 1927, was present for the occasion.

On September 5, after two years of construction, the new Mebane Post Office opened on South Third Street, replacing the old post office, which was built in the 1930s and located on Center Street in the middle of the town's business district. The new site was the result of an extensive search process to identify a location that would best serve the city's future needs. Although the new post office was well south of downtown and far removed from its former location, the new site truly reflected the city's growth and where the town was headed.

People who gathered in the Mebane Arts Center on October 14, 2000, weren't concerned with where Mebane was headed, but rather where it had been. Mebane High School ceased to exist in 1962 and disappeared from the landscape in the 1970s, but it could not be erased from the memories of those who passed through its doors. The Blast from the Past, a two-day celebration honoring all graduating classes, attracted more than six hundred people from all over the country. The event did more than bring former classmates together, as the reunion served as a springboard for the creation of the Mebane Historical Society.

The year 2000 was an election year, and by November, Mebane's landscape was littered once again with fallen leaves and the usual campaign signs that dotted every street corner. The presidential race captured everyone's interest as Vice President Al Gore ran with hopes of keeping the Democratic Party in the White House while Republican George W. Bush, governor of Texas, looked to follow in his father's footsteps as president. Votes may have been cast on November 7, but the outcome of the election was not known until December 12. It came down to Florida, as recounts and examinations of ballots held the election in limbo. The U.S. Supreme Court ultimately decided the outcome, determining that the recount process was unconstitutional and declaring George W. Bush the winner.

Those looking to buy a house in this new century were winners, too, as mortgage lending hit the ground running. First Savings rode a hot streak, averaging $8.9 million in loans annually for the first three years of the new decade. A closer look at the data confirmed that First Savings did well with its loyal customer base, as 56 percent of the refinances made in 2000 were to existing customers. By 2002 the number of loans made to existing customers reached 81 percent. From 2000 to 2002 construction lending fell from 28 percent of total loans to just 12 percent, and lending to purchase a house dropped from 16 percent to just 7 percent. In the war with mortgage lenders, First Savings was clearly losing the battle to attract new business. These declining numbers were an omen of things to come.

Mebane was a real estate hot spot, offering a varied menu of homes in traditional and rural residential subdivisions as well as plenty of new construction.

Home buyers had their choice of homes in established neighborhoods starting in the sixty-thousand-dollar range to five hundred thousand dollars and higher in upscale subdivisions. Old traditions were changing along with the city's demographics, and so did housing demands and preferences. Single-family dwellings were joined by apartment complexes, and more condos and townhouses were being built. Familiar residential streets like North Ninth, Carr, Fifth, Emerson, and New London Lane were joined by newer ones with names like Briarwood, Fieldstone, Springforest, Saint Andrews Drive, and many more.

Charlotte's First Union and Winston-Salem's Wachovia, which had battled each other for the better part of the twentieth century, shocked the financial world in 2001 with the announcement of a merger of the two rivals. The newly formed Wachovia Corporation would have its work cut out for it, going head to head with Charlotte's Bank of America. Bank of America was now the second-largest bank in the nation, and its growth had been remarkable. Their branches and ATMs seemed to be everywhere, prompting one bank executive to predict that Bank of America would be the first bank to "have a branch and ATM on the moon if they haven't done so already."

With the stock market faltering, housing remained the true bright spot in an economy that was on the ropes. It didn't take long for investors and consumers to realize that the new decade would be much different than the good times of the 1990s. North Carolina's manufacturing base continued to suffer, as unemployment climbed from 3.5 percent in 2000 to 6.1 percent by 2001. Mebane was hit again when R.L. Stowe announced in early September that it would close by the end of the year with the loss of 115 jobs. Stowe had purchased the former Dixie Yarn textile plant just three years earlier, and its closing, for all practical purposes, ended any significant textile presence in Mebane. Within one year's time, the city had seen the tobacco warehouses and now textiles, two key areas of its commercial heritage, disappear. With White Furniture long since closed, Craftique was the town's remaining link to the furniture industry. As one local resident put it, "At this rate, I don't think there will be a tobacco field, furniture factory, or textile mill left in North Carolina ten years from now."

The news was worse on Wall Street. By September 1, the Dow Jones Industrial Average had managed to recover 85 percent from its 2000 plunge but was still firmly in the red for the year, closing on that day at 9605. The NASDAQ continued its free fall, closing in August at 1804, off 64 percent from its highs in March 2000. It had been a horrible summer in the markets, but horror of a different kind was about to strike America in a form that it had never known before.

Tuesday, September 11, 2001, was a beautiful day on the east coast of the United States. There was not a cloud in the sky; it was a perfect day to travel. President Bush boarded Air Force One and flew to Florida to push an education agenda. Before the day was over, the agenda for President Bush and the nation changed forever. A day that started out with such beauty and promise ended in terrible human tragedy.

Terrorism had been something Americans viewed on television from the safety of their living rooms, never really feeling its raw pain until the Oklahoma City bombing in 1995. Most Americans felt removed if not immune from car bombs and other tragedies that occurred with regularity halfway around the world. That thinking changed in the time it took for two hijacked airliners to slam into New York's World Trade Center. Fear had been something generations of Americans knew quite well during the days of the Depression and the uncertainty of World War II. But those emotions had been replaced by confidence and strength that postwar America's prosperity promised. The fear and anger were stoked as another plane struck the Pentagon and a fourth slammed into a field in Shanksville, Pennsylvania. As with other national tragedies—Pearl Harbor, the Kennedy assassination, and the *Challenger* explosion—everyone remembered where they were and what they were doing that September morning.

Lower Manhattan is a long way from Mebane, North Carolina, in more ways than just geography. That didn't seem to matter. Churches held prayer vigils, and local schools organized balloon releases, planted trees, and created other memorials to honor those lost. Volunteers from Mebane went to the Pentagon and Ground Zero in New York, assisting in rescue and recovery efforts. The Mebane City Council met on September 17, drawing a crowd of 140 people, and 9/11 was the primary topic.

The human loss in the attacks of September 11 was compounded by the economic uncertainty of its aftermath. The New York Stock Exchange closed for the remainder of that historic week, and as expected, stocks plummeted when the markets opened the following Monday as the fear of more attacks kept investors on edge. The Office of Management and Budget confirmed that the nation's economy had been in a recession since March 2001, and the attacks only exacerbated the slowdown. Investors quickly opted for the safety of conservative investments as the markets continued their slide. Like most FDIC-insured institutions, First Savings showed increased deposit inflows from 2001 through 2003.

The nation responded militarily in Afghanistan as the War on Terror became the nation's top priority. The Department of Homeland Security was established, and airline travel would never be the same. Congress passed the USA PATRIOT Act, strengthening the Bank Secrecy Act and requiring closer background checks on customers.

As the country entered an uncertain conflict, the Federal Reserve was fighting a war of its own against a slumping economy. The Fed pumped billions of dollars into the economy and lowered the federal funds rate to levels not seen since the 1950s. Mortgage rates soon followed, and by November they hit a forty-year low at 6.5 percent.

The Fed's response to 9/11 ushered in a period of record low interest rates and high liquidity, which is important to note. The low interest rate environment that began in 2001 and which continued through the decade instilled in Americans that low interest rates were the norm. This period redefined the credit environment for the remainder of the decade and the pending financial crisis.

The economic slowdown facing the country had very little effect on Mebane. From its earliest days to the present, Mebane's path to success was its access to transportation and its central location in the state. One hundred years earlier, the town owed its existence and prosperity to the railroad that cut through the heart of the town. In those early days, shoppers came from rural areas on dirt roads and wagon trails to buy goods at the Mebane Store or Tyson Malone Hardware, and farmers brought tobacco for auction in the fall. Businesses of all types lured people to town.

That trend reversed itself as the town took its business to the people. With hundreds of thousands of cars traveling down I-40/I-85 every day, the commercial potential along the interstate seemed unlimited. Sam and Will White must have had the same feeling about the railroad when a steam locomotive pulled into the depot one hundred years ago. Back then, Mebane's businesses were owned and operated by local people, a trend that held true until the 1980s. By 2002, national chain stores and company franchises that saw profits in Mebane's location joined the local entrepreneurs.

As commercial ventures located on the city's south side, some pondered the future of two of Mebane's most familiar landmarks. Over the years many of Mebane's historic places were lost to time and progress, including Mebane High School, Bingham School, and the depot. Two key landmarks were saved in 2002, fittingly purchased by the city they called home. The recently closed R.L. Stowe/Dixie Yarn building at the corner of East Washington and South Second streets was a link to Mebane's rich textile history. After extensive renovations the century-old building became the Mebane Public Library. The transformation from textile mill to library took eighteen months and $2 million before the ribbon-cutting ceremony in November 2006, and the results were simply stunning. Its open, two-story interior with weathered brick walls and rich hardwood floors was lined with bookshelves that housed a different kind of yarn. One could only imagine what the original Reviewers literary club that started the first Mebane Library in a spare room at Mebane High School in 1936 would have thought.

The city of Mebane purchased the former post office on Center Street for its growing police department, and like the Dixie Yarn building, the old post office needed extensive work. These two projects were the first of many rehabilitation and recovery projects by the city that would occur during the decade, restoring some of the community's most distinguished architecture.

While these commercial ventures added to the city's appeal, residential real estate was clearly stumbling. The recession that lingered after 9/11 finally caught up with Alamance County's housing market as home sales hit a four-year low in 2002. Although the number of homes sold in Mebane fell 11 percent during the year, the sales price managed to climb to a record $152,625. Any apparent slowdown in sales didn't seem to deter tract builders, who were buying land and putting up houses. The City Council approved more than nine hundred home sites for development, including three hundred on South Third Street Extension that eventually became Governor's Green.

The mention of tract builders draws mixed reactions, yet Mebane's housing boom during the 2000s owed its momentum to these out-of-town developers. During the real estate explosion of the 1990s and 2000s, tract builders became the one-stop-shopping destination for the nation's home buyers, offering traditional homes, condos, and townhouses and often providing their own mortgage financing. Local home builders loathe tract builders, as the volume of these projects undercuts the construction prices that smaller builders offer. Love them or hate them, tract builder projects altered the way large housing developments were constructed, and in turn, determined how communities and cities expanded.

As Mebane continued to transition, so did First Savings and Loan. To say that First Savings had a veteran staff in 2002 was an understatement, as the length of service for its employees averaged twenty-three years. Two important changes occurred in June 2002 that brought one career to a close and began another one. Amy Edwards (Cannady) graduated from East Carolina in May with a degree in accounting and joined the staff on June 12. Edwards was the granddaughter of President Neal Smith and began her career as a teller and assistant for comptroller Gail Jordan.

One of the most important dates in the association's history occurred on June 30, 2002, when Neal Smith officially retired after forty-nine years. A reception was held in his honor, and hundreds of customers attended. A portrait of Smith by award-winning photographer and painter Harriet Lynch was unveiled during the event and is permanently displayed in the association's lobby.

Many individuals during the association's one hundred years have impacted the institution. Neal Smith's leadership and longevity put him at the top of that list. Under Smith's direction, First Savings truly became the institution it is today and remains a reflection of his conservative style. From the good times of the 1950s and 1960s through the constant turmoil of the 1970s and 1980s, Smith stuck to his guns with the firm conviction that a small-town association could be successful.

Of all the qualities Smith possessed, none was more important than his unwavering loyalty to the savings and loan concept. Leading is easy when times are good, and only when challenges arise is true leadership revealed. The pivotal times during the inflationary environment of the 1970s and the savings and loan crisis of the 1980s convinced Smith more than ever to stay the course as a savings and loan, as others ran from it.

First Savings never followed the conventional path of most institutions, and fittingly its CEO of forty-seven years didn't either. First Savings was not your run-of-the-mill institution, and Neal Smith didn't fit the usual mold of a financial executive.

He didn't play golf and was more comfortable driving a tractor than a golf cart. Smith enjoyed hunting quail with a bird dog rather than hunting for a lost golf ball. He admittedly was not a banker and never wanted to be, and he never apologized for not having a cell phone or not knowing how to use a computer. Neal Smith enjoyed people and was more at home with country folk than members of the country club. He always said that "it was the little guy that made [First Savings]" successful.

Neal Smith might have officially retired, but he was far from leaving the association permanently. Smith was named chairman of the board and remained on the association's loan committee. Rick Smith was named as the association's president effective July 1, 2002.

Neal Smith's accomplishments and management of the association did not create a stir in banking circles or make waves on Wall Street. The important thing was the notice and appreciation of generations of customers. In 2002 First Savings was voted as Best Mortgage Company in Alamance County by the readers of the *Burlington Times-News*. This was quite an accomplishment considering the competition from much larger institutions in Burlington. The association was also named Best Mortgage Company by *Mebane Enterprise* readers in 2006 and again in 2008.

Consolidation of the banking industry claimed another local institution in 2002 when Community Savings Bank merged with Raleigh-based Capital Bank. Three years later, Capital would come calling again, taking First State Savings Bank into its fold.

North Carolina was once referred to as the "Rip Van Winkle State," as change came very slowly in every sector of Tar Heel life. Now the state and Mebane were changing at a torrid pace. Once the nation's leader in textiles, North Carolina was now home to multinational companies with diverse products and services, and Mebane reflected that transformation. North Carolina Industrial Center shrugged off the economic slowdown, expanding its Third Street Extension campus north to West Holt Street. Tobacco and dairy farming were two more North Carolina industries going through their own evolution. Vacant and aging tobacco barns that dotted the countryside suffered the same fate as empty and rusting feed silos that once towered over thriving dairy farms which had long since gone out of business. Many of these domed silos disappeared and were replaced by tall cellular phone relay towers that stood high over fields where cattle once grazed.

North Carolina agriculture was still very strong, leading the nation in tobacco, Christmas tree, and sweet potato production. Many of its tobacco fields now sported alternative crops, including grapes. The largest of four wineries in Alamance County, the Winery at Iron Gate Farm, opened on Lynch Store Road north of Mebane, and the number of wineries in North Carolina tripled during the 2000s.

David Freshwater, owner of Freshwater's Store, passed away on November 10, 2002, and sadly an era in Mebane disappeared with him. In a time of grocery store chains and superstores, Freshwater's was a throwback to when general stores were the mainstays of local communities. Since his father Thad opened the store in 1914, Freshwater's had served generations of customers. Unlike the experience in supermarkets and convenience stores, most folks didn't run in and out of Freshwater's Store, but lingered to socialize. In return, David Freshwater was loyal to his customers, working fifty-six straight years behind the counter and rarely taking a vacation or day off. First Savings and D.L. Freshwater had a lot in common; both faced increased competition, yet each managed to carve out a successful niche market of loyal customers who desired a quality product and customer service. The business closed after Freshwater's death, and the once-busy store at the corner of Crawford and North First Street sat vacant, its peeling paint and distressed appearance looking much the same on the day the store closed as it did in decades past when the store was a thriving business.

Another weathered and decaying Mebane landmark down the road from Freshwater's was the home place of Giles Mebane, situated in the middle of twelve acres of prime real estate on the corner of North First Street and Stagecoach Road. A nineteenth-century legislator, Mebane was remembered for bringing the railroad through the town of Mebane in the mid-1800s and for introducing legislation separating the county of Alamance from its beginnings in Orange County. As Freshwater's Store passed into history, a new shopping center was approved for the Mebane property, anchored by a Food Lion grocery store.

The economic road had been rocky since the bursting of the tech bubble in 2000 and the attacks of 9/11. The Dow Jones Industrial Average had declined more than 4400 points since the decade began, closing at 7286 in October 2002. After three years of struggling, the economy began to rebound by 2003, and like most postwar economic recoveries, it began with housing. Mortgage rates fell into the 5 percent range for the first time in nearly half a century, igniting a firestorm of activity from home buying, commercial lending, and construction lending. The historic rates sent refinancing into overdrive. The economic recovery had the same look and feel as every other, but the next cycle would be like no other in American history. The nation was on the verge of another strong economic surge that would end in the near collapse of its financial system.

Since World War II, First Savings had benefitted from every housing boom that cycled through, but this economic recovery would be very different for the association as well as the country. The town of Mebane and First Savings grew up together, and for the great majority of the prior ninety-four years, they depended on each other. Local folks turned to the association to save and borrow the money to purchase or build a home, and although First Savings still depended on Mebane, Mebane no longer depended on First Savings. The reason was simple: the area's population was changing, and the days when everyone knew everyone else in the town were slipping away. The incredible growth of the previous thirty years brought people from all parts of the country, and most of these folks had few ties to Mebane or North Carolina. Many newcomers blended in, embraced the local culture, and often took leadership roles, while others didn't identify with Mebane at all. The Census Bureau estimated that by 2000, 25 percent of Alamance County workers commuted to jobs outside the county. Newcomers who commuted to a job in another city related more with where they worked than where they lived, creating "Two Mebanes." The Old Mebane comprised those who either grew up in town or had spent most of their lives here, while the New Mebane were folks who were new to town and spent little time getting to know the city they now called home.

Attorney Charles Davis related a story about one New Mebane couple who lived south of town but knew very little about the community. That lack of knowledge was exposed when they contacted Davis for legal advice. When asked about setting up an appointment, they asked for directions to his office on Center Street, admitting they had lived in Mebane for two years but had never been to downtown. Like everything else, the definition and perception of community and hometown were changing.

The differences between Old and New Mebane were having a definite effect on First Savings. Commercial banks and credit unions attracted the New Mebane customers, and while First Savings' limited product line was a hit with the Old Mebane crowd, that too was changing. Up until the 1970s, nearly 90 percent of the association's depositors also had their personal homes financed with First Savings. By 2000, less than 10 percent of its customers had both a mortgage and deposit account with the association. Most of the association's depositors in the twenty-first century were retirees with little or no debt, enjoying the simplicity of a hometown institution. Borrowers, on the other hand, were usually younger, with credit cards, kids, and cars to pay for, and with little or no ties to the institution. Relationships had been the key to past success, but the illusion of a loyal customer base was eroding as finance in the twenty-first century was a rate-focused and product-driven business. First Savings, once the center of home lending for Mebane, had become just another face in a growing financial crowd.

Both Mebanes certainly shared international concerns at this time. Convinced that weapons of mass destruction were in the hands of Saddam Hussein, the United States invaded Iraq in 2003. Operation Iraqi Freedom, coupled with Operation Enduring Freedom which began in Afghanistan in 2001, would dominate U.S. foreign policy well into the next decade. These two wars cost the United States over $12 billion per month by 2009 and nearly five thousand American lives. The cost of this military action, entitlement programs, and the severe recession that surfaced later in the decade placed monetary strains on a U.S. federal deficit that approached $12 trillion by 2009.

No one knew it, but by the early 2000s, the financial crisis of 2008 was gaining speed down the fast track toward an eventual train wreck. The crisis remains a multilayered and complex disaster that was years in the making and which will take years to correct. This financial tragedy continues to unfold as this history is being written, and although its causes are many, the early indications suggest that the odd combination of assumptions, good intentions, and greed were central to its formation. This economic crossroads is covered extensively in this history, as this catastrophic event changed First Savings, the nation, its banking system, the financial values of Americans, and the government's role in private enterprise.

The crisis, like others that came before, was born out of the nation's prosperity. The rapid escalation of real estate prices that began in earnest in the 1990s exploded during the 2000s, reinforcing the assumption that real estate always appreciates in value. Since the Great Depression, with few exceptions, this notion had proven to be true. This conventional thinking was a key element to the crisis, as investors in the mortgage, construction, and financial industries took risks and formulated business strategies centered around this basic assumption. Likewise, Americans came to believe that real estate appreciation was the one true constant in an otherwise unpredictable financial world, and they amassed debt with homes used as collateral.

Following World War II, housing had its boom times, but the rise in home values during the 1990s and 2000s outpaced anything in the postwar era. From 1997 to 2006 the average price of a home rose 124 percent. This rapid rise priced more and more people out of the housing market, making the American Dream virtually unattainable for first-time home buyers and low-income borrowers. To some observers, the financial prosperity of the day was turning America into the land of the free and the home of the haves and have nots, and real estate was at the center of the debate. Reasoning surfaced that if low-income and first-time borrowers could buy houses, they could raise their standard of living while establishing a base for building wealth, benefitting not only themselves but the overall economy.

Upper- and middle-class Americans had achieved the American Dream for generations. Shouldn't low-income borrowers be given the same opportunity? The problem was that many of these would-be borrowers could not qualify for a conventional mortgage loan under existing lending standards. Once again, hard and fast changes came to a mortgage industry that had always adapted to its environment. But there was a price, as the good intentions that lowered the bar for loan qualifications opened the door for riskier loans.

The reality was that the incomes of first-time home buyers were stretched to the limit, and buying homes seemed unrealistic as many individuals simply could not qualify for home loans under most underwriting standards. But this was the twenty-first century, and there had to be a way to transform these renters into home owners. Just as Gordon Gekko stated, investors saw an opportunity, and it wouldn't take long for mortgage lending's "evolutionary spirit" to find a way to tap a new market.

Legislative changes, market forces, and demand altered mortgage lending, and a variety of different and creative loans made home financing more attainable. A significant change had come about two decades before, in 1982 amid record-high interest rates, when Congress passed the Alternative Mortgage Transactions Parity Act (AMTPA), creating a host of nontraditional mortgages, including adjustable-rate mortgages, interest-only mortgages, and balloon-payment loans, among others.

In 2003 it wasn't interest rates that prevented first-time home buyers from entering the market as they had in 1982. In fact, rates were at record lows. The culprit was loan qualification standards themselves, and the timing seemed right for a change. Consumer confidence had returned, as the country was moving forward after 9/11, and housing led the charge. Investors saw low-income home buyers as an untapped and potentially lucrative market, and the exotic and flexible loan products born out of the 1980s served as the platform in a new credit environment.

These loan options were used in the form of subprime mortgages as an alternative to traditional home financing. Subprime loans were designed for applicants with poor credit, high debt, and other factors that prevented them from obtaining conventional home mortgages. Although subprime lending had been around for years, it was risky and was never considered mainstream lending. In the past, lenders had steered clear of subprime investments because default rates by borrowers were high. As mortgage products changed, the stigma of subprime loans changed with them. In 1994 the subprime market made up just 5 percent of all mortgages. By 2006 subprime loans accounted for 20 percent of the entire mortgage market.

Many of these loans—with names like "Alt-A," "low-documentation loans," "stated-income loans," and a host of others—allowed buyers to enter the housing market for the first time. Variations of adjustable-rate mortgages (ARMs) were used extensively in the subprime arena and would come back to haunt investors and borrowers alike. Many of these ARMs provided a borrower with an initial low interest rate that could adjust or reprice with a different rate in the future. With the assumption that real estate values always rise, the thinking was that buyers with an initial ARM could refinance in a year or two, locking in a more favorable long-term fixed rate. In 2005, 23 percent of all mortgages generated were adjustable-rate mortgages.

And then there was greed. Many analysts believed the risk associated with subprime mortgages was reduced and even eliminated by securitization, the process of buying and selling mortgages. Securitization, unlike subprime mortgages, was mainstream lending. The process by which loans are bundled together and sold in the form of mortgage-backed securities (MBSs) and collateralized debt obligations (CDOs) was the powerful engine that financed homes in America.

Securitization, like the mortgage industry, had morphed into a complicated investing process that included derivatives and securities with complex risk structures in which investors could make higher returns by assuming more risk. Designed to create liquidity for lenders while spreading risk among investors, securitization worked well in a conventional lending environment, and it was assumed it could work with subprime loans. Fannie Mae and Freddie Mac were banking on it. These government-sponsored enterprises bought, packaged, and sold subprime mortgages in the form of MBSs and CDOs, adding credibility to these risky securities.

The upside of increased returns attracted investors to what was always considered the boring and safe arena of home lending. As profits rolled in, it wasn't long before subprime investing strategies became the centerpiece of investment portfolios of many financial institutions. Large investment banks on Wall Street purchased subprime MBSs and CDOs, often repackaging these instruments with other investments and reselling them to other financial entities.

Although the subprime meltdown was several years away, some observers saw the potential for problems. A September 30, 1999, *New York Times* article stated, "The Fannie Mae Corporation is easing the credit requirements on loans. The action ... will encourage ... banks to extend home mortgages to individuals whose credit is generally not good enough.... Fannie Mae ... has been under increasing pressure from the Clinton Administration to expand mortgage loans among low and moderate income people ... borrowers whose incomes ... credit ratings and savings are not good enough.... Fannie Mae is taking on significantly more risk.... The government-subsidized corporation may run into trouble ... prompting a government rescue."

On the other side of the equation were first-time and low-income borrowers whose chances of owning a home diminished every time home prices climbed. Subprime lending changed all that. Low rates and easy credit terms and qualification standards lured folks who never dreamed they could own a home. Lenders, afraid to stick their toe in the risky waters of subprime lending, felt more confident when the nation's two largest mortgage lenders, Countrywide and Washington Mutual, became major players in the subprime market.

With a strong market of investors willing to buy subprime loans, the only thing mortgage brokers had to do was originate the loans. This was, after all, mortgage lending, and most investors felt that there wasn't really a downside. But indeed there was. If defaults did occur, investors who had assumed more risk by purchasing these MBSs and CDOs could lose money, and lots of it. Most observers felt that this double-barreled scenario was highly unlikely and could happen only if real estate values fell and unemployment rose. They were right.

By the mid-2000s, all the assumptions that drove mortgage lending were working, and the results were paying off. A new era of easy credit had arrived, and mortgage lenders and investors from Wall Street to Charlotte rode the housing bandwagon down the road to profitability. In 2005 and 2006, there were no bank failures in the United States, and everything was right with the financial world. Subprime lending, once considered risky, had become a major conduit for housing finance. The time bomb began to tick.

As the lending world charted its new future, First Savings celebrated part of its past. Attorney Lee Settle had been a close and dear friend of the association for more than fifty years. From loan closings and legal advice to serving on the board of directors, there was not a part of First Savings and Loan that Lee Settle did not know intimately. The board honored Settle at the monthly meeting in May 2004 for his many years of service. The meeting was more of a standup comedy hour as Settle kept the board entertained with stories and memories in his unique and unabashed style. It would be the last time Lee Settle would meet with the board, as he passed away in September at age eighty-five. First Savings had lost one of its pioneers. Neal Smith commented that Settle was "someone you could trust and what he told you, you could hang your hat on. He always looked out for First Savings, and I trusted him with anything."

One afternoon in October 2004, someone new to the area came into First Savings to open a savings account. When asked how he found out about First Savings, the customer replied, "You have the highest rating of any institution in this area by Bankrate.com." Surprised, Rick Smith followed up and found that the association was rated "Five Stars" by the Internet company for safety and soundness. The closest any other area institution scored was "Four Stars." The conversation with this individual revealed not only something positive about the association but also showed where the next generation of customers was getting its information. Simple Internet business applications that began in the 1990s exploded during the 2000s, yet the 'Net was something First Savings had never utilized, other than opening a basic informational Web site in 2003. The Internet was obviously the future, and First Savings would have to embrace it sooner or later.

The first waves of the financial crisis came ashore for First Savings in 2004. From 2003 to 2006, when subprime mortgage lending was at its peak, the association's loan production fell to its lowest levels in twenty-five years. It wasn't subprime loans that First Savings was missing out on; it was the easy credit environment. Mortgage brokers, armed with easy credit terms and products, ate local lenders for lunch, luring away once-loyal customers. By the end of 2003 the association's mortgage portfolio had fallen nearly 20 percent as refinances and payoffs placed the institution in a dilemma, raising a difficult yet familiar question. Should the association cut interest rates and lower credit standards to compete with mortgage brokers or stay its conservative course? The rate swings of the 1970s and 1980s had doomed institutions that kept mortgages in-house, revealing the downside of the savings and loan concept.

First Savings had seen rates fall before, but had never in its history lost this much mortgage business. Higher rates in the long run could offset any short-term gains made by drastically lowering mortgage rates. The association's equity capital or reserve crossed the $9 million mark in June 2003, and it did so through sound and conservative decisions, not by taking unnecessary risks. It wasn't easy, but the association once again bit the bullet, remaining conservative and keeping interest rates and lending standards at an acceptable level.

Some small associations were not as fortunate to have a strong financial reserve. In 2008 Rick Smith received a call from a small-town thrift's CEO whose institution was in dire straits. The CEO stated that he had reduced mortgage rates during the mid-2000s to compete with mortgage brokers. When interest rates rose later in the decade, the institution was on the brink of failure and looking to merge its operations with a healthy institution.

National trends in retail also affected local conditions in Mebane. One word that strikes fear in the hearts of small business owners is "Walmart." Just as downtown Mebane was claiming its new identity, the announcement came in 2003 that Walmart and Lowe's Home Improvement were coming to town. These retail titans would certainly place pressure on traditional Mebane businesses, but downtown was no longer the retail center it used to be. Reliable Furniture and others, once part of that era, had closed, and in their places were specialty shops and service-related businesses. Undaunted, Lacy Bennett joined downtown's renaissance, opening the Elegant Relic on Fourth Street. Bennett later moved the store to its now-familiar location on Clay Street.

Walmart opened ahead of schedule in January 2006, becoming the anchor store for Garrett Crossing on Mebane Oaks Road. Business and store openings that once garnered front-page coverage in the *Mebane Enterprise* were occurring with such rapidity that they were often relegated to smaller articles in the back pages of the town's weekly newspaper. One article that appeared in the *Enterprise* in 2006 recognized the new businesses that had opened during the year, which totaled thirty-one. Many folks still living in Mebane could remember when there were hardly thirty-one businesses in the entire town.

Walmart was an American success story, one that the banking community sought to imitate. Banks applied the business model of the Arkansas retailer to the financial world by redesigning themselves to be the one-stop shop for all financial needs. By the 2000s it was evident that this approach was working. Banks offered an array of financial services, from car loans and mortgages to mutual funds. But something was lost in the process when quantity replaced quality, and try as they may, banks could not substitute the days gone by when one-on-one service brought people through the door. Financial institutions were caught in a balancing act between speed, efficiency, and individual customer needs. That, too, was changing as customers were drawn to the convenience of ATMs and online bill paying, thus avoiding bank lobbies altogether.

While the American economy is hard to understand and even more difficult to predict, one thing is certain: the country's economic health is tied directly to consumer spending as more than 60 percent of the nation's economic activity is connected to the pocketbooks of American consumers. The Greatest Generation, by necessity, was forced into saving money during the Depression and World War II, and these lessons shaped their financial choices later in life. First Savings Director Ned Gauldin commented about his experiences growing up in rural

Virginia, "You really didn't have money anyway, but if you did, you didn't spend it. Everybody grew their own food, made their own clothes, so you didn't really spend money for anything you needed."

The difference between needs and wants changed over the years as America prospered. Baby boomers and Generation Xers grew up in a completely different consumer culture, learning to borrow and spend as tremendous borrowing potential became available through financial products and options unavailable to their parents. By the 2000s, the double-edged sword of debt became another factor in the coming financial crisis. As the savings rate of Americans slipped closer to zero, ways to borrow and spend became easier.

The process of home refinancing changed dramatically over the years, and by the 2000s, like the credit card, the home equity loan transformed one's house into an all-purpose loan option. As home values soared and interest rates fell, home owners often tied multiple mortgages to their houses, pulling out increased equity. Cash from home equity loans more than doubled from $627 billion in 2001 to $1.428 trillion by 2005, driving both consumer spending and the economy. Americans enjoy a wealth of freedom in every sector of life, including financial choices. Many of these choices came back to haunt Americans as consumers found themselves drowning in debt. Credit card defaults rose, and home foreclosures increased at an alarming rate. Alamance County foreclosures increased 250 percent between 1998 and 2003.

Any thought of an economic crisis was the last thing on the minds of Mebane citizens as the city continued to march to the steady drumbeat of commercial and residential development. Although most new ventures came from outside investors who speculated in the city's future, perhaps the town's best success story was the Mebane Company itself: Kingsdown. For over a century, one could not talk about Mebane without mentioning White Furniture and Kingsdown in the same breath. For the majority of the twentieth century, the mattress maker often lived in the shadow of White, which had developed a national and worldwide reputation in its early years. Although the two companies operated just across the railroad tracks from each other, in some ways they were light years apart.

The closing of White during the 1990s left Kingsdown as the city's oldest employer. Unlike White, Kingsdown thrived on the cutting edge of both technology and innovation in a rapidly changing world of manufacturing. Thriving long after White Furniture had closed its doors, Kingsdown earned its own place as a world leader in mattress production, serving retailers in twenty-five countries. In 2003 Kingsdown opened its first Sleep to Live retail store at Southpoint Mall in Durham. The mattress maker celebrated one hundred years in operations a year later with the purchase of the former Royal Home Fashions building on Oakwood Street Extension. Unlike its century-old downtown building, the one-hundred-thousand-square-foot facility was on one level and conducive to high-speed manufacturing. At full capacity Kingsdown's Mebane plant could produce one thousand mattresses a day, quite a long way from its humble beginnings on the second floor of Cook's Mill. Kingsdown's iconic downtown facility is now used mostly for office and storage space.

Kingsdown's move in 2003 brought to an end the long and storied manufacturing presence in downtown Mebane. Lured again by transportation, the town's manufacturing base had reestablished itself south and east of the city, beginning in the early 1970s, predominantly in two key industrial areas. South Third Street Extension was home to Kidde Corporation, Sandvik, and the companies that populated two industrial parks. Oakwood Street Extension was anchored by Armacell, AKG, Meadwestvaco (Mebane Packaging), and now Kingsdown.

In 2004, financial institutions expanded their exposure on Mebane's south side when both Truliant and the State Employees Credit Union (SECU) built new branches across the street from each other on what was now a very busy Highway 119 South. The exception to this southern expansion came when First State Savings Bank (Capital Bank) moved from its familiar Fifth Street location to the vacant Fidelity Bank building one block to the west on Fourth Street.

The strong presence of Truliant and SECU demonstrated the growth and popularity of credit unions in an increasingly crowded financial world. For decades, credit unions were content with taking a backseat to banks and other financial institutions by serving a select membership, such as teachers or federal workers. That changed during the 1990s when credit unions broadened their identity and membership possibilities and offered an array of financial services. The once-passive credit union industry took an aggressive approach, becoming a financial force that gave banks a run for their money, no pun intended. Credit unions made no bones about it: they directly challenged banks for the consumer dollar while enjoying a tax-exempt advantage over the banking industry. An expanded product line and lenient membership requirements led to the tremendous growth of credit unions, and North Carolina's State Employees Credit Union became the second-largest credit union in the nation. The banking industry believed that the expansion and increased competition from tax-exempt credit unions gave the latter an unfair competitive edge. "If it looks like a bank and acts like a bank, it should be taxed like a bank," said one North Carolina banking executive. The loyal following of credit unions included legislators on Capitol Hill, and any calls for credit union taxation fell on deaf ears.

First Savings Director Dr. David Jones spent his entire medical career in the town of Mebane, practicing first with the Aycock Mebane Clinic and later the Kernodle Clinic. In December 2003 Jones opened the Mebane Medical Clinic at the Brookhollow Shopping Center, seeing more than thirty patients the first day. The increasingly complicated world of health care never seemed to phase Dr. Jones's dedication to his patients, and this loyalty didn't stop when folks left his clinic. Jones routinely visited patients in their homes, and he could be seen walking the sidelines every Friday night, volunteering at Eastern Alamance football games. Jones's presence was known in community activities and organizations, including local schools, and he guided the association's funding of numerous education projects. As a physician, Jones was interested more in people than the details of copays or insurance coverage. His dedication to others can be detailed in countless ways, but one example illustrates his willingness to help anybody, anytime, anywhere.

Dr. Jones came to the rescue of John Forlines, an executive with the Bank of Granite, during a convention in Puerto Rico in 2001. Forlines suffered a severe fall and was transported to a hospital in San Juan. Being out of the country and needing immediate health care can be a nightmare in itself, but Forlines was in his eighties at the time, further complicating the problem. Dr. Jones accompanied Forlines to the hospital and stayed with him for a few days. Jones later described the hospital conditions as deplorable, and he was genuinely concerned for Forlines's care and safety. John Forlines made a full recovery from what could have been a life-threatening situation and never forgot the kindness that Dr. Jones showed him. The doctor's personal attention to Mr. Forlines earned Jones the unofficial title of "Surgeon General" of the North Carolina Bankers Association by President Thad Woodard. Sadly, Dr. Jones was not nominated as a director at the association's shareholders' meeting for 2004, ending fifteen years of service. The number of board directors was reduced to five as Jones's seat was left unfilled.

Mebane's rush toward the interstate finally decided the future of the Arrowhead Golf Course. Situated squarely in the middle of the town's commercial expansion, the course was for sale by its owners, the Robert Bosch Company, but had remained open for local golfers. The land off Mebane Oaks Road was just too valuable to remain a golf course, and on September 16, 2003, Arrowhead's last foursome played the course's final round.

Arrowhead was more than just a golf course. Its friendly social atmosphere had attracted golfers young and old since the early 1960s. Like many locals, First Savings Director Ned Gauldin had played for decades with the same group of golfers and voiced his sadness over the course's closing. Some who didn't play golf at all also found the course appealing; folks would flock to Arrowhead when a deep snow came, as its steep hills made for great sledding. Although the course closed, no immediate announcements about its future were forthcoming, and the golf course sat idle until 2005 when the City Council approved a long-range plan for the property that included both commercial and residential development. What had people talking the most was the fifty-two-acre project to be developed by Tanger Outlet Center that would bring big-name retail stores to town. Elements and specifics of the proposed development changed numerous times, but what affected the project more than anything was a deteriorating economy. The construction of roads and infrastructure began by the mid-2000s, but the recession that emerged in 2008 put the brakes on the project. With so many intangibles surrounding the nation's financial system and economy, some thought the project would never come to pass. Tanger never wavered from its commitment, moving forward with the project in 2009.

With the announcement of the Arrowhead project came the news that the North Carolina Industrial Center had landed Florida-based Badcock. The home furnishings company expanded operations into North Carolina and Virginia in the midst of the country's housing explosion, and Mebane was the perfect place for a distribution center. The opening of Badcock was a prime example of what occurred in Mebane during the late 1990s and 2000s. If one company closed—or another, like Mercedes, chose a different city—it seemed that another company was there to take its place.

Still one firm decided to pass on moving to town. Synthon's on-again, off-again commitment to bring its pharmaceutical headquarters to Mebane had been plagued by lawsuits and zoning issues for six years. The company felt that the Research Triangle Park was a better fit, ending its attempts to relocate south of the city.

As new manufacturing reshaped Mebane's future, some forgotten structures disappeared that reflected the town's industrial past. The ongoing renovation of the new library in the former Dixie Yarn / Stowe building saw the demolition of two large water towers that had been part of the textile operation. People hardly noticed these old rusting structures that once towered above the thriving textile mill, although hundreds of pigeons flew routinely from the towers to the feed silos at Rice's Feed Mill on North Sixth Street. The silos, part of the once-active mill, were also torn down in 2004. The former feed mill had long since closed and was home to Griles Heating and Air.

The only thing that seemed to match the extraordinary commercial and industrial development of the mid-2000s was the town's seemingly unstoppable housing market. Many of the same factors that brought industry and commercial development to Mebane drew in home buyers. Still, home owners were looking for more than just price and location. Besides small-town charm, one of the first things newcomers with children look for in a community is the quality of the school system. They were not disappointed, as Hawfields Middle, Woodlawn Middle, South Mebane Elementary, and E.M. Yoder Elementary were all named Schools of Distinction by the State Department of Public Instruction in 2003.

Many of these newcomers were drawn to housing developments offered by tract builders who continued their influence on local home building. In 2004 one of Mebane's largest subdivisions was approved east of town on a 138-acre tract that was once part of the Mebane Lumber Company. What became Ashbury was typical of subdivisions of the 2000s as the 525-home development offered a variety of options, including single-family homes, duplexes, and a retirement center for seniors. Home owners were now looking for more than just a neighborhood, and amenities such as clubhouses, pools, and health clubs became common in new developments.

After celebrating the twenty-fifth anniversary of its Mebane plant a year earlier, A.O. Smith laid off 60 of its workers. Still one of the town's biggest employers, the company's workforce had dwindled to just 385 from its glory days when the company employed more than 800. The company cited the economy and foreign competition for the layoffs. In some ways, A.O. Smith was a reflection of what seemed like a daily occurrence in North Carolina manufacturing. The state had been losing industry to cheap foreign labor for years, and the problem was not only getting worse, it was accelerating. More and more U.S. companies were sending jobs to Mexico and other countries, and imports from China were exploding. North Carolina's unemployment figures told the story, as 5.2 percent of Tar Heel workers were now out of work.

Mortgage loans weren't headed to Mexico, but they surely weren't coming to First Savings either. The topic of discussion at the association's annual shareholders' meeting in February 2005 was First Savings' plummeting loan production. Competition from mortgage brokers resulted in a second straight year of poor loan originations. From 2004 to 2006, loan originations fell nearly 35 percent as the association averaged $5,808,000 in mortgage volume per year. Put in perspective, mortgage loans that made up 69 percent of the association's total assets in 2000 made up just 45 percent of total assets by 2006.

For the first time in its history, First Savings seemed to be on the outside looking in, as borrowers routinely bypassed the association for better terms from mortgage brokers and other lenders. By far, the hardest-hit loan product for First Savings was construction lending. Mebane had more houses going up than Carter had liver pills, and more were being built every day as speculation building was at its peak. Banks rolled out the red carpet for builders, large and small, with incentives and favorable loan terms that First Savings simply could not match.

This cold, hard reality hit home in 2004 when First Savings did not originate one construction loan during the entire year. Although it is hard to interpret some of the association's earlier minutes, an entire year with no construction loans had to be a first for the association, at least in its post-Depression history. This was a bitter pill to swallow, and with lending changing so rapidly, it looked like construction lending—the reason the institution was founded—might be a thing of the past. With builders defecting to other lenders, the association ended its forty-year relationship with the Home Builders Association of Alamance County.

But there was a bigger picture here. The association wasn't just losing construction loans. A new credit environment now existed in America, and obtaining a loan for virtually anything from a house to a computer was simple. First Savings watched nervously as its loan portfolio walked out the door, wondering how any conservative lender could compete in this anything-goes mortgage environment.

The tug of war that existed between the lucrative bottom line and the risks associated with subprime lending seemed justified by the virtues of an ownership society, a philosophy that had floated around for years and was encouraged by the actions of both the Clinton and Bush administrations. The initial success of the subprime mortgage experiment further reinforced the argument, and the nation seemed on the verge of a new era of prosperity.

In his second inauguration speech on January 20, 2005, George W. Bush gave his endorsement, stating, "In America's ideal of freedom, citizens find the dignity and security of economic independence, instead of laboring on the edge of subsistence. This is the broader definition of liberty that motivated the Homestead Act, the Social Security Act, and the GI Bill of Rights. And now we will extend this vision by reforming great institutions to serve the needs of our time. To give every American a stake in the promise and future of our country, we will...build an ownership society. We will widen the ownership of homes and businesses...preparing our people for the challenges of life in a free society. By making every citizen an agent of his or her own destiny, we will give our fellow Americans greater freedom from want and fear, and make our society more prosperous and just and equal."

With Wall Street and now Washington firmly in its corner, the mortgage industry's assembly line shifted into overdrive. Loan approval took seconds instead of weeks as automated loan underwriting became common. Hungry investors from Wall Street pumped billions into the mortgage market, buying subprime loans and keeping the money pipeline flowing to the lenders. But there was a small problem. The loan pool of acceptable applicants began to shrink as more Americans jumped into the housing market. To entice more loan applicants in the door, loan qualifications were lowered even further, allowing applicants with poor financial histories and low credit scores to obtain mortgage loans. Loan standards eventually became so bad that mortgages were approved to borrowers who, in some cases, had "no income, no job or assets," referred to as "Ninja loans." As one mortgage broker said of these mortgages, "The only real qualification for these loans was that you had to have a pulse." By 2005, borrowers, lenders, investors, and real estate agents were on board with a lending product that was reshaping home ownership in America. Subprime mortgages hit their peak that year with more than $625 billion in loans extended nationwide.

With a variety of loans available for almost any and every applicant, it appeared that the mortgage industry was poised to accomplish what the savings and loan industry had set out to do in the first place: making the American Dream of home ownership a reality for everyone. Low-income borrowers were enjoying the fruits of owning a home, many for the first time. Many of these new home owners had been renters, and this new wave of home buying was taking its toll on landlords. A First Savings customer who owned several rental houses complained that half of his houses were now vacant, stating, "I've cut my rent and even quit asking for a deposit, but people can buy a house now with no money down. Why would anyone want to rent when they can buy a house?" The sign of the times could be seen at apartment complexes that offered free rent for six months and other incentives to attract tenants.

Consumerism had consumed the nation. Ironically, at a time when money was plentiful, consumers struggled to save money. In 2005 the savings rate in America went negative for the first time since the Great Depression as Americans now spent more than they were making in income.

Mortgages of every kind, from subprime to jumbo, were in big demand in Mebane as the area's housing market steamed ahead. The average price of a house in Mebane reached a record high of $171,450 in 2005, an 11 percent increase in just one year. Mebane home prices had doubled in the past eleven years, and owning a home in Mebane seemed a sure bet.

On another gambling note, state lawmakers passed the North Carolina Education Lottery in 2005. No more day trips to Danville, Virginia, or stopping at a convenience store in South Carolina on the way home from the beach to buy a lottery ticket. Tommy's Mini Mart, across from First Savings, sold a ticket worth $1 million to a lucky customer in 2008.

Historically real estate had been a good wager, and the odds of winning seemed to grow every day. Commercial development along Mebane's new business district at Mebane Oaks Road and Highway 119 South took on a life of its own with the completion of Walmart and Lowe's Home Improvement. More restaurants were on the way, including Ruby Tuesday, Sonic Drive-In, Smithfield's, and Blue Ribbon Diner. But a few speed bumps were found amid this building fast track. In 2005 Winn-Dixie Food Stores closed all its North Carolina locations, including the anchor store in Mebane Oaks Market Place. Lowe's Foods followed later that year, closing its Fifth and Washington Street location, now Z-Bowl. Peaches N Cream, a Mebane tradition since 1970, closed as well. Originally part of May Apparel and known in its early days as Kidswear, Peaches N Cream developed a regional following for its line of children's clothing.

It seemed that change was occurring at light speed in 2005 as some of Mebane's best-known and oldest companies were bought and sold. Hawkins-Tripp Realty became part of real estate giant Coldwell Banker. Crawford Amick sold Amick Ford to Durham car dealer Bell Ford, and Warren's Drug Store was sold as well. Although the Amick name disappeared from the front of the dealership on West Center, the Warren's name lived on. Warren's Drug had been a Clay Street fixture since the 1930s and had operated in its familiar corner store at Clay and Fourth streets since the 1960s. Gone were the days when Doug Issac, Calvin Oakley, and Ken Capes stood behind the pharmacy counter. Gone, too, was the store's soda fountain, which attracted everyone from high school kids ordering milk shakes after school to retirees for morning coffee. As that generation passed, so did the business itself, which moved to its new building in the Oak Manor Shopping Center on North First Street. Warren's legacy grew again in 2008 when its owner Stephen Joyce opened a second store in Kingsdown Commons Shopping Center south of town.

CVS Pharmacy opted for a new location, purchasing the McClure Funeral Home property at the intersection of South Fifth and Mebane Oaks Road. The older two-story home was replaced by a modern drugstore next to popular breakfast spot, Biscuitville. McClure wasted little time breaking ground for a new funeral home on South Third Street near the new post office.

The year 2005 affected Mebanites, and all Americans, in a climatic sense as well. Summertime in the South means tropical storms and an occasional hurricane. Most folks who live along the southern coastlines learn to live with the warnings and occasional evacuations. Many of these storms pass by harmlessly while others change the lives of those who experience their fury. Hurricane Hazel in 1954 still generates stories for many North Carolinians, as does Hugo from 1989. Most recently the 1999 devastation left by Hurricane Floyd remains fresh in Tar Heel memory.

The unusually active and deadly storm season of 2005 packed its biggest punch when Hurricane Katrina slammed into the Gulf Coast on August 29. Katrina's storm surge quickly overwhelmed the levee system of New Orleans, flooding 80 percent of the city. From Texas to Florida, the storm leveled areas of Gulfport and Biloxi, Mississippi, and forever changed the state of Louisiana. The storm took the lives of 1,836 people, causing $81.2 billion in damage. Like other cities and towns across the country, Mebane opened its wallets and hearts to those in need. Local churches and schools held fund-raisers, and many volunteers went to the Gulf to assist in cleanup and rebuilding.

Hancock Bank is a large regional institution with its home office in Gulfport. Katrina devastated many of the bank's branches throughout Mississippi and Louisiana. Amid the destruction at one branch, bank management worked under a makeshift tent and were surprised to see President George Bush looking over their shoulders as they struggled to put the pieces of their bank back together.

Regardless of change, there are things that some folks expect to remain the same, particularly in a small town. White Furniture, Kingsdown, the Dogwood Festival, and the annual Christmas Parade are just a few places and events that are synonymous with Mebane. One constant for customers of the association was walking in the front door and seeing Shelby Murphy and Janice Wright at the teller line.

Wright joined the association in 1980 after several years with CCB (now Suntrust) while Murphy began her career in 1958, working most of her life at First Savings. That kind of longevity is rare in most businesses and virtually nonexistent in the banking industry. These ladies came into the financial world at a different time, when banking was truly a relationship business, not just an advertising slogan. Wright and Murphy knew customers by name and spent more time talking about family and events around town than mortgage balances or interest rates. Relationships are still quite common in small-town institutions but are often lost on larger banks that stress the importance of getting people in and out as quickly as possible. After twenty-six and forty-eight years, respectively, Janice Wright and

Shelby Murphy both retired in 2006, bringing to a close two of the longest careers in the association's history.

Most financial institutions would not give a second thought to filling a teller position, where turnover is extremely high. Job turnover for First Savings is rare, and incredibly a vacancy had not occurred on the teller line since the 1980s. Finding the right fit for these two key positions was crucial. In January 2007 Rhonda Bowling joined First Savings with an impressive resume. Bowling began her career at Graham Savings and Loan in 1987, witnessing the changes brought on by conversions and buyouts when the thrift was bought by CCB and again when Suntrust purchased CCB itself. In August 2008 the transition of First Savings' teller line was completed when Denise Snead joined the association after a career with First State and Capital Bank.

Mebane's two business districts had opposing philosophies that were as different as their contrasting styles and customer base. Mebane Oaks Road had come a long way from the days when Junior Madden's Texaco and Arrowhead Restaurant were favorite stops along I-85. Merchant success along this busy corridor depended on volume and speed. Downtown merchants were betting that a slower-paced atmosphere would make a trip to Clay Street a shopping destination rather than a quick stop for customers. The formation of Destination Downtown had that purpose in mind as this committee organized seasonal and holiday festivals, such as the Spring Shoppers Stroll, Sunfest, the Mebane Autumn Festival, and the Hometown Holiday Celebration. By the mid-2000s Clay and surrounding streets had evolved into a curious mix of eclectic specialty shops, antique stores, restaurants, and bars. Brick Alley Antiques opened on Clay Street, offering an upscale flare that fit downtown's elegant appeal. The former Warren's Drug Store building didn't sit idle for long, opening briefly as the Market on Clay, which had a strong but short run as a downtown wine store and eatery. The Warren's building eventually returned briefly to its roots as a pharmacy in 2009 when Mebane native Ike Brady opened the Mebane Drug Store next to Dollar General, which occupied the forgotten Colonial Store building. In this modern era in which shopping malls and bank centers were the high rollers in attracting customers, downtown Mebane and First Savings were both niche players. Accepting that role and making it work would be the challenge.

Those businesses that succeeded downtown had patient and thick-skinned owners willing to take risks. Another element in the mix was the City of Mebane's restoration of historic places to make downtown more inviting. The completion of the library and renovations to the new police station were the latest additions, but the city's crowning achievement was the construction of the Veterans Garden.

The busy corner of Third and Center streets had been the perfect home to several filling stations over the years, including the Eagle Oil Company and Jeffreys and Lancaster's Texaco, among others. In 2006 the city purchased the northeast corner lot of Third and Center from its latest owner, Don Crawford Automotive, and erected one of Mebane's most recognizable and favorite landmarks. Surrounded by flowers and shrubs, Veterans Garden is a peaceful and reverent place to reflect and remember those who served in the armed forces. A brick-lined pathway, with many bricks engraved with names of local veterans, leads visitors to a waterfall set inside a five-pointed star that serves as its centerpiece. In 2007 the Garden Clubs of North Carolina dedicated the Blue Star Highway Marker at the Garden, honoring all veterans who served in the military. A similar marker had been erected at the corner of Washington and Fifth streets in the 1950s, honoring veterans from both World Wars and Korea.

Over five hundred people attended the formal dedication of Veterans Garden on September 10, and the memorial quickly became the capstone to downtown, and with it, new and lasting community traditions. Mebane always flew the Stars and Stripes from downtown power poles during the Fourth of July and other national holidays. Now flags honoring the VFW, POWs, and the United States were permanently displayed in the Garden. Formal ceremonies for Veterans Day and Memorial Day took on deeper meaning, and events such as the annual Christmas tree lighting held during the Hometown Holiday Celebration brought more folks to downtown.

Maybe it was Veterans Garden that did it, or the renovations and openings of Clay and Center street businesses, but the atmosphere downtown was certainly different. Eastern Alamance High School thought so, reviving the traditional homecoming parade in the fall of 2006. Local farmers, once a familiar sight on city streets when the tobacco warehouses were in their heyday, returned to the corner of Third and Clay streets as a weekend farmers market sprang up during the spring and summer months. Ironically the market made its home where the tobacco warehouses had thrived for half a century.

Mebane has had its share of horrific fires that changed the course of the city's history, but the human sides of these events provide the real story. Harold Sykes, Sammy Wilson, and Tim Bradley are three names that Christina Lindsay will likely never forget. In October 2006 fire claimed Lindsay's home on Ben Wilson Road, south of town. The loss of her home was bad enough, but it could have been much worse. Sykes and Wilson spotted the blaze and alerted the Mebane Fire Department while assisting Lindsay to safety. Veteran firefighter Tim Bradley arrived on the scene before emergency vehicles and learned that Lindsay's young son, Nathan, was still trapped inside the burning structure. Time was crucial, and Bradley knew it. Without proper equipment or backup, Bradley entered the smoke-filled home alone, searching for signs of the boy. Bradley discovered the unconscious child on the floor and managed to lift him through a window to awaiting EMTs. Nathan survived the experience but was badly burned, and Bradley himself suffered injuries during the rescue.

Both Wilson and Sykes received Life Saving Awards from the Mebane Fire Department. Two years earlier, Bradley had been named North Carolina's Fireman of the Year. For his lifesaving actions in October 2006, Bradley received the Medal of Valor from the Mebane Fire Department and the National Firehouse Heroism Award. Tim Bradley will humbly tell you that he was just doing his job that day and that God was doing His. For those who live in Mebane, the distinctive sound of the town's fire siren is as common as the diesel horn of a passing train. Yet both are often tuned out as folks go about their busy day. Thankfully, people like Tim Bradley, with uncommon courage, hear something very different when that alarm sounds.

Not all actions are lifesavers, but some still carry great consequence. Neal Smith has had some pretty good ideas over the years, but perhaps none like the hunch he had in November 2006 that saved the association hundreds of thousands of dollars. Smith walked into his son's office one day and sat down, and what he said next caught his son Rick Smith totally by surprise. "Son, we need to go ahead and sell a large chunk of our Freddie Mac stock before the end of the year."

One of the responsibilities the younger Smith assumed when taking over as CEO in 2002 was handling the association's investment portfolio. With interest rates at all-time lows, the portfolio was struggling, with the exception of the Freddie Mac stock that was now worth almost a half a million dollars. Neal Smith's suggestion of selling such a prime asset seemed outrageous.

"Dad, you cannot be serious?"

"I am very serious, and I think we should sell another large block of it after the first of the year. This will give a boost for your bottom line at the end of the year, and when we sell some more of it in January, you'll get a shot of income to start the year."

"Dad, Freddie Mac is the best thing we have right now and kicking off a lot of income. We can't do this right now, not with interest rates so low!"

Neal Smith punctuated his argument with a chilling statement. "Rick, I have a gut feeling that something very bad is going to happen with the Freddie Mac stock someday, and we need to sell it while we can."

Neal Smith had no idea how prophetic his statement would be. Securitization had transformed mortgage lending into big business with big profits. Freddie Mac and Fannie Mae were at the pinnacle of their success, due in part to the exploding subprime mortgage market. From 2002 to 2006 the combined purchases of subprime mortgages by Fannie Mae and Freddie Mac rose from $38 billion to $175 billion per year. Securitization of subprime lending increased from 54 percent to 75 percent of all mortgage loans by 2006, and nearly all of these loans passed through these two mortgage giants. Of the $12 trillion mortgage market in 2006, $1.3 trillion were made up of subprime loans, and the demand was rising along with Freddie Mac and Fannie Mae stock.

First Savings followed Neal Smith's advice in December 2006 and again in January 2007, selling most of the association's Freddie Mac stock for around seventy dollars per share. In less than eighteen months, the government would take control of both Freddie and Fannie as the financial crisis surfaced, and the stock of both companies became worthless.

The financial crisis of 2008 was still more than a year away, and the sale of the Freddie Mac stock came at the best possible time. The financial crisis that emerged in late 2007 will continue well into the next decade. The short-term impact of the crisis and the recession that followed were devastating, and the long-term effects of the crisis are not yet fully known.

The crisis itself was not one specific event but rather a series of events that worked in concert to create the perfect financial storm. The first wave of that storm, starting a chain reaction within the financial system, was the collapse of the subprime mortgage market. Complicated by a severe recession and high unemployment, the crisis mushroomed to all areas of the economy, threatening the entire financial system. Once these forces were set in motion, the crisis intensified, moving from the subprime sector to the conventional mortgage market by 2009.

Initially, when the crisis surfaced, the generally accepted perception was that this entire fiasco resulted from low-income borrowers who defaulted on mortgages they never should have received under lowered underwriting standards. This explanation is absolutely true, but not the entire story. Low-income borrowers weren't the only folks getting loans that went bad. Easy credit standards permeated all levels of mortgage lending, allowing middle- and high-income but debt-laden borrowers to obtain loans as well. Many of these high-risk loans were stated-income mortgages (often referred to as "overstated-income loans") where the borrower's actual income is never verified; therefore, applicants simply lied about their income. Another loan used extensively for borrowers who could not qualify for standard mortgage loans was the Alt-A mortgage. Like stated-income mortgages, Alt-A loans grew in popularity, requiring little financial documentation and by 2006 accounting for 13 percent of all home loans extended nationwide. That same year, Alt-A loans represented 86 percent of all approved mortgages in California.

The rubber-stamp approval of thousands of mortgages to borrowers who could not pay them back was just the tip of the iceberg. The profitable and powerful engine of mortgage lending ran on securitized loans sold to investors. But by the 2000s, even securitization itself had changed. What had been simple buying and selling of packaged loans had morphed into a complicated investment strategy, offering more reward to investors willing to assume more risk. These lucrative but risky investments transformed subprime lending into an important driver of mortgage lending and were built on the assumptions of appreciating real estate values and stable employment. If these assumptions worked, as they had in the past, the risk of default on these subprime loans remained low while investor profits could be very high.

What delighted everyone, from investors and lenders to buyers and home-builders, was that these assumptions had worked and drove housing demand to new levels. Some areas of the country were so hot that investors purchased speculative condominiums and homes, making huge profits by flipping or selling them prior to their completion. The Las Vegas housing market was so strong that buyers were required to enter a lottery just for the chance to buy a house in the many speculative subdivisions under construction. The downside was that this incredible demand fueled speculative development that created overbuilt housing markets. Since 22 percent of all homes sold in America in 2006 were bought for investment purposes and 14 percent of homes sold were vacation homes, it is hard to accept the argument that bad loans made to low-income borrowers were the only cause of the financial crisis.

Another misconception is that banks created the crisis by making these sub-prime loans. By the late 2000s, 68 percent of all home loans were made by less regulated mortgage brokers. Banks certainly made mistakes and poor choices, but they weren't the cause of this financial disaster.

The timing of this crisis could not have been worse for the American consumer. By 2008 the average American family had thirteen credit cards, and 40 percent of these had recurring balances, up from just 6 percent in 1970. Household debt went from $705 billion in 1974 to $7.5 trillion in 2000, and rose to $14.5 trillion by 2008.

The upside to this spending frenzy was that Americans enjoyed the highest standard of living in the history of the planet, and in turn, the cycle of borrowing and spending drove the nation's economy. Financial institutions were certainly enjoying the ride as profits for U.S. banks reached a record high of $145 billion in 2006. With all the assumptions that led to this crisis, perhaps the worst one of all was that this perpetual prosperity could and would continue indefinitely.

The prosperous ride Americans had enjoyed ended as the fundamental principles and assumptions that drove the subprime mortgage market unraveled. First, the interest rate cycle reversed; mortgage rates climbed, and the dominos began to fall. Higher rates caused adjustable-rate mortgages to reprice, forcing some home owners to fall behind on their mortgage payments. Second, and critical to the coming crisis, jobs were being lost at an alarming rate as the U.S. economy cooled off. National unemployment more than doubled from 4.5 percent in 2006 to 10.2 percent by late 2009. The final nail in the coffin came in 2007 when home appreciation values, thought to be the one true real estate constant, began to fall and default rates on mortgage loans began to rise.

Although a massive financial storm was brewing, the only waves pounding the shores of the Mebane community seemed to be the unending wave of growth. Mebane was now the eighth-fastest-growing city in the state, with a population topping ten thousand for the first time.

Still, with all the change facing the city, the closing of White Furniture Company in the 1990s left a huge void in the heart and soul of those who grew up in Mebane. The mammoth factory had been reduced to little more than a storage facility and home to a few small businesses—quite a fall for a magnificent structure that once defined Mebane's industrial age. A Durham developer proposed a massive makeover for White's that would breathe life in the eighty-four-year-old building. The plans were similar to successful ventures in Durham, Greensboro, and other cities where vacant factories and mills were transformed into modern residential and commercial developments. The project created a lot of public interest, but like the Tanger project, the slumping economy in the late 2000s pushed the future of the proposed White development into the next decade.

Another Mebane icon searching for a new identity was the former Melville Chevrolet building. Located next to the Veterans Garden at the corner of Clay and Third streets, the building had struggled in recent years to find its niche in downtown's revival. The building had been the site of several small businesses and briefly made a go of it as Food Deals, sporting a truly forgettable pink exterior. By 2007, major renovations were under way on the building that would become Melville Trading Company, blending with Clay Street's unique style.

The city's unstoppable growth seemed to be a sure sign that the local economy was stable. Subtle hints of a cooling real estate market surfaced in 2005, but most folks shrugged it off, and with good reason. Mebane's commercial and residential growth had been stuck in high gear for two decades, displaying an incredible resilience in nearly every economic cycle. Even the recessions of 1990 and 2001 never slowed the demand for housing or commercial projects. But the country was on the verge of a major economic disaster that no city could escape.

The nation's real estate market came to a screeching halt in 2007 as new home sales fell 26 percent and long-term prospects for a turnaround were bleak. This sudden and abrupt drop in real estate sales was shocking not only to Americans but the economy as well, as problems in the subprime mortgage market accelerated. The economic downturn finally caught up with Mebane when the average price of a house dropped for the first time in a quarter century, falling 11 percent. The news was worse for Alamance County, as home sales dropped 23 percent for the year and construction permits fell 9 percent.

The connection between the growing subprime problem and rising unemployment could be seen in Alamance County's skyrocketing foreclosure figures. When the 2000s began, 239 Alamance County homes were in foreclosure. By 2007, that number had reached 1,149. Delinquent loans for First Savings rose sharply, and by 2008 the association had one foreclosure on its books, something it had avoided since 2003. The housing slowdown could be seen in the association's home lending, which fell 29 percent in 2007. Despite increasing problems in the housing market, Wall Street plowed ahead as the Dow closed at an all-time high of 14,154 in October 2007.

Traditional southern manufacturers continued their exodus, and many towns witnessed entire economies change overnight. North Carolina's textile industry was dying as foreign competition and plant relocation eroded traditional factory jobs. In 2007 Mebane found out that the foreign job threat was not limited to textiles and furniture when A.O. Smith and Kidde Corporation moved the bulk of their operations to China and Mexico. A.O. Smith, Kidde, GE, and Sandvik broke new industrial ground for Mebane during the 1970s, and with A.O. Smith and Kidde leaving, nothing seemed safe. "We don't make anything in America anymore," said one Mebane resident on hearing the news. "If this keeps up, we'll be crossing the border into Mexico to find a job one day."

Some towns adapted to plant closures, while others simply could not. Haw River felt this pain when the Cone Mills Granite Plant shut its doors in the 1990s. The shock of two major employers like Kidde and A.O. Smith closing at the same time would devastate most small towns. The news was disturbing but by no means fatal to Mebane's strong, diverse, and stable business environment. Had these announcements come years earlier, perhaps the response and consequences would have been different.

With so many U.S. manufacturers headed south of the border or overseas, many wondered which company would be next. One company that pioneered Mebane's industrial revolution during the twentieth century wasn't going anywhere, and in fact invested for the future. Sandvik had quietly become one of Mebane's leading employers and one of the area's most resilient companies. The Swedish tool maker found Mebane a good fit, and despite a slowing economy, Sandvik broke ground in 2008 on a four-year, $85 million expansion, restoring confidence in Mebane manufacturing.

For decades, Ben Corbett had been part of the First Savings family, cleaning the offices and mowing the yard. These were just a few of the jobs Corbett did with endless energy from sunup to sundown. From tending vegetable gardens in the summer to cleaning offices at night, nothing seemed to slow him down, even at age seventy-nine. In October 2007 Corbett was struck from behind by a car while driving his tractor on Highway 70. Ben Corbett never recovered from the accident, passing away a year later, and First Savings and Mebane lost a good friend.

The pivotal year of 2008 began on a high note for Mebane, despite the housing slowdown. Since the 1990s, the city of Mebane had embarked on one restoration project after another, and the result was a pleasant mixture of new construction standing alongside the city's most recognizable and historic buildings. Downtown had seen more visible changes in the last decade than in the previous thirty years. Fresh off the successes of Veterans Garden, the public library, and the police station, the city closed the decade in a flurry, altering three of Mebane's most familiar structures.

Having functioned as a municipal building, police and fire station, community meeting place, and town hall, Mebane's old fire station at the corner of Fourth and Washington streets had a long and storied history. This building, along with what is now the Five Star Center, are considered the most likely places that the first meeting of the Mebane Home Builders Association was held in 1909. Over the years, the building has undergone numerous improvements. Two bays were built for the fire department in 1950, with two more added in 1960. Topping the two-story structure was the fire department siren that still sounds today. Now nearly a century old, the structure was showing its age, and the east side of the building facing Fourth Street was rebuilt.

The renovation of this historic structure, which served as the main municipal building in the town's earlier years, was minor compared to the plans for Mebane's reigning city hall. Located in the shadow of the old fire station on Washington Street, the Municipal Building, like its predecessor, was antiquated for the growing city. During 2009 the building was remodeled, as interior offices were redone and a new and inviting entry was created. The results were simply spectacular, leaving little evidence that the Mebane Municipal Building was once the home to the children's clothing outlet Peaches N Cream.

The city's next stop was the former site of Mebane High School, which remained a sweet memory in the hearts and minds of generations that grew up in Mebane prior to the 1960s. Located at the corner of Lee and Second streets, what physically remained of the iconic school was the old gymnasium, library, and a few classrooms. The city's recreation department had made its home there since the 1970s, but had long since outgrown the small gym along with Walker Field, as the demand for recreation exploded during the 1990s. The construction of the Mebane Arts Center and the subsequent development of surrounding athletic fields propelled the city to another level in recreation. By the mid-2000s, Mebane boasted facilities that would be the envy of much larger cities. From basketball leagues in the winter to baseball and softball in the summer, the Arts Center and surrounding ball fields on Corregidor Drive were the center of Mebane sports and recreation. Soccer fields were added in 2004. Youth soccer grew so rapidly that by decade's end the MYSA (Mebane Youth Soccer Association) had become one of the strongest associations in the state. The Lee Street facilities were not up to par for the recreation demands of the city and needed a facelift. A makeover of the gym that began in 2008 also included a two-level home for the Mebane Historical Museum.

These improvements added to Mebane's struggle to hold on to its small-town charm while being tugged into the future by inevitable change. Sidewalks stretched from one end of the city to the other, and the city's investment in these older buildings and the exploding commercial development said a lot about the town's continuing transition from bedroom community to thriving city.

As Mebane transitioned, so did First Savings as three important changes occurred during 2008, solidifying staff and director positions. On March 27, Ned Gauldin was named director emeritus, joining Calvin Oakley and Paisley

Nelson as the only directors in the association's one-hundred-year history to ever receive this honor. Gauldin's declining health prevented him from attending monthly meetings, and James R. Guthrie was appointed to serve out Gauldin's term. Gauldin was honored again in August 2008 by the North Carolina Bankers Association with a sixty-year service certificate. Jim Guthrie was no stranger to the financial industry, having served on the board of directors at Graham Savings and Loan during the pivotal 1980s and worked on an advisory board after the merger of Graham Savings with CCB (Suntrust).

Ned Gauldin's tenure at First Savings lasted thirty years, and his impact was long lasting. Gauldin came to First Savings in 1978 and followed a long line of directors like Sam Hupman Sr. as the ultra-conservative voice on the board. As such, Gauldin had a difficult time adjusting to the easy credit environment that emerged during the 2000s. He had been highly critical of the mistakes made by both the financial industry and the government during the savings and loan crisis of the 1980s and felt the same way about this latest financial fiasco. Gauldin often remarked, "This country is going to hit another depression one day, and it will start with the banks." People have a tendency to smile politely and nod their heads when someone from an older generation makes doomsday comments like this, discarding them as old-fashioned pessimism. By late 2008 Gauldin's prediction seemed to be coming true.

Gail Jordan retired on May 30 after fourteen years with First Savings. To say that Jordan paid close attention to detail was an understatement, and although she received good-natured kidding from the staff for this quality, it made her the perfect bookkeeper. Amy (Edwards) Cannady, Jordan's assistant for the previous four years, was appointed as the association's comptroller.

The year 2008 might have started on a positive note, but it certainly would not end that way. Home sales plummeted for a second year in a row, confirming a bear real estate market. Home sales in Alamance County fell 29 percent while Mebane saw a 10 percent drop to its lowest levels since 1996. The only bright spot was that the price of a house in Mebane actually rose a modest 4 percent, reaching an all-time high of $181,803.

Oddly, as residential real estate stumbled, commercial ventures plowed ahead, highlighted by the news that Lowe's Foods, after leaving Mebane a few years earlier, was returning in a big way with a total renovation of the vacant Winn-Dixie store in the Mebane Oaks Market Place.

The wavering economy forced consumers to cut back, but it didn't seem to keep them from the great American pastime of eating out. From old favorites like the A&M Grill and Huey's to newly built franchises near the interstate, Mebane had a host of eateries to choose from, with more opening all the time. Pomodoro's opened in the Five Star Center, and Grill Worx became an instant success on West Center Street in a building that seemed cursed as a restaurant location. Then there was Nita's. With umpteen years at the old Arrowhead Restaurant and Nita's Café on North Second Street, chances are pretty good that Nita Harwood had cooked at least one meal for most folks in Mebane at some time or another. After Nita's husband passed away in 2009, Nita's Cafeteria closed, and so did a Mebane dining tradition.

Nita's business sign, like most in small-town America, is known very well by the locals, and such signs often have a unique style and flare. From the Rose's 5-10 sign that once graced Center Street to the T-shaped Hollywood Theater marquee, Mebane has seen signs of every shape and size. By the 2000s, Mebane had signs of local interest blending in with the golden arches of McDonald's and KFC's familiar Colonel Sanders' bucket. There was the distinctive red sign at Sheetz, Cracker Barrel's universal logo, and the red, white, and blue ReMax balloon, among others. Even a local watering hole, the Stumblin' Pig, had its own mural. And, of course, First Savings and Loan had the time and temperature sign.

The association introduced its first electric time and temperature sign in 1965, which quickly became a local landmark. One reason for its popularity at that time was that no one else had a sign quite like it. Over the years as technology changed, so did the association's sign. The first-generation signs of the 1960s were crude by today's standards, using individual bulbs on the sign board. Burned-out lights and vibrations from passing trains frequently loosened the bulbs and left folks to guess at both the actual time and temperature. The inconsistency of bulb technology was abandoned during the 1990s and replaced with a separate round temperature sign and clock. Although its design was stylish in appearance, it frequently broke down and was very inaccurate. The sign was down so often that one customer commented, "Well, at least the time on your sign is right twice a day." In 2008 a computer-generated digital message board was erected, drawing rave reviews and compliments from everyone, with the exception of a few members of the Mebane City Council. Somehow digital signs at First Savings and the Blue Ribbon Diner became an issue and front-page news for the local press. After much debate, the City Council revamped its sign ordinance, hoping to tone down what some referred to as a "Las Vegas" image.

The sign that most Americans were paying attention to in 2008 was a sign of instability in the nation's banking system as the subprime mortgage problem intensified. By spring the pieces of the financial crisis of 2008 finally came together and fed off each other. The failure of Wall Street investment firm Bear Stearns and California's Indymac Bank sent shock waves through financial markets, shifting the crisis into high gear. The collapse of both institutions was directly linked to subprime mortgage investments, and throughout the summer the world watched nervously as stunning events occurred with painful rapidity. Mortgage-related investments were thought to be safe and secure, and were routinely bought and sold by just about every financial institution from small-town banks to Wall Street titans. The value of these mortgage-backed securities fell as rising foreclosures created havoc in the stock market. The damage was not confined to Wall Street, as Americans nervously watched the value of their homes and retirement funds plummet. As Americans pumped four-dollar-a-gallon gas into their cars, anger grew, and few had any sympathy for problems occurring on Wall Street.

The turning point came in September when the focus turned to the center of the mortgage industry, Fannie Mae and Freddie Mac. Speculation over the safety of the two government-sponsored enterprises culminated in the government seizing control of both mortgage giants. But the damage was done. By now, many of the nation's largest lending institutions and investment firms had amassed large portfolios of mortgage-related instruments, and many were imbedded with subprime loans. For those institutions, the takeover of Freddie and Fannie was just the beginning. The government guaranteed Fannie and Freddie's mortgage-backed securities, hoping to restore confidence in the collapsing mortgage market and keep money flowing for home loans.

Wall Street finally crumbled under the weight of these toxic assets when Lehman Brothers filed bankruptcy and both Goldman Sachs and Morgan Stanley converted to bank holding companies. In a controversial move, Merrill Lynch was purchased by Bank of America. Officially the U.S. economy had been in a recession since late 2007, and now its financial system was headed off a cliff.

The news from Wall Street was confusing to some and downright frightening to others. Like the popular Las Vegas advertisement, many were hoping that what happened on Wall Street stayed on Wall Street. But that was not to be as the crisis intensified and moved to its next victim, the commercial banks. Fear and uncertainty sent investor confidence in the nation's financial system out the window as bank stocks began a rapid and painful slide that continued well into 2009. Guilt by association left no one unscathed, and the sell-off of financial stocks spread to small-town community banks as the crisis took no prisoners.

First Savings was besieged with phone calls and visits from worried customers, many of whom had been children during the Great Depression and vividly remembered the pain of that era. Younger folks had no perspective or concept of a severe economic crisis. One worried First Savings customer, who worked as a construction subcontractor and entered the building business during the 1990s, confessed that he had never known anything but good times and wasn't sure that he was going to make it financially.

Credit for home lending slowed to a trickle as banks, fearful of risk, shut the door on contractors whom they openly courted just a few years earlier. From large developers to small local builders, speculation construction virtually died as tract builders, the dominant force in home construction, shut down. Unfinished residential subdivisions dotted the county with their white plumbing taps protruding out of the ground—a sign of the times. Many of these incomplete subdivisions were financed by banks, both large and small, and the potential of these investments going bad was a lender's worst nightmare.

Comparisons of the financial meltdown were quickly drawn to the savings and loan crisis of the 1980s and the Great Depression of the 1930s. It is difficult to compare the archaic financial system of the 1930s and the fragmented banking environment of the 1980s with today's complex financial system. This latest situation and the savings and loan crisis were both chock-full of bad decisions driven by greed, poor economic conditions, and lapses in government oversight. One big difference, however, in the crisis of the 1980s was its limited scope, as there was no systemic risk that threatened the entire financial system.

Most observers used the Great Depression as the best yardstick, although this latest fiasco paled in comparison to the economic disaster of the 1930s. At the height of the Depression, one in four American workers were unemployed, compared to 10.2 percent unemployment by November 2009. More than ten thousand banks failed between 1930 and 1933, while fewer than two hundred banks closed in 2008 and 2009. Still the current crisis is only a year old, as the time line of this history concludes in November 2009, and its long-term impact remains far from over.

One banking phenomenon that grew out of those Depression years did play a critical role in this modern crisis. If a bank failed, prior to the creation of deposit insurance, customers often lost most if not all of their savings. Comfort was found in larger institutions as few small banks were strong enough to make it through the 1930s. Over time, depositors came to trust the perceived safety of larger institutions, convinced that bigger was always better. That notion grew over the years and was shared not only by the public and investors but apparently by regulators and Congress, becoming an accepted and informal measure of an institution's safety and soundness. Following the savings and loan crisis, the industry witnessed twenty years of mergers and acquisitions that radically changed the financial environment, creating regional, national, and international banking giants. By the turn of the century, the largest investor down to the smallest of savers believed that the nation's megabanks, by their sheer size and sophistication, were immune to major economic shocks and were simply "too big to fail."

The nation's banking system is truly the lifeblood of American and world commerce, made possible through multiple relationships with other financial institutions, nonbank entities, corporations, and investment firms, creating a mini-economy within the industry itself. These relationships perpetuated the "too big to fail" phenomenon. The term "bank failure" seemed absurd in today's financial world, conjuring up thoughts of old black-and-white photos from the 1930s when bank runs symbolized a completely different era in finance. But the emerging crisis did more than just strip Americans of wealth when the stock market tanked. When the financial crisis surfaced, something more frightening was revealed. Hidden within this complex financial economy was exposure to systemic risk, and the collapse of one or two large banks could trigger multiple bank failures. By September 2008 the conventional wisdom of "too big to fail" fell apart as events snowballed. What started out in the subprime sector of mortgage lending quickly escalated into something bigger than anyone ever imagined. Multiple bank failures were a real possibility, with catastrophic and far-reaching consequences well beyond investors and depositors. Whatever long-term changes that were sure to come through financial reform had to wait as the panic and the bleeding first had to stop.

Just like the Great Depression, all eyes turned from Wall Street to Washington as history repeated itself. In early October, Congress reluctantly passed the Economic Stabilization Act of 2008, which was unpopular with lawmakers and the public alike. The controversial bill was complex and expensive, and it extended powers to the government on many levels. In a series of unprecedented events, the government took partial ownership of some of the nation's largest banks and institutions. The U.S. Treasury bought many of the bad assets held by troubled financial institutions. Participation in the government's plan, for some institutions, was not an option, and many banks were forced to go along with the program. There was even talk of nationalizing the country's banks.

Money and power are deeply rooted in Washington, and the government unleashed both in heavy doses to fight the escalating crisis. Lawmakers took control and threw around billions and trillions of dollars like there was no tomorrow, and many felt that if they didn't, tomorrow might not come for the nation's financial system. Funds were "loaned" to financial institutions through the Troubled Asset Relief Program (TARP). The federal funds rate was cut to near 0 percent, and the Treasury flooded the economy with cash. The FDIC raised the insurance level on deposits from $100,000 to $250,000, restoring some calm to worried savers.

Like the 1930s, the financial crisis of 2008 altered and expanded the role of government into the realm of private enterprise like never before. The crisis went well beyond the nation's financial system, threatening other sectors of the economy. But unlike the Depression era, Washington stepped in to rescue some of America's oldest and most well-known institutions and companies. Critics of the government's actions argued that tinkering with markets and economic forces would prove fatal in the long run, and in a capitalistic society, market forces should be allowed to play out without intervention. Others thought there was no choice, and that a government solution was the only solution to prevent a major meltdown of not only the financial system but the country's economy.

With so much uncertainty, customers fled, as in times past, to the safety of FDIC-insured institutions with what was left of their investments and retirement funds. But this time it was different. The same fear that drove depositors to the perceived safety of large institutions during the Depression now drove them to smaller banks as money left Wall Street for the refuge of smaller community institutions. First Savings welcomed customers of much larger institutions who questioned the stability and safety of these financial giants. As one customer put it, "I don't care if I make anything [on my savings]. I had to get it [the IRA] out of the stock market to keep from losing it all." Insured institutions attracted plenty of money and paid almost nothing for it, as interest rates fell to historic lows. In the fourth quarter of 2008, savings deposits for First Savings climbed 13 percent, its largest one-quarter growth since the early 1960s.

Despite government guarantees and assurances, lenders grew increasingly paranoid, taking little if any risk. Credit markets froze. Those still in the housing market hit a brick wall when looking for a mortgage as credit virtually shut down. The easy-credit days were over, and those who would have easily qualified for a mortgage a few months earlier found out quickly that the financial world had changed. First Savings seized on this opportunity, continuing to make prudent loans, and of the nearly $8 million of mortgages originated in 2008, 41 percent of these loans were made in the last three months of the year.

As credit dried up, consumers pulled back on spending through the fall and into the prized Christmas season as America slipped deeper into a recession. The one-two punch of a stock market free fall and plummeting real estate prices had been devastating. The Federal Reserve reported that from October to December 2008, U.S. household wealth fell by a record $5.1 trillion.

Although the painful year of 2008 came to an end, what was now a broader economic crisis had not. Washington managed to subdue some of the initial panic through rescue packages and stimulus bills, but the crisis took away something that money just couldn't fix. As bank stocks continued to fall, more was lost than just a company's equity. When the curtain was pulled back—revealing how much the quest for profits, greed, and assumptions had played in this disaster—consumer fear quickly turned to outrage, and the public overwhelmingly viewed government assistance to these institutions as nothing more than a bailout. Struggling with financial problems of their own, Americans had no sympathy for troubled financial institutions that apparently had gambled big and lost.

This reaction was natural, but there was even more to this crisis than met the eye. The general notion that Wall Street banks and Main Street institutions were one and the same is false. In fairness, the great majority of community institutions were sound and conservative, and the only thing they were guilty of was being a bank. In the fourth quarter of 2007, just before the crisis hit, the American Bankers Association conducted a survey of 248 community banks and found that most institutions were engaged in conforming loans, considered prime lending, rather than risky subprime mortgages. The survey revealed that these institutions kept 68.5 percent of their mortgage loans in-house, with the remainder being sold on the secondary market. Most of these institutions had absolutely nothing to do with subprime lending or the financial crisis itself, but like the thrift debacle of the 1980s, the innocent paid for the sins of the guilty. Now the financial crisis bore another dubious characteristic of the Great Depression, as corporate America and its financial system quickly lost the trust and confidence of the American people.

For many people, TARP is obviously a four-letter word in more ways than one. With the panic and uncertainty of the period, the Troubled Asset Relief Program, rightly or wrongly, became the informal barometer that most Americans used to judge the safety and, more important, the trustworthiness of the banking industry. If an institution took TARP money from the government, the public just assumed the institution was either on the brink of failure, dishonest, or both, adding to the public relations ordeal facing the industry. Banks that received TARP funds defended their actions, while those that declined the money proudly acknowledged this decision to an increasingly skeptical public. One reason for the suspicion was that many banks which participated in TARP or received other financial assistance did not immediately lend these funds out when credit markets froze, infuriating both the public and the government. The reflection of the industry's hesitancy to lend can be seen in the statistics, as the FDIC reported that banks experienced their sharpest decline in lending since 1942.

In hindsight, banks that pulled the plug on lending in this unprecedented time of crisis acted prudently. If this sounds like a shameless defense of the banking industry, it is. In 2008 and 2009 the financial sky was falling after the collapse of Wall Street. With the entire banking system apparently not far behind, nothing seemed safe. Banks were afraid for their own existence, and keeping funds offered to them by the government in the bank, so to speak, as a safety net rather than risk lending the money appears to be a sound decision. With the economy and the nation's financial system in shambles, why should banks take more risk by lending money to an individual who may or may not have a job next year or to a business that might fail in six months? While critics blasted the industry for not lending, banks contended that creditworthy borrowers were hard to find. The banking industry was understandably circling the wagons for what became one of the worst financial disasters in their history, although neither an impatient government nor angry consumers saw it that way. Foolish lending and bad decisions had landed some institutions in trouble in the first place, and they were not about to make the same mistake again in an unstable economy. The tightening of the belt by institutions was controversial and didn't sit well with most folks, only making banks look worse in the eyes of the public—if that was possible.

By 2009 the crisis was no longer about subprime lending. The focus was now a deep recession that compounded every bank's bottom line. Many of the institutions that accepted TARP were in deep trouble, and this assistance allowed some banks to get back on their feet. Over time these institutions made it through the storm and paid the money back to the government with interest. For other unfortunate institutions, however, the damage was done—TARP or no TARP. Questionable decisions and a poor economy sealed their fate, and failure or merger was just a matter of time.

Whether banks took federal money or not, they did take the heat. The uncertainty of the nation's financial sector and a worsening recession kept investors on edge, and the sell-off of bank stocks continued. The Dow Jones Industrial Average hit its low for the crisis in February 2009 at 6547, off 54 percent from its all-time high in October 2007, prompting more consolidation of banks and fueling rumors of takeovers. Citigroup, one of the nation's largest financial institutions, saw its stock price fall to one dollar per share. San Francisco–based Wells Fargo purchased slumping Wachovia, and a North Carolina banking pioneer disappeared.

First Savings and Loan did not enter the conversation when it came to TARP, although some folks assumed that all institutions were either required to accept TARP or needed financial assistance. Ironically, as everyone called for heads to roll within the banking industry, those who played by the rules paid a heavy price anyway, proving once again that "no good deed ever goes unpunished." Reminiscent of the savings and loan crisis, the association was penalized for doing the right thing and was assessed more than $330,000 by the FDIC to help pay for the mistakes of troubled institutions.

If anyone had any concerns about the condition of First Savings during the financial crisis, they certainly didn't show it. Customers frequently called with general questions about the overall crisis, but few questioned the safety and soundness of First Savings itself. President Rick Smith sent a letter to customers assuring them of the institution's strength and safety, along with an annual proxy in early January. The association anticipated and prepared for a large crowd at its February annual shareholders' meeting, but surprisingly, only ten people showed up, and eight of them were either association employees or directors. Then again, maybe it wasn't that much of a surprise after all. The all-important trust factor that now eluded many institutions was by far First Savings' strongest weapon in fighting a tough economy and an industry under assault. Trust had been one of the intangibles that pulled First Savings through the turbulent 1980s and once again proved to be its saving grace.

From the economy to politics, these were indeed historic times, and America wanted change. Two hundred years ago, if a black man traveled to Washington, D.C., he mostly likely did so as the personal property of someone else. On January 20, 2009, Illinois Senator Barack Obama came to Washington to become the first African American president of the United States. Ten days earlier, the elections of 2008 made history in North Carolina when Beverly Perdue was sworn in as the state's first female governor.

President Obama and Governor Perdue both had their hands full as the unemployment picture, which had deteriorated in 2008, accelerated in 2009. Snowballing unemployment changed the face of the financial crisis, and the economic downturn had been simply brutal to the Tar Heel State. North Carolina's jobless rate, which began 2009 at 8.1 percent, climbed steadily through the year, reaching 10.2 percent by November 2009. From 2007 to 2009, North Carolina lost 248,000 nonfarm jobs, and not surprisingly, manufacturing dropped 95,500 jobs while construction cut 65,800. The financial sector, still weak in the knees, now braced for a worsening scenario. As the unemployment picture shifted the nation's foreclosure problem from the subprime to the conventional mortgage market, lenders were sure that more loan defaults were on the way. Although foreclosures across America reached historic levels, First Savings foreclosed just twice the entire year.

The deadly combination of job losses and millions of homes for sale across the country further depressed home values. Median home prices had dropped 29 percent by 2009 from their peak in 2006 and were still falling. In 2009 alone, home prices fell 12 percent, and one out of every four mortgage borrowers carried loan balances that were higher than the values of their homes. In Nevada, California, and Florida, 65 percent, 48 percent, and 45 percent of borrowers, respectively, were underwater, owing more in a mortgage than the value of their home. Real estate prices fell so rapidly in 2009 that 11 percent of borrowers who took out loans that year wound up owing more than the home's value by year's end.

The foreclosure epidemic was the newest front on the war against a recession that would not let up, and the government encouraged lenders to modify existing mortgage loans by offering extensions to borrowers facing foreclosure. Although lenders modified 680,000 home loans in the third quarter of 2009, delinquencies still rose to 6.2 percent, and the number of mortgages in foreclosure passed 1 million. One Washington idea that caught on was an eight-thousand-dollar tax credit for first-time home buyers. This tax incentive kept the struggling real estate market alive for the remainder of the year. Despite the slumping housing market, the back-to-back years of 2008 and 2009 were First Savings' strongest years in the entire decade for new construction loans. Construction lending accounted for 21 percent and 18 percent, respectively, in those years, up from a woeful 4 percent in 2005.

The foreclosure problem meant the terms "REO" and "short sales" were regular topics of conversation in every financial institution. REO is short for "real estate owned," meaning an institution has foreclosed or obtained title on property usually under distressed circumstances. The term "short sale" is a property that is on the market, with the lender's permission, for less money than is owed on the mortgage.

Securitization made mortgages accessible for the masses, but when it came down to foreclosure, the process became a nightmare for lenders. Stuck with bad loans, lenders took big losses. The perfect financial storm caused 140 banks to close their doors in 2009, and the FDIC reported that 702 more institutions were in danger of failing.

During the panic of 2008 and 2009 the association was fortunate to have only three foreclosures and no short sales at a time when bank-owned properties became a national epidemic. Extending only 80 percent loans instead of the industry norm of 90 percent and 95 percent certainly was a factor in these low numbers. But during those two volatile years, home values dropped more than 20 percent in some cases, and any equity position of the association and home owners had vanished. One defensive tool that First Savings had in its arsenal was allowing home loans to be assumed by qualified borrowers, thus avoiding foreclosure action. Loan assumptions are impossible for troubled mortgages that are sold to other lenders and investors. Ironically, after decades of living with the risk of holding loans in-house, the once-common lending policies that built the savings and loan industry were again paying off.

Although First Savings took the conservative road, the association found out firsthand that no institutions could escape the financial crisis, no matter how safe they thought they were. First Savings and Loan never engaged in subprime mortgages or made risky investments, but a bank that the association had a relationship with did. Since the 1990s, the association bought and sold securities with Banker's Bank, an Atlanta-based institution that worked strictly with the investing and financial needs of other banks. Banker's Bank changed its name to Silverton Bank during the 2000s and, like many institutions, invested heavily in the booming real estate market. By 2009 those investments were going bad and taking the bank down with it. First Savings had over $20 million invested with Silverton when the FDIC took control of the bank in May 2009. Silverton acted as a safekeeping bank for First Savings, and the association's investments were never exposed to loss. Silverton's failure forced First Savings to form another banking relationship, moving its securities to San Francisco–based Pacific Coast Bankers' Bank later that summer.

The fact that Mebane endured the economic downturn with only minor damage was simply remarkable. Not surprisingly, the sector hardest hit was housing. The slight rise in home prices seen a year earlier was erased in 2009 as home sales for Mebane hit a fourteen-year low, with prices falling 6 percent. Still there was a silver lining. Despite these numbers, homes in Mebane sold faster than in other sections of Alamance County. According to the Alamance Multiple Listing Service, it took an average of 101 days for a home in Mebane to sell, compared to 206 days countywide. This was the fastest homes had sold in Mebane since 1995, revealing that despite the overall slowdown, Mebane real estate was still in demand.

Commercial development along the I-85 corridor managed to hold its own during this period, while downtown clearly stumbled. One of Mebane's most recognizable businesses, Ace Hardware, closed in March on the heels of Bell Ford's shutdown in late 2008. Southern States became the third major business to leave West Center Street when in 2009, under very different circumstances, it expanded its operations in a new facility on Highway 119 South. Southern States, formally known as FCX, had operated in its Center Street location since the early 1960s.

The closings of Ace Hardware and Bell (Amick) Ford were another story, marking the end of an era in downtown. Although some blame can be attributed to the recession, the closings of these two businesses were in many ways reflective of twenty-first-century commerce in small-town America. Once upon a time, Melville Chevrolet and Amick Ford were marquee car dealerships that flourished alongside several used-car lots that also did a brisk business. In today's market, car dealers often struggle in older downtown locations without the exposure of high-volume traffic. Rodney Weaver, like his father Gary, spent decades at Amick Ford before the buyout by Bell. The younger Weaver opened an auto dealership in 2005 on a street he knew very well, West Center Street. A decade ago, that tried-and-true formula probably would have worked as it had in decades past. Weaver saw the writing on the wall and followed the trend set by other dealerships, moving Weaver Auto Sales to the now densely traveled Highway 119 south of I-85/I-40.

Hardware stores that thrived as staple businesses in communities all across America during the twentieth century were disappearing, and Ace's closing was another statistic. Competition from home improvement centers coupled with the recession was too much to take. For decades, Newlin Hardware and McPherson's Hardware were as well known to Burlington residents as a Zack's hot dog, yet both had closed their doors in the previous five years. Ace Hardware's rich history dated back to 1906, when the company was known as Tyson Malone Hardware. One of the original owners, W.Y. Malone, was also one of the association's founders in 1909. Demographics and shopping preferences had changed Mebane, and Mebane changed with them.

Two major events took place in 2009 that demonstrated not only how far the city had come but gave a glimpse of where it was headed. Alamance Regional Medical Center (ARMC) committed to Mebane, initially breaking ground in 2005, on a multimillion-dollar medical park off Mebane Oaks Road. ARMC's expansion brought a variety of medical services, including an urgent care and surgery center. ARMC stood by that commitment and in September 2009 dedicated a cancer center, giving Mebane a wide range of medical services typically found in larger cities.

On the cold morning of December 10, 2009, four hundred people gathered a stone's throw from ARMC on the former Arrowhead Golf Course property. The chilly weather, however, could not quell the excitement taking place in the city that day as Mebane residents, city and county leaders, along with Governor Perdue celebrated the groundbreaking of Tanger Outlet Center. The recession briefly delayed Tanger's initial construction but never deterred Tanger's long-range plans. With unemployment topping 11 percent in Alamance County, Tanger's announcement was the best news the city and county could possibly hope to hear. The center was completed and opened in November 2010, creating an estimated eight hundred full-time jobs, and Mebane joined Tanger's thirty-three-outlet empire in twenty-two states.

In some ways, Tanger's announcement brought Mebane full circle. There was a time when folks traveled for miles to spend most of their day shopping in Mebane's downtown business district, which offered everything from food to furniture. A *Mebane Enterprise* article published in 1919 stated that one could find virtually anything in the wide variety of shops and stores, earning the town the reputation as the "Biggest Little Town on Earth." Although commercial evolution and industrial transition over the years forever changed Mebane's downtown business district, the city never quit. Downtown survived with a renewed vision and business environment much different from a generation ago when the railroad and Highway 70 brought jobs and people. Now an eight-lane interstate fed a city with two versatile business districts, and with Tanger on the way, Mebane would have even more to offer visitors.

Tanger's groundbreaking had everybody thinking *green*, but what truly captured the attention of every Mebanite in December 2009 had them thinking *green and gold*. After capturing the East Region Championship, Eastern Alamance High School's quest for a state football championship took them to Carter Finley Stadium in Raleigh. That same weekend, Eagle cross-country standout Jake Hurysz headed to San Diego to compete for a national title. Although few locals made it to California to watch Hurysz blow past the competition, placing sixth in the nationals, the entire town showed up in Raleigh. That's the kind of town Mebane is. John Kirby's Eagles came up on the short end of the score that day, but like the town they represented, they never quit. That's the kind of team they were.

After one hundred years, Mebane and First Savings were very different, yet both had a lot in common. Mebane was still a town where total strangers spoke and waved to each other and, like a century earlier, "y'all" was still heard on the street along with midwestern and northern dialects. Ironically, as many of the nation's financial institutions contemplated an uncertain future, First Savings and Loan had a lot more to celebrate in 2009 than just its centennial. Throughout its history, First Savings rarely followed the financial crowd, a stance that offered rewards and consequences. Just as Tanger redefined Mebane's commercial identity, the financial crisis clarified the mission of First Savings, and in a strange twist, answered many open-ended questions that the association had pondered for years.

First Savings survived the savings and loan crisis of the 1980s by sticking to its conservative roots and admittedly sat on the sidelines, making few changes, while the rest of the financial world evolved for twenty years. To be honest, the association often second-guessed itself for staying a wallflower while the rest of the banking world enjoyed the dance. One of the consequences of this lone-ranger approach was that the association became more isolated from mainstream banking. This strategy may have kept the association financially sound but limited the institution from building broader customer relationships outside its conservative base. At times the association contemplated becoming more bank-oriented, offering different products and services. One of those periods occurred just before the financial crisis unfolded, when the association nervously watched one-third of its loan portfolio walk out the door during the easy-credit environment of the day.

But that never was First Savings and Loan's market. Although financial institutions share many common traits and goals, what works well for one institution may not be suitable for another. Each institution much choose its own direction and take its own financial road. As the financial crisis of the late 2000s painfully demonstrated, success is not defined by how large or diverse an institution becomes. The anything-goes lending spree of the 2000s not only caused financial institutions to take pause, but consumers followed suit. "Too big to fail" indeed failed, and the nation's largest banks weren't immortal after all. Like an old tie that hung in the closet for twenty years, small community institutions were suddenly back in style. The savings and loan crisis, and more important the financial crisis of 2008, dispelled any self-doubt that the association had about its conservative philosophy, confirming that First Savings had been on the right road all along.

For over half a century, Neal Smith took the association down that road, and his road map had been the age-old concept of mutuality. The American Bankers Association reported that just 689 mutual associations were still in existence in 2009. The contribution of mutuality to the success and longevity of First Savings has been mentioned numerous times in this history. It is somewhat fitting that an institution which didn't follow the crowd would embrace a concept that few thought could survive.

But survive it did. Looking back over the association's first one hundred years, perhaps the biggest challenge for First Savings was not found in the threat of economic shocks or the evolution of the banking industry. The real challenge just may have been overcoming its own internal struggles and accepting the rewards, however large or small, that come with remaining a small-town thrift. In its infancy the association tried its best to grow, but simply could not. "Contentment" is a word seldom used in business and frowned upon by most experts, who equate it with apathy and complacency. Many argue that the blueprint for success must constantly change, when sometimes a simple and proven formula is all that's needed. The management at Coca-Cola would probably agree. Maybe First Savings' former chairman, Calvin Oakley, was on to something when he said, "If it ain't broke, don't fix it."

First Savings spent 2009 celebrating its one hundredth anniversary, getting as much mileage as it could out of this special milestone at a time when good publicity in this business was hard to come by. The year-long celebration culminated in a catered gala on November 2 and 3, complete with a harpist, and the event drew hundreds of well-wishers. The association revived a few popular ideas that were successful in past celebrations to mark its centennial. During its fiftieth birthday in 1959, the association gave out numbered coins to customers when they opened savings accounts. The new coins used for the centennial featured the association's building engraved on one side of the coin with "100th Anniversary" minted on the other side. The numbered coins were given out when savings accounts were established or a home loan was closed. Those receiving a coin were entered into a monthly drawing for one hundred dollars, with a five-hundred-dollar grand prize awarded on the anniversary date of November 3. Like the ninetieth birthday bash in 1999, the centennial's two-day gala saw the association's staff adorn period costumes from the early twentieth century.

After two days of festivities, the crowds wore thin, and quite frankly, so did the patience of the staff who were ready to shed the hot and cumbersome costumes. A century had passed since twelve Mebane businessmen faced an unknown future when they met to form the Mebane Home Builders Association. At 3:00 in the afternoon on Tuesday, November 3, 2009, exactly one hundred years to the day and hour of that first meeting in 1909, a simple ceremony took place. Those in the association's lobby that day were Neal Smith, Rick Smith, Janis Murray, Jamie Park, Amy Cannady, Rhonda Bowling, Denise Snead, and Gail Jordan. Also in attendance were guests Pearl Poole, Glenn Wallace, Beth Katosic, Bonnie Bach, and Marg Cobb. A simple toast was made to First Savings' first one hundred years and with the hope of a successful second century.

The story of First Savings obviously does not end here. Its first one hundred years is just the end of one chapter and the beginning of another. As this chapter concludes, First Savings was enjoying the best years in its history, proudly carrying the banner of a mutual savings and loan in a banking industry under tremendous pressure. Like those businessmen who took a chance in 1909, First Savings now faced an unknown future as massive financial reform was under way. Few would argue that changes were needed, yet history has shown that financial reform can result in unintended consequences.

Likewise, a different era had dawned in America. The 2000s began with high economic expectations and ended with the nation mired in what was now the Great Recession. This period of history, like the Great Depression, profoundly affected the country and its financial values, altering everything from employment to individual finances. Accepted principles in American life had changed, and what was once considered sound financial wisdom didn't seem to apply anymore. This new chapter is just beginning.

Mebane ended the decade on the verge of yet another commercial explosion as Tanger estimated that 4.5 million customers would visit the eighty stores on Arrowhead Boulevard each year, assuring that Mebane would again retain its lost legacy as a shopping destination. The fact that Tanger's announcement came during one of the most challenging economic times in the nation's history proved that the company saw in Mebane the same thing people saw in First Savings for a century. Despite crisis periods and changing economies, people believed in First Savings and Loan and Mebane, North Carolina. Both are success stories, yet each has taken different paths. Much of the industry that put Mebane on the map has been replaced with a much different manufacturing and commercial environment than existed a century earlier. First Savings didn't embrace the monumental changes that have occurred within the nation's financial system over the past century, and in reflection, it didn't need to. The success of a financial institution cannot be defined by its size and sophistication, any more than a city can be judged by the size of its population. First Saving and Mebane have always shared many common denominators, perhaps none more important than the ability to adapt to change.

A surprised Neal Smith is presented with a portrait by award-winning artist Harriet Lynch at his retirement in June 2002.

Directors Steve Troutman, Neal Smith, Bobby Massey and Ned Gauldin at Smith's retirement reception.

While customers head for refreshments, Neal Smith shares a moment with his dog Brutus.

Staff celebrate First Savings 100th anniversary in November 2009. FRONT ROW Rhonda Bowling, Denise Snead, BACK ROW Jamie Park, Gail Jordan, Neal Smith, Rick Smith, Amy Cannady and Janis Murray.

The completion of Veterans Garden, the Mebane Public Library and renovations of City Hall (top right photo) in 2009 changed downtown's appearance and was a reflection of a city poised for the future.

Mebane Oaks Road and Highway 119 south hit full stride as a primary business district by the 2000s.

ARMC's opening of a cancer center on Arrowhead Boulevard in 2009 reflected the health provider's long term commitment to Mebane.

Ashbury subdivision was one of the many residential communities that opened during the 2000s reflecting the influence of tract development.

Mayor Glendel Stephenson, Governor Beverly Perdue and Stephen Tanger celebrate Tanger Outlet Center's ground breaking in December 2009. *Courtesy Mebane Enterprise*

Customers crowd the stores at Tanger's as the "Biggest Little Town On Earth" regains its legacy as a shopping destination. *Courtesy Mebane Enterprise*

Traffic backs up on I-85/40 on Tanger Outlet Center's opening weekend in November 2010. *Courtesy Mebane Enterprise*

First Savings board of directors in November, 2009. L-R Neal Smith, Bobby J. Massey, James R. Guthrie, Steven E. Troutman and Rick Smith

The Association's staff, November 2009, Rick Smith, Rhonda Bowling, Amy Cannady, Denise Snead, Janis Murray and Jamie Park.

In writing this book, I have referred to many publications and organizations for information. I was also fortunate to have the cooperation and input from a number of individuals who contributed their time and, in many cases, documents and/or images to help me put this story together.

SOURCES

Alamance News
American Bankers Association
Banking In North Carolina, A Narrative History by T. Harry Gatton–1987
Bankrate.com
Bloomberg.com
Centennial History of Alamance County by Walter Whitaker-1949
City Of Mebane
Closing: The Life and Death of An American Factory by Bill Bamberger & Cathy N. Davidson-1998
The Congressional Research Service
Encyclopedia of North Carolina by William Powell–2006 UNC Press
Federal Deposit Insurance Corporation
Federal Reserve
First Savings and Loan Association
Freedom From Fear–The American People in Depression and War by David M. Kennedy–1999
The History Channel
Kingsdown, Inc
Library of Congress
The Mebane Enterprise
Mebane Historical Museum
Mebane Historical Society
Mebane Public Library
North Carolina Bankers Association
North Carolina Through Four Centuries by William Powell–1989 UNC Press
Office of Thrift Supervision
PBS
U.S. Census Bureau
U.S. Department of Labor
Silverton Bank
Times-News
Wall Street Journal

CONTRIBUTORS

Amy Altese
Mike Baptiste and IT Express
Don Bolden
Rhonda Bowling
Jackie Brown
Penny Butler
Amy Cannady
Betty Carroll
J.J. Carroll
Karen Carter
Amy Clement
Jim Covington
Charlie Davis
Joanne Doberstein
Ned Gauldin
Sam Hupman
Lib Hurdle
Bill Humbert
Bob Hupman
Mrs. W.R. "Kitty" Hupman
Doug Isaac
Jane Iseley
Jimmy Jobe
Debbie Lynch and William Lynch Studios
Steve Mills
Shelby Murphy
Janis Murray
Luanne Jobe Nicholson
Ron Oakley
Jamie Park
Algernon Primm
Virginia Sellew
Judy Settle
Lee Settle
Denise Snead
Juliana Smith
Neal Smith
Jim Thomas
Joe Thompson
Sam White
Robert Wilson
Thad Woodard
Janice Wright